D0267639

Michael Schofield

The Sexual Behaviour of Young Adults

A follow-up study to
The Sexual Behaviour of Young People

Allen Lane

First published in 1973

Allen Lane
A Division of Penguin Books Ltd
21 John Street, London WC1

ISBN 0 7139 0605 7

Printed in Great Britain by
Ebenezer Baylis & Son Limited
The Trinity Press, Worcester, and London

Contents

1 Research Plan

1.1 *The Earlier Research* 11
1.2 *Tracing Seven Years Later* 12
1.3 *The Refusals* 14
1.4 *The Original Sample Compared with the Interviewed Groups* 15
1.5 *The Interviews and the Questions* 17
1.6 *Analysis and Presentation* 18

2 Sex Education

2.1 *Results from the Previous Research* 21
2.2 *Sex Education Now and Then* 22
2.3 *Was It Helpful?* 23
2.4 *The Demand for Information* 26
2.5 *The Source of Information* 27
2.6 *The Best and the Usual Way* 30
2.7 *Parents or Teachers* 33
2.8 *The New Generation of Parents* 36
2.9 *Inadequate Knowledge* 37
2.10 *The Effect on Behaviour* 38
2.11 *The Effect on Attitudes* 42
2.12 *Adequate and Poor* 44
2.13 *Reasons for Ineffectiveness* 47
2.14 *The Changing Sexual Scene* 49
2.15 *Do We Need It?* 51
2.16 *Motivation is Not a Problem* 54
2.17 *Reasons for Official Resistance* 56

3 Venereal Diseases

3.1 *Sexually Transmitted Diseases* 61
3.2 *Possible Reasons for the Increase* 62
3.3 *Knowledge and Names* 65
3.4 *The Symptoms* 67
3.5 *Incidence and Type of Disease* 72
3.6 *Those Most Likely to be Infected* 73
3.7 *Contacts and Treatment* 75
3.8 *The Attitude to Clinics* 77
3.9 *Ideas from Informants* 80
3.10 *Future Campaigns* 83
3.11 *The Fear of Success* 86

4 Contraception

4.1 *The Earlier Research* 90
4.2 *Knowledge and Information* 91
4.3 *Obtaining Advice* 93
4.4 *The Extent of Use* 94
4.5 *The Various Methods* 97
4.6 *Supply and Demand* 100
4.7 *Fears about the Pill* 104
4.8 *Reasons for Rejection* 109
4.9 *The Mythology* 112
4.10 *Identifying the Non-User* 117
4.11 *The Gap between First Intercourse and Contraception* 122
4.12 *Whose Responsibility?* 124
4.13 *Distribution* 126
4.14 *Publicity and Education* 129
4.15 *Eight Basic Steps* 131

5 Premarital Pregnancies

5.1 *The Incidence in This Research* 134
5.2 *The Consequences* 135
5.3 *The People At Risk* 137
5.4 *Terminations and Miscarriages* 141
5.5 *Aborting and Abortionists* 145

5.6   *The Cost of an Abortion*   146
5.7   *The Fear of Premarital Pregnancy*   148
5.8   *Negative Attitudes to Premarital Pregnancies*   150
5.9   *Abortion as an Adjunct to Contraception*   153
5.10 *The Right to Choose*   158

6   Sexual Intercourse

6.1   *The First Experience*   160
6.2   *The Reaction to the First Experience*   162
6.3   *Second and Subsequent Experiences*   164
6.4   *Premarital Sex*   166
6.5   *Frequency*   169
6.6   *Sexual Enjoyment*   171
6.7   *Sex Problems*   174
6.8   *Fidelity*   178
6.9   *The Inexperienced*   181
6.10 *Marriage*   185
6.11 *Marital Problems*   190
6.12 *Attitudes to Premarital Sex*   193
6.13 *Variations in Sexual Behaviour*   199

7   Social Policy

7.1   *A Review of the Results*   202
7.2   *Sex Education*   203
7.3   *Venereal Diseases*   205
7.4   *Contraception*   207
7.5   *Premarital Pregnancies*   210
7.6   *Sexual Intercourse*   212
7.7   *A Situation of Instability*   214
7.8   *Population and Sex*   215

Appendix A. Tables   219

Appendix B. Methodology

B.1   *Finding the Informant*   227
B.2   *The Refusals*   229
B.3   *Possible Bias from Lost Informants*   232

8   Contents

B.4   *Selecting the Questions*   236
B.5   *The Interviews*   237
B.6   *Validity*   239

References   241

Index   245

Acknowledgements

Understandably it is difficult and expensive to set up a unit for only a short period. In fact the administrative costs of this research were small, largely because we received excellent cooperation from the Health Education Council. Baroness Birk and Mr G. W. H. Woodman provided maximum support and encouragement. This was particularly valuable because the decision to go ahead with the research was made only four weeks before the starting date, consequently administrative arrangements and staff appointments had to be made with rapidity. Mr D. G. Freeman and Mr J. F. Pottinger made it possible for the administration to be efficient and inexpensive. I much appreciate the way all members of the HEC staff helped us; in particular a special word of appreciation should go to Mrs Crane and the staff of the Document Reproduction Centre. The Health Education Council is not, of course, committed to an endorsement of the conclusions and recommendations in this report.

Ken Plummer was the research organizer and Ann Thompson was the secretary; the eight interviewers were Jenny Browett, Rosemary Cond, Jeremy d'Agapeyeff, Malcolm Davies, Randall Kinkead, Carla Murkette, John Turner and Wendy Young. Together they made an enthusiastic and enterprising research team, and I am much indebted to them.

Two people have been particularly helpful, as they have been during the preparation of all my recent books: Anthony Skyrme for precise and detailed help with the manuscript, and Bryn Ellis for valuable assistance throughout the research.

1. Research Plan

1.1 The Earlier Research

The report on *The Sexual Behaviour of Young People* is based on 1,873 interviews chosen from a representative sample of teenagers. It is the most thorough and valid sexual research ever carried out in this country. I make this statement not as the immodest author of the report but because sufficient time (supplied by the Central Council for Health Education) and money (supplied by the Nuffield Foundation) were provided to do the job thoroughly.

There were suggestions that a similar investigation into the sexual activities of the new teenage generation should be carried out again and there is much to be said for this idea because a comparison between the two generations would be both interesting and useful (although my own guess is that there would be many more similarities than differences).

But I thought it would be more rewarding to conduct a longitudinal research by attempting to trace and re-interview some of the same young people seen seven years ago. It was agreed that I should train and lead a team of young interviewers to trace as many as possible of the 790 boys and girls aged about eighteen at the time of the first interview. This research was to be under the auspices of the Health Education Council and financed partly by that organization and partly from the royalties that had accrued from the previous report.

The objectives were to obtain descriptive information about residence, schooling, occupation, leisure, group activities, marital situation, sex education, knowledge of sex, attitudes towards sex, sexual behaviour, incidence of venereal diseases and use of contraceptives. As the original interview schedules were still available, it was possible to compare the old and new information and thus study the sexual development of these men and women over the last seven years. A follow-up research of this kind nearly always produces some interesting information. Even if some of the factors have not changed over the years, that in itself is interesting.

1.2   Tracing Seven Years Later

The interviewing was carried out over a period of three months and eight interviewers were employed (not all of them were able to work the full twelve weeks). Tracing these young adults after seven years proved to be a difficult task. The interviewers found that they were wasting a great deal of time visiting people when sometimes the house, even the whole street, had been demolished. It was therefore decided to employ an agency to make the first call. This showed that 84 per cent had moved since the last interview. The agency reported back what little information they were able to find. In many cases all the interviewer had to work on was a seven-year-old address.

If a person had moved elsewhere in the same town we had some chance of finding him, although it involved a fair amount of detective work, such as inquiring at his old place of work or from neighbours or trying to trace him from the register of electors. It was particularly difficult to find the girls because most of them had married and changed their names. Sometimes a study of the old interview schedule provided a clue. For example one boy had said that his ambition was to be a policeman and although he could not be found at his old address, he was traced after an inquiry at the local police station. But it is strange that some people can leave an area and quickly lose all contact with the neighbourhood. From the original sample of 790, 117 (15 per cent) were never traced at all.

Another 188 (24 per cent) were traced in the sense that we had some idea of their whereabouts but for a number of different reasons it was impossible to interview them. 7 (1 per cent) of these were dead, disabled or in a mental hospital and could not be interviewed. 11 (1 per cent) more now lived abroad and a further 106 (13 per cent) lived so far away from the main interviewing centres that it was impossible to contact them with the money and time available. Self-administered postal questionnaires which included many of the questions asked during the interview were sent to some of the people beyond our range, but this method was soon abandoned because information obtained in this way was found to be less valid and reliable than the answers obtained during a face-to-face interview. (Table B/1 in Appendix B sets out these results in tabular form.)

We felt fairly sure we knew where 19 (2 per cent) people lived, but were never able to find them at home despite several calls both during the day and in the evening. Another 45 (6 per cent) people had been traced but were away from home for long periods, for example, working abroad during the summer, on lengthy holidays (we were prepared to wait for them to return from a two-week holiday) and two were in prison. Interviewers called sometimes as many as eight or nine times, never less than three times. There have been occasions when interviews have been obtained after five or six calls, but as these 64 cases show, even dogged persistence does not always produce an interview.

As long as there was an interviewer in the area calls would be made, but after a while it was necessary for the interviewers to move on to other parts of the country so that the sample might be representative. It is certain that we could have obtained more interviews from this large group of 170 (21 per cent) if time and money had been limitless. In some cases the interviewer might spend more than a day attempting to trace a person and then discover that he or she had moved too far away. The resources of the research made it essential to set a limit on the number of towns and countries to which interviewers could be sent.

It is not simply a matter of sending someone to Newcastle, for example, to obtain an interview and return the next day. More likely the interviewer would have to go there, spend a day or more before establishing contact with the person required, then wait perhaps a few days until an appointment for an interview could be arranged, because it seldom happens that someone agrees to a long interview at the first meeting. A letter sent beforehand does not often reduce the time and sometimes produces an outright refusal.

It can be seen that as soon as an interviewer was required to go away from his base, living and travelling expenses more than doubled the cost of each interview. I calculated that some of these interviews cost more than £50. Others, of course, were much less expensive. Nevertheless, the cost per interview of this research is high (nearly £20) and a responsible researcher must balance the advantages of a high response rate with the cost of eliminating a bias which may not in fact be very important.

1.3   The Refusals

Altogether 109 (14 per cent) people were contacted but refused to agree to an interview. The number of refusals is higher than expected considering that they had all agreed to a second interview seven years ago. Of course many of them had forgotten this and a few of them said they had never been interviewed in the first place; sometimes it required several germane questions from the early interview record to convince the person that he really had been interviewed seven years ago. Sometimes it was the husband or wife of the original informant who refused to allow his or her partner to participate. Only a few refused because they objected to the first interview.

People who were reluctant to be interviewed were pressed hard by the interviewers and many were persuaded to change their minds, but there is a limit to this kind of persistence. The problem about refusals for the social scientist is that it may be a particular type of person who refuses and this may bias the results. Fortunately in this case we are better placed than most researches because the record of the early interview contains much information about the people who would not agree to be interviewed again. An analysis of this information is given in Appendix B. This shows that there is a slight tendency for the less well educated and those with less sexual experience to refuse. This bias is small and never more than 5 per cent, but the reader should remember that the results of the research tends to exaggerate the views of the better educated and of the sexually more adventurous.

1.4 *The Original Sample Compared with the Interviewed Groups*

Despite the refusals and those who could not be traced, not a large number considering the experience of others who have done follow-up researches on this age group which is the most mobile section of the population, it seems likely that we have managed to obtain a fairly representative sample of the population, because there is a quite remarkable similarity between the results obtained from the original 790 and the 376 we interviewed again. Tables 1/1, 1/2 and 1/3 compare the original sample with the groups which were interviewed a second time and it can be seen that there is very little difference between them. Table 1/1 gives estimates of social

TABLE 1/1. Father's occupation: the original sample compared with the extracted group (i.e. those who were re-interviewed).

Father's occupation	BOYS			GIRLS		
	Original sample %	Extracted group %	Difference %	Original sample %	Extracted group %	Difference %
Professional and managerial	7	9	+2	8	7	—1
Intermediate	19	22	+3	19	20	+1
Skilled non-manual	13	12	—1	7	5	—2
Skilled manual	37	36	—1	42	45	+3
Partly skilled	16	15	—1	14	13	—1
Unskilled	6	5	—1	7	8	+1
NK	2	1	—1	3	2	—1
No. (100%)	393	219	—	397	157	—

TABLE 1/2. Parental background: the original sample compared with the extracted group (i.e. those who were re-interviewed)

| Parental background | BOYS | | | GIRLS | | |
	Original sample %	Extracted group %	Difference %	Original sample %	Extracted group %	Difference %
Father dead	9	9	—	9	10	+1
Mother dead	2	2	—	3	1	—2
Divorced	4	4	—	4	5	+1
Separated	2	1	—1	4	5	+1
Other	2	1	—1	3	1	—2
Two parents	81	83	+2	77	78	+1
No. (100%)	393	219	—	397	157	—

TABLE 1/3. Number of girls/boys dated more than six times: the original sample compared with the extracted group (i.e. those who were re-interviewed)

| Number of girl/boy friends | BOYS | | | GIRLS | | |
	Original sample %	Extracted group %	Difference %	Original sample %	Extracted group %	Difference %
None	17	18	+1	6	8	+2
1	18	19	+1	13	10	—3
2	19	21	+2	13	16	+3
3	13	12	—1	16	15	—1
4	7	6	—1	9	11	+2
5	4	4	—	10	11	+1
6–10	9	10	+1	17	17	—
10+	7	5	—2	13	10	—3
DK/NK	6	5	—1	3	2	—1
No. (100%)	393	219	—	397	157	—

class based on the father's occupation and Table 1/2 shows the parental situation at the time of the first interview. Table 1/3 is included here because it shows that even when there is a larger number of categories and such a wide spread in the percentages, the differences are rarely more than 2 per cent. In Appendix A Table A1/1 gives the age at which each group left school, Table A1/2* shows the religious denominations, Table A1/3* lists the source of knowledge about conception and Table A1/4 shows the extent of sexual experience. These tables, and many others that have been studied, show that the differences are very slight and never more than 5 per cent.

It is clear that the replies which the 376 people in our interviewed group gave seven years ago do not differ markedly from the replies given by the whole sample of 790. I am unable to say if this striking result is simply a matter of good luck because one would not expect such a close resemblance, especially as the group of girls was quite small. In any event it does seem probable that our 376 informants are representative of the teenage population of seven years ago.

1.5   The Interviews and the Questions

We adopted the same principles as in the first research. All eight interviewers were specially recruited and trained for this work; men interviewed men, and women interviewed women; and they were all about the same age as the informants so that it was easier to build up a large measure of *rapport* before questions were asked on intimate sexual behaviour. All the information was obtained direct from the persons previously interviewed and no one else was allowed to be present during the interview. Care was taken to exclude all moral implications or value judgements during the course of the interview. Nearly all the people we met were friendly and cooperative, happy to talk about themselves and willing to take the interviewer completely into their confidence. After each interview the informants were asked to fill in an attitude

* Tables A1/2 and A1/3 also show how the replies have changed during the course of seven years and these will be referred to again later in this report.

inventory consisting of twenty-eight statements and this gave the interviewer the chance to check his schedule and clear up any inconsistencies and ambiguous answers.

There were 205 questions on the interview schedule, although no one was asked every question since some only applied to particular groups (e.g. married men and women were asked several extra questions). Some (70) of the questions were similar to the questions that were asked seven years ago. But this time we usually allowed them to give more than one answer if they wished.

For example, many people wanted to give more than one answer to the question: What do you think is the best way to learn about sex? Anyone unfamiliar with methods of analysis and computer programming would scarcely believe the added complexities of allowing a person to give more than one answer to this question. In the earlier research the question was especially framed in such a way as to reduce the possible answers to one. But for some people there is more than one 'best way'. In most researches the interviewer presses for only one answer so as to fit in with the technical limitations of the computer. In this research we decided to fit the analysis to accord with human flexibility. To this question about the best way of learning, over half the men and women gave more than one reply.

In addition to the 70 repeated questions, there were 135 new questions, to elicit information about contraceptives, marital adjustment, attitudes to premarital and extramarital sexual relations, the most frequent sexual problems that young adults encounter, and the way these problems are resolved.

1.6   Analysis and Presentation

When all the interviews had been completed, the schedules were checked, coded and prepared for the computers. The information obtained from the 219 men and 157 women was analysed in two ways: the new answers were compared with the replies given seven years ago; but as many new questions were asked in the second interview, there was scope for several correlations based on their more recent replies. Altogether 650 tables were studied and the report is divided into six main sections: Sex Education; Venereal Diseases; Contraception; Premarital Pregnancies; Sexual Intercourse. The final chapter considers the implications for future social policies.

The group under study actually spans the age range from seventeen years six months to nineteen years six months, so seven years later their age will vary from twenty-four to twenty-six. But for the sake of convenience they are referred to as eighteen-year-old boys and girls, and twenty-five-year-old men and women.

Some chapters, especially the next one, report negative results – that is to say, hypotheses were tested and found to be null. I am aware that a page reporting negative results does not make for interesting reading and so I have limited these to cases where the hypothesis has often been assumed to be valid despite the lack of factual evidence. Many more statistical associations were tested and found to be negative, but are not reported here.

Some of the more important tables are in the text and others are in Appendix A. But on many occasions I have summarized the results of a table in the text without setting out the figures in tabular form. This is not for the benefit of readers who dislike columns of figures, but it is intended as a caution to others who, like me, prefer to get more of the information from the statistics and then draw their own conclusions. Such a procedure, to be recommended in a large-scale research, would be unwise in this case; the inclusion of a large number of tables in this report would give a false impression of accuracy not justified by the size of the group, nor by the way the material has been collected.

Percentages given in the text and tables are usually based on the whole group of 376. Where this is not the case it is made clear in the text. Although the results have been subjected to an extensive and sometimes complex analysis, the percentages are intended to give an idea of approximate proportions and to support general statements or tentative suggestions; they should be regarded as indicators, not as exact measurements.

The earlier research was a large-scale descriptive investigation involving multi-variate analysis of many factors. This follow-up research involves a smaller number of informants but the problems are studied in greater depth. It is not, of course, a sex education book, still less a manual to help people to develop their sexual potential. It is addressed to those people who accept that improvements can be made in the type of sex education given in schools, in the campaign to prevent the spread of venereal diseases, and in the provision of contraceptive advice and supplies.

2. Sex Education

When the boys were eighteen, they were all asked if they had ever received any sex education at school, and over half (55 per cent) replied in the negative. Seven years ago schools were more likely to give sex education to girls than to boys. Altogether 84 per cent of the girls compared with 45 per cent of the boys had received some kind of formal sex education when they were at school.

The girls more often received sex education than the boys in all types of schools except for private schools. Boys who attended grammar schools were no more likely to be given sex education than other boys who went to secondary modern or comprehensive schools. The lack of sex education was exactly where it was most needed. It was the working-class boys who were least likely to learn about sex from their parents and were least likely to receive sex education at schools.

There were signs of a lack of frankness in the teaching. Sex education, when it did occur, seemed to concentrate on biological and physiological matters and seemed to be unrelated to human affairs, except when it was wholly concerned with putting across a particular moral point of view, as was often the case with the girls.

Sex education did not appear to have any immediate effect on the sex behaviour of the teenagers. Those boys who were given some form of sex education were neither more nor less experienced in their sexual activities; similarly there is no association between girls who received sex education and the level of their sex activity. The sexually active teenagers tended to find out about sex from their friends and to eschew information or advice from their parents or teachers. Sex education given in the schools did not seem to inhibit sex activities nor did it seem to encourage them by 'putting ideas into their heads', as some have feared.

2.2   Sex Education Now and Then

When we saw them seven years later the men and women were again asked about the sex education they had received at school. In five cases it was the same question so that I could compare their replies with their earlier answers. In addition they were asked ten other questions about sex education.

When we first interviewed them as teenagers, about half the boys (45 per cent) said they had received some kind of sex education: now this has dropped to 32 per cent. Among the girls 84 per cent said they had received sex education: this time it is 50 per cent. So 13 per cent of the men and 34 per cent of the women think so little of the sex education they did get that either they have forgotten about it, or more likely, they no longer think our inadequate attempts to teach them are worth the name of sex education. Indeed this became clear when they were asked to describe the sex education and in many cases it was confined to one session, either an outside speaker or a teacher devoting just one period to it.

Those boys who did not get any sex education were more likely to have missed GCE, left school at fifteen and to have come from a working-class home. Among those who had taken GCE, 62 per cent did not receive sex education, whereas 72 per cent of those who did not take GCE did not get any sex education either. Among the boys who left school at eighteen or over, 58 per cent did not have sex education, whereas 72 per cent of those who left school at fifteen did not get sex education. When social class is judged by the occupation of the father, 60 per cent middle-class, 70 per cent non-manual working-class, and 73 per cent manual workers did not receive sex education.

A similar trend is not reflected amongst the girls. Indeed the tendency is slightly the other way. Girls who had taken GCE were less likely to have had sex education than those who had not taken it (54 per cent compared with 47 per cent).

Girls who left school at eighteen or over were less likely to have had sex education than those who left at fifteen (57 per cent compared with 45 per cent). More middle-class girls (53 per cent) did not have sex education compared with girls whose fathers were non-manual working-class (46 per cent) or manual workers (also 46 per cent).

This trend among the girls is surprising and it may reflect a fear among teachers at schools in working-class areas that girls are so vulnerable that they must be warned of the dangers. If this speculation has any foundation, then the teachers would be more helpful if they put the emphasis on birth control. This is clearly not the case, for only 1 per cent of the group had ever discussed birth control with their teacher and protection for the girls is limited to warnings about the dangers of giving in to the desires of boys or to admonitions about the immorality of premarital sexual intercourse.

There is little cause for satisfaction with the situation even for the girls when half of them maintain that they have not received any sex education. But they do seem to be better off than the boys. Middle-class girls may be less likely to get sex education at school, but they are more likely to get help and advice from their parents, especially from their mothers. Working-class boys, in contrast, are less likely to get information about sex from their parents and are also less likely to get it at school.

2.3 Was It Helpful?

The girls were not only more likely to receive sex education, but it was also more likely to be given at an appropriate age. Table 2/1 shows that 8 per cent of the girls but only 2 per cent of the boys were given sex education at primary school. By the age of fourteen, 39 per cent of the girls and 16 per cent of the boys had received sex education. After this age nearly all boys and girls have learnt about sex in other ways and the most the teacher can do is to correct misinformation. It seems likely that sex education was not very valuable for the 14 per cent of the boys and 10 per cent of the girls who did not get it until fifteen or over.

TABLE 2/1. Age received sex education

Age	Boys %	Girls %
Under 12	2	8
12–14	14	31
15–16	10	9
17+	4	1
DK	2	1
None	68	50
No. (100%)	219	157

Although it is possible to get some idea of the amount of sex education, it is far more difficult to get a qualitative assessment. If we use age as an indication, it seems possible that only a third (39 per cent) of the girls and less than a fifth (16 per cent) of the boys received useful sex education. The informants were also asked to describe their sex education and their replies were put into three categories. Most often (15 per cent boys, 26 per cent girls) it was one session only, sometimes from a teacher and at other times from an outsider. The most usual outside speaker was a doctor. It is hard to understand why doctors should be thought to be especially suitable; few of them have received training about sexual problems and there is no reason to believe that they have any particular knowledge beyond anatomy. It is even harder to understand why clergymen should be chosen for this task because inevitably they will start from assumptions that a large number of pupils do not accept. It is also probable that an outsider would not have the teaching skills to hold the attention of the class and present information on a subject that most of them will think of as a giggle. Even when it is given by an experienced teacher, it is often no more than one short talk to the fifth form or a welcome diversion after O levels.

The one-session approach is probably the least satisfactory form of sex education. Next in our descriptive categories were those (8 per cent boys, 4 per cent girls) who were allowed to discuss it informally in class when it fitted in with the subject being taught. This might have been very good, depending a great deal on the personality and the training of the teacher. But it was more likely to be haphazard and was unlikely to cover all the ground in a systematic way.

Finally, it appears from answers to our questions that 9 per cent of the boys and 20 per cent of the girls had a formal course in sex education. Again this obviously varied in quality, but it is probably fair to suggest that only one in ten of the boys and one in five of the girls can be said to have received adequate sex education.

It may be better to judge the quality by asking for the subjective views of the pupils. So we asked everyone to look back on their sex education and tell us if they thought it had been helpful. Just 3 per cent of each sex were enthusiastic and another 8 per cent of the boys and 9 per cent of the girls said it was helpful.

In contrast 20 per cent of the boys and 36 per cent of the girls thought it was unhelpful; 11 per cent of these boys and 24 per cent of these girls were quite positive in their condemnation, some even suggesting that the information they were given was actually misleading. The percentages given in the last two paragraphs are based on the whole group. Considering only those who had received some kind of sex education, 28 per cent found it helpful and 68 per cent did not.

The sex education being described here was given about ten years ago and it is reasonable to suppose that things are better today. It is certainly true that more schools have decided to give sex education, but it is less certain that the quality has improved with the quantity. There is still considerable controversy about what should and should not be included. We asked this group if they could suggest ways in which their sex education could have been better and it is not unfair to suggest that the views of the client should be given some weight.

Of course there were many different opinions, although there was not much difference between the men and women. A very few (3 per cent) said it could not have been better; another 5 per cent could not think of any improvements. The most frequent (11 per cent) complaint was about the teacher, who was thought to be at fault in some way. Others (7 per cent) said the information was given too late with the result that they thought they knew all about it (mistakenly, most of them now ruefully admit) and so were not inclined to listen. Others (7 per cent) felt they should have been told more about the physical side of sex and in particular they wanted to be told about the physical features of the opposite sex; boys wanted to know how to arouse girls, and girls wanted to know what excited men.

There was much less demand (1 per cent) for more information about emotional or moral aspects of sexual activities. A further 7 per cent suggested other areas where they felt they had not been given enough information.

Here are some of the things they want to learn about before they leave secondary school. What are the pleasures and dangers of sexual intercourse? What are the different ways of doing it? Do girls have an orgasm? What does it feel like? Does a condom stop sex from being enjoyable? Is the pill safe? What other kinds of contraception are there? The wonder of child-birth is a fascinating subject for primary schools, but later on they want to know how to stop having a child, not how to have one. Of course they want to know if it is really wrong to have sex before marriage. What is an abortion? Is it dangerous? What causes a miscarriage? What are the symptoms of VD? Can VD be easily cured? Boys as well as girls want to know about menstruation.

There were also requests that pupils be taught the 'correct' words because sometimes they had questions they would like to have asked but they only knew the 'rude' words. A similar but more unfortunate situation occurs when a pupil genuinely wants to know the answer to a question but he does not ask it because he fears his teacher will be shocked by the question.

2.4   *The Demand for Information*

So far I have reported on the 40 per cent (32 per cent boys, 50 per cent girls) who have received sex education. When we asked the whole group if they thought they should have been told more about sex at school, a large number (80 per cent) wanted more information and only 17 per cent replied in the negative; 3 per cent were undecided.

Of the 32 per cent men who received sex education, 23 per cent were discontented and only 8 per cent were satisfied; those who received it late tended to be the most dissatisfied. Of the 68 per cent who did not receive sex education, only 9 per cent were content with that situation and 58 per cent were dissatisfied.

Among the women who received sex education (50 per cent), 43 per cent wished they had been told more and only 5 per cent were satisfied; those who received it late tended to be the most dissatisfied. Of the 50 per cent who did not receive sex education, only 12 per cent were content and the other 37 per cent were dissatisfied. Another 3 per cent were unsure.

So it is clear that among both men and women there is an overwhelming demand for sex education, especially from those who did not get any information at school. But even those who received some form of sex education were not satisfied and it is certain that the overall demand is not being met.

2.5 The Source of Information

Seven years ago we asked how they found out about conception and we asked a similar question again this time. In the original question they were restricted to naming only one source of knowledge, but this time they were encouraged to name all the people who had helped them to find out about sex.* Consequently the percentages in the replies from the second interview are higher but the proportions are similar with a few striking exceptions.

Table A1/3 (in Appendix A) gives: first, the replies from the original sample of 790 eighteen-year-old boys and girls; second, the replies of the 376 extracted from the original sample, which are quite remarkably close to the larger sample as noted in section 1.4; third, the replies from the same men and women obtained seven years later.

* For a note on the advantages and disadvantages of questions permitting more than one answer, see section 1.5.

The number of times each source of knowledge was mentioned has increased in every case except for the teacher and to a much smaller extent for the mother as far as the girls are concerned. In the first interview the teacher was named by 11 per cent of the boys, but now only 5 per cent mention the teacher; originally 18 per cent of the girls named the teacher, now it is only 8 per cent. As they were allowed to name more than one source this time, it would not have been surprising if more had mentioned the teacher, but in fact the number of times the teacher is named is less than half. The only explanation that seems to fit such a remarkable change is that seven years later the men and women decided that the information they received from the teacher was unimportant or unnecessary. When they first gave this information at eighteen, like most people of that age, they may not have looked back on their school days with much favour, but by the age of twenty-five when they answered the question again, they thought even less of the help they had received at school.

At the second interview girls named more sources than boys; 157 girls mentioned 282 sources (an average of 1·16 per girl) and 219 boys mentioned 336 sources (an average of 1·05 per boy). This probably accounts for the sharp rise in the number of girls who mentioned school friends; it was originally far the most frequently mentioned source (40 per cent girls, 62 per cent boys) and now there is a rise of 25 per cent among the girls at the second interview when two thirds of both sexes mentioned school friends (65 per cent girls, 63 per cent boys).

There is a noticeable increase in the number who mentioned their fathers as a source of information, but the figures are so small that it cannot be regarded as significant. Perhaps it might add a little statistical weight to the remark by Mark Twain that when he was young his father was painfully ignorant but by the time he was past twenty he was delighted to see how much the old man had improved.

But far more significant is the striking rise in the number of men and women who mentioned workmates and books as a source of information. In the first interview 3 per cent of the boys named workmates but at the second interview this had gone up to 11 per cent; 2 per cent of the girls mentioned it the first time, now it is 16 per cent. Of course some (18 per cent) of them were not at work when they were first asked this question, but this does not altogether account for the four-fold increase. A possible reason is that as they grow up, the young men and women have a vague worry about their capability for sex and feel that they do not understand it quite well enough, and even perhaps wonder if they are getting as much as they should out of sex. So they discuss it with their workmates and in some ways this can be quite educative, but it is also a way of acquiring a mass of misinformation. Many sexual myths are spread at work, sometimes when the older workers intentionally mislead or frighten the new entrants. The initiation ceremonies for apprentices and other new-comers often have rather unpleasant sexual connotations.

There is an even greater increase in the number who mentioned books as a source of information; originally 8 per cent boys, now 26 per cent; and 4 per cent girls, now 20 per cent. This large increase confirms the suspicion I had seven years ago when I suggested that the many thousands of books on this subject printed for adolescents are read after they have heard about conception from other sources, if indeed they are read at all. It is possible that these books are a useful aid to correct the misinformation and myths obtained from other sources. But they are of limited value for two reasons. For many of the less well educated group, books are expensive and not the usual form of communication. Unfortunately it is also true that many of the books are not good; two teachers (Hill and Lloyd-Jones, 1970) examined forty-two books on sex education, all those obtainable at that time, and they found that most of them were obscure, inaccurate and often badly written, and that nearly all of them confused factual information with moral exhortations.

At the first interview some boys and girls answered that 'they just picked it up as they went along', but this and similar answers were not accepted by the interviewer who was instructed to probe for a more accurate source. However, this may have put too much pressure on the informant, so in the second interview this type of answer was accepted and put into the category 'self-taught'. Altogether 24 per cent said they were self-taught, 64 per cent said they had learnt from school friends and 13 per cent from workmates. This suggests that what they are learning is sexual folklore rather than knowledge. In most sections of the community discussions among young people about sex are frequent, some would say too frequent, but it is still true that the information they are acquiring is limited, misleading and inadequate.

2.6   The Best and the Usual Way

When the men and women were asked what is the best way to learn about sex, there were many suggestions.

'They should have TV programmes at school. Children are more interested in TV than anything else.'

'It's better to leave it to the schools.'

'Wait until they ask questions and then answer them truthfully.'

'Give them a book to read.'

'Have a chat with the doctor.'

'Experience.'

'It requires more publicity. Take a minute in the middle of *Coronation Street*. Take a full page in the *Daily Mirror*. It's mainly a problem with the working classes.'

'I think you only learn from example. I think you learn about sex after you're married. Nothing you learn at school sinks in.'

It is difficult to quantify these various ideas, but when they are asked to name the best person to learn from, it immediately becomes clear that there is a wide divergence between the kind of help they would have preferred and the kind they got.

Most of the women (66 per cent)* chose the mother, but there were also many others who mentioned the father (47 per cent) and the teacher (50 per cent). The number who mentioned the parent of the opposite sex reflects the idea

* This is another question in which they were allowed to name more than one person, so the percentages add up to more than one hundred.

widely held (noted in section 2.3) that girls feel that they do not know enough about boys, and vice versa.

The men were overwhelmingly in favour of the teacher (63 per cent) and quite a large number also chose the father (33 per cent) and the mother (30 per cent). Taken together it is clear that the majority would rather learn from the teacher (57 per cent) than from parents (42 per cent). So if we are to consider the views of the adolescent, and we should, then sex education at school is more often preferred to learning from parents.

The only other group of any significance in Table 2/2 consists of those who maintain that the best way to learn about sex is from experience. As modern education puts the emphasis on the 'discovery method', that is, learning through experience and investigation, we should not be too abashed if some

TABLE 2/2. The best way to find out about sex compared with the way they actually found out*

Source of knowledge	MEN		WOMEN	
	Method preferred %	Actual method %	Method preferred %	Actual method %
Mother	30	8	66	24
Father	33	10	47	7
Teacher	63	5	50	8
Sibling	0	1	1	4
Clergyman	0	0	0	1
Experience	16	24	9	24
School friends	2	63	3	65
Workmates	1	11	1	16
Books	7	26	4	20
TV/Films	5	0	6	0
Others	5	4	8	10
DK	2	0	1	0
No. (100%)	219	219	157	157

* Informants were allowed to give more than one answer to each question so percentages add up to more than one hundred.

pupils want to apply this method and decide to find the answer to their sexual questions from experiments. But there are two points to notice about the 16 per cent boys and 9 per cent girls who want to find out about sex in this way. First, it is not the result of sex education because nearly all (83 per cent) of those who chose this method had not had any sex education. Second, it is not a method to be recommended because the evidence shows that experience in this case is not a good teacher. Indeed it is one of the central conclusions of this study that sexual knowledge is something most people have failed to pick up from experience.

No other item is chosen with any frequency. There is a small demand for books (6 per cent), TV and films (6 per cent). Hardly anyone mentioned siblings or workmates, and only one person in the whole sample thought that a clergyman was the best person to help him learn about sex.

It is significant that only 2 per cent boys and 3 per cent girls preferred to find out from school friends. In Table 2/2 it can be seen that in fact 63 per cent of the boys and 65 per cent of the girls learnt this way, but this is not what they want. The younger generations emphatically reject the idea that it is best to pick it up from friends and it is reasonable to assume that they found out about sex in this way because we adults did not provide a better method before their curiosity was aroused. The preferred and actual source only coincides in one group of any size: those girls, about a quarter of the total number, who were informed by their mothers.

Neither the actual source of information nor the preferred source seems to be related to social class. But many of those who thought that the teacher was the best source of knowledge had not had any sex education and, not surprisingly, those who had found their sex education helpful named the teacher; those who had received sex education but thought it had been unhelpful were more likely to choose mother, father or experience.

Of the 215 who said the teacher was the best source, 185 (86 per cent) thought they could have been told more about sex at school. Even those who chose mother or father as the best person felt they should have been told more at school. Of the 168 who chose mother, 139 (83 per cent) wanted more information at school; and of the 146 who chose father, 121 (83 per cent) wanted more information at school; but of the 49 who chose experience, 32 (65 per cent) wanted more information at school. So even among those who feel that the best way was to find out for themselves, many wanted more help at school and nearly all those who preferred to learn from their parents felt that the school should have told them more about sex.

This section has shown that despite the increase in the amount of sex education, we are failing to provide for the needs of young people. Modern educationalists who maintain, with some justification, that young people learn best from others of their own age should accept that this is an exception to the educational tenet, and this is not difficult to understand. In this whole new world of mystery opening up before these children, they do not want to be led by the blind. They may not wish to be told what they may, or may not do, but they do want to get factual information from someone who knows his way around this new world so that they can be helped to avoid the obstacles and discover the pleasures.

2.7   Parents or Teachers

There are still people who maintain that school is not the right place to give sex education. They argue that children mature at different ages and any large classroom will contain children of such wide levels of maturity that what is right for one child cannot be right for another; therefore the only satisfactory way to give sex education is for the parent to give the information when the child is ready to receive it. In this way sex education can start early and will be a continuous development carefully and lovingly carried out over many years.

This is an attractive argument and indeed it is an almost ideal programme for moral education. At present it is still an unrealistic programme, but certainly could be a legitimate aim for future generations. The people we interviewed were more practical and were not so positive that parents were the best people to give sex education. Although the earlier

2

research had shown that 48 per cent had never at any time received any advice about sex from either their father or mother, a surprisingly high number (37 per cent) did not feel dissatisfied with the help they had received from their parents.

All the men and women were asked if they felt they could have been told more about sex at school and by their parents. Table 2/3 compares their replies to these two questions.

TABLE 2/3. Do you feel you could have been told more about sex at school and by your parents?

Need more information	At school %	By parents %
Yes	80	60
No	17	37
DK/NK	3	3
No. (100%)	376	376

There is little difference between the replies given by men and women, so the results are given together. These show that the strong demand for information from the school is greater than the demand that parents give more help. It is still a majority, indeed nearly two out of three, who feel they could have been told more about sex by their parents, but it is clear that most people expect more from school than from the home.

For years we have been saying that parents are the best people to give their children sex education, if only they would. This may still be true for the child before puberty, but after that it is possible that there is too big a barrier in some families. It is not always easy for a teenager to ask mother or father for help with sexual problems. In some families it is impossible to discuss such things in the home. This has always been true to a certain extent, and it may be truer today than ever before because our ideas on sexual morality are changing so fast that what was disallowed in one generation is permitted in the next.

But it is false to think of it as a dichotomy – a choice be-

tween parents and school. In ideal circumstances sex education will be carried on in both the home and the school. At
the first elementary stages when the child is learning how
babies are born, most people would want the parents to play
a major part because the information can be given simply and
naturally as the child asks questions.

In fact we seem to have got the emphasis the wrong way
round. At present it is the schools that are likely to be teaching the simple facts on conception, often too late. Most of the
sex education books and the classes in school concentrate on
the straightforward anatomical details of the male and female
genitals leading up to the sex act. I suspect this is because it is
the least difficult and least controversial part of sex education. But this is the part that can best be done by parents
because most children will ask how babies are born long
before they get to secondary school age.

The school should be concerned about teaching the more
complex and more debatable aspects of sex education. Even
in ideal circumstances it is probably better if the parents are
not left to do the whole task on their own and the assistance
of the school is almost sure to be needed at the post-puberty
stages of sex education. Furthermore my earlier research
shows quite clearly that circumstances are a long way from
the ideal and many parents cannot help their children with
their sexual problems. At the very least sex education has the
function of supplying information parents have been unable
to give, and preparing the children so that they can be more
helpful when they become parents.

The Longford Report on Pornography (1972) contains a
special section on sex education. The committee objects to
much of the sex education that they imagine is going on in
schools and in particular to books and broadcasts which
'describe techniques of sexual congress, especially when, as
so often happens, it is accompanied by, or given through, the
medium of visual presentation'. They conclude that 'sex education is primarily an affair for parents'. This chapter, and
particularly this section, makes it obvious that the ideas of the
Longford Committee are quite impractical. The choice is
between learning about sex at school, or from dirty jokes. If

we had to rely upon our parents to educate us about sex, most of us would still be waiting.

2.8 The New Generation of Parents

The men and women were asked if they thought they would be able to help their children to learn about sex. Nearly all of them (91 per cent) said they would; only 3 per cent said they would not and another 6 per cent were not sure. This shows a high level of confidence despite the dissatisfaction with their own sex education, or possibly because of it.

Perhaps the wording of the question was wrong. It is reasonable to assume that almost every parent will be able to provide some help, but it is doubtful if many of these men and women will be very good at providing all the help their children will need. Indeed a later question makes it clear that more than one in three felt that they did not know all they needed to know about sex. There were 152 (40 per cent) who felt their sexual knowledge was inadequate and 137 of them (i.e. 36 per cent of the whole group) still felt that they could help their children to learn about sex.

Of those who felt satisfied with the help given by their own parents, 91 per cent say they are ready to help their children; of those who were dissatisfied with the help given by their parents, 92 per cent are going to help their children. So it makes no difference whether their parents were helpful or not.

There is some slight indication, however, that helpful sex education made them more likely to say they would help their children. Only a very few (2 per cent) who had sex education which they regarded as helpful, said they could not help their children; but 9 per cent who had what they regarded as unhelpful sex education said they could not help their children, and 11 per cent with no sex education said they could not help. This suggests the possibility that some of the sex education was valuable, but the figures are small because the great majority felt they could be helpful whether they had received sex education or not.

In this group 45 per cent had children and another 26 per cent were married, so within a few years most of them will have to fulfil their commitment to help their children about sex. When it gets to the point, the number who actually do so may not be quite as high as 91 per cent, but even so it is evident that this generation of parents are going to be less reserved and more outspoken than earlier generations.

But it is a limited consolation that more parents are willing to try, for there are considerable difficulties caused by ignorance and language. Indeed there is the possibility that many of these people are over-confident and may provide misleading information, or may implant fears instead of confidence.

This again raises the question of how much help we can provide for the parents. Inevitably there is the problem, common to many health education courses, that those who need the help will not take part and any scheme to help parents will be filled by those who do not really need to be helped. But this is not a strong enough reason to abandon such a scheme. Even those who are said not to require such a course would almost certainly gain something from it. Much could also be learnt from inquiring why others who need help do not come. More encouraging still, the fact that more than nine out of ten parents say they intend to help their children learn about sex indicates that the response from this generation of parents is likely to be much greater than in the past.

2.9 Inadequate Knowledge

Everyone was asked: Do you feel you know all you need to know about sex? Only 56 per cent of the men and 64 per cent of the women thought they had an adequate amount of knowledge. Women are more confident than men; males may like to give the impression that they have nothing to learn, but privately 44 per cent admitted that they wished they knew more. Some women may be less inquisitive about sex than men, nevertheless 36 per cent were prepared to admit to a stranger that they did not know all they needed to know.

So in every ten young adults of twenty-five, four feel their knowledge of sex is inadequate. If these figures are representative of the whole population, no one can claim that our sex education programme is a success.

When they were asked this question seven years ago, more girls (57 per cent) than boys (51 per cent) said they needed to know more about sex. So over the years there has been an increase of 14 per cent which reflects either more knowledge, more confidence or both.

Where were the gaps? When they were asked about things they felt unsure about, many different answers were given. The main demand was for concrete factual information (11 per cent). There was not much demand for discussions about emotional or moral problems (3 per cent). Quite often sex education programmes are criticized because there is not enough emphasis put on love, but these people felt they knew enough about romantic love and wanted rather more practical down-to-earth information. The men wanted to know more about women and the women more about men. They wanted to learn how to get more out of their sexual activities.

2.10 The Effect on Behaviour

Until recently there was surprisingly little research on the effects of any kind of education. Some of us may still be able to recite the names of Plantagenet kings, but there is a growing suspicion that most of the material fed to us at school is not retained or used later in life. This may be just as true of sex education as most of the other subjects taught at school. If sex education is said to be effective, it should mean more than the ability to remember and recall the facts imparted in the classroom; it should continue to act as the basis for future development. A simple test of sexual knowledge would not be a good measure of the effectiveness of sex education. If it is of some value, it should be possible to find some demonstrable effect both on behaviour and on attitudes. This is what I tried to find when I compared those who had received sex education with those who had not over a whole range of subjects.

It seemed to have had little effect on early sexual activities. Those who had received sex education were neither more nor less likely to have had sexual intercourse before the age of nineteen. This finding may be important to those who believe that sex education encourages young people to experiment and so leads to promiscuity. Table A2/1 (in Appendix A) shows that sex education has no effect on the age when a boy or girl first has sexual intercourse.

In Table 2/4 the first partner is put into one of four categories and the table is given in numbers instead of percentages. The table shows that:

Of the 78 people who first had intercourse with their spouse, 42 (54 per cent) had received no sex education.
Of the 72 who had premarital sexual intercourse with their spouse, 40 (56 per cent) had received no sex education.
Of the 129 who had their first intercourse with a 'steady' friend, 81 (63 per cent) had received no sex education.
Of the 71 who first had sexual intercourse with an acquaintance, 51 (72 per cent) had received no sex education.

TABLE 2/4. The type of partner at the time of first intercourse: those who received sex education compared with those who did not

| Type of first partner | BOYS | | GIRLS | | |
	No sex education	Sex education	No sex education	Sex education	Total
Spouse	18	8	24	28	78
Later spouse	13	8	27	24	72
Steady	61	27	20	21	129
Acquaintance	48	19	3	1	71
NK or NA	9	8	4	5	26
	149	70	78	79	376

Table 2/4 does suggest that sex education may have some influence on the choice of the first partner. Those who received sex education were more likely to have premarital intercourse with the person they married if they had any sexual experience before marriage.

Towards the end of the interview we asked all those with sexual experience to tell us how many people they had had sexual intercourse with during the last year. Not everyone answered this question, but 65 per cent of the men and 85 per cent of the women claimed to have had one partner, 19 per cent of the men and 6 per cent of the women said they had had intercourse with more than one person, and 17 per cent of the men and 3 per cent of the women had had more than two partners. Table A2/2 compares those who did have sex education with those who did not. (For the definitions of 'adequate' and 'poor' sex education, see section 2.12.) The table shows that 98 out of 149 (66 per cent) men who did not have sex education, and 45 of the 70 (64 per cent) who did receive sex education had one partner; 69 of the 78 (88 per cent) women who did not receive sex education and 65 of the 79 (82 per cent) women who did have sex education had one partner. So those who received sex education were not more likely to be promiscuous or more faithful.

All the men were asked if they had ever made a girl pregnant before marriage. In reply 34 (16 per cent) of the men had been responsible for a premarital pregnancy and 32 (20 per cent) of the women said they had become pregnant before marriage. Among the men, 21 of the 34 (62 per cent) had not had sex education; this compares with the 68 per cent of the whole group who had not received sex education. Among the women 18 of the 32 (56 per cent) had not had sex education; this compares with 50 per cent in the whole group. This demonstrates that those who have had a premarital pregnancy are neither more nor less likely to have received sex education.

The girl friends (or wives) of 17 (8 per cent) of the men and 12 (8 per cent) of the women had had an abortion. Of these 60 per cent of the men and 58 per cent of the women had not had sex education. This proportion is not significantly different from the whole group.

Among the men, 44 (20 per cent) thought they had caught one of the venereal diseases at least once, but 13 of these were not infected; 6 (4 per cent) girls thought they had caught it but 3 were not infected. Of the 34 men and women who were definitely infected, 20 (60 per cent) did not get sex education at school. This does not support the claim made by some people that sex education is helping to spread the venereal diseases.

Similar calculations show that sex education had no influence on the number of steady girl friends or boy friends each individual had before marriage, no influence on the age that they got married, no influence on the number of times that they had sexual intercourse, and no influence on the number of children they had.

One type of behaviour where sex education appears to have had some slight effect is on the use of contraceptives. The extent that the different birth control methods are used is discussed in Chapter 4.

For these purposes the group is simply classified into four categories; 54 per cent of the men and 62 per cent of the women said they always used some type of contraceptive; 17 per cent of the men and 7 per cent of the women said they occasionally used one; 21 per cent of the men and 25 per cent of the women said they never did; the remaining 8 per cent of the men and 6 per cent of the women did not have sexual intercourse.

Table 2/5 shows that 34 of the 47 (72 per cent) men never took precautions and did not have sex education, but 76 of the 118 (64 per cent) who always used contraceptives did not

TABLE 2/5. Sex education and the use of contraceptives

	MEN			WOMEN		
Extent of contraceptive use	No sex education	Some sex education	Total	No sex education	Some sex education	Total
Always	76	42	118	46	52	98
Occasionally	26	11	37	5	5	10
Never	34	13	47	22	18	40
NA	13	4	17	5	4	9
Totals	149	70	219	78	79	157

have sex education. A similar trend can be observed among the women; 22 out of 40 (55 per cent) who never took precautions had no sex education compared with the 46 out of 98 (47 per cent) who always used contraceptives. Or to put the same information in another way, 44 per cent of those who always used contraceptives had received sex education, whereas 36 per cent who never used contraceptives had received sex education.

But these figures do not show significant differences and it would be surprising if they did because sex education is unlikely to have much effect on the use of contraceptives when birth control is hardly mentioned in most programmes of sex education. It is possible, however, that discussions about population problems and other related topics may have an indirect influence. Although sex education may have very little effect on behaviour, it may have some influence on the attitudes to sex.

2.11   The Effect on Attitudes

In section 2.6 it was reported that most (57 per cent) of the group named the teacher as the person from whom they would prefer to learn about sex. It might be expected that those who received sex education in their youth are more likely to prefer the teacher, but it does not seem to have made much difference to the replies whether they received sex education at school or not. Those who rejected teachers or parents as a good source of knowledge but felt the best way to learn about sex was from experience were not more or less likely to have received sex education.

Those who felt that they had an adequate knowledge of sex did not appear to have gained this confidence from receiving sex education; 61 per cent of those who felt they had an adequate knowledge had had sex education, and this compares with the 60 per cent without sex education who felt they knew all they needed to know. Nearly all (91 per cent) the men and women felt they would be able to help their children and this does not seem to depend on the extent of their own sex education.

During the interview the men and women were questioned about their attitudes to sex and were asked if they had particular sexual problems. In every case their replies were divided into two groups according to whether they had received sex education or not. It was found that the proportions did not differ greatly from the proportions found in the whole group. In the following lists it will be seen that about two out of three men and about half the women did not have sex education no matter what opinions they held.

Of all those men who took a very tolerant attitude to premarital sexual intercourse   70 per cent had not received sex education.
Of all those men who had disliked their first sexual intercourse
66 per cent had not received sex education.
Of all those men who reported serious sexual problems
69 per cent had not received sex education.
Of all those men who had sexual problems after marriage
67 per cent had not received sex education.
Of all those men who expressed a tolerant attitude towards homosexuals   64 per cent had not received sex education.
Of all those men who had a tolerant attitude to sex activities between different races
67 per cent had not received sex education.

Of all the men in the group
68 per cent had not received sex education.

Of all those women who took a tolerant attitude to premarital sexual intercourse   46 per cent had not received sex education.
Of all those women who disliked their first sexual intercourse
47 per cent had not received sex education.
Of all those women who reported serious sexual problems
46 per cent had not received sex education.
Of all those women who had sexual problems after marriage
50 per cent had not received sex education.
Of all those women who expressed a tolerant attitude towards homosexuals   53 per cent had not received sex education.
Of all those women who had a tolerant attitude to sex activities between different races
50 per cent had not received sex education.

Of all the women in the group
50 per cent had not received sex education.

So it does not seem as if sex education has any effect on their views about sex before marriage, nor does it prepare them for their first experience of sexual intercourse. Information obtained at school did not appear to allay or banish sexual problems, nor does sex education seem to make a person more or less tolerant of other people's sexual activities.

In only two areas was it possible to trace any statistical association between sex education and attitudes to sex. First, those who had received sex education were more likely to be aware of the dangers of venereal disease, but were not more likely to know the symptoms. This is not very surprising because in most programmes the horrifying effects of advanced syphilis (a fairly rare disease) are emphasized, but the fact that VD is a curable disease if treated early is not mentioned so often. Second, those who received sex education were more likely to say that they felt the need for more information about birth control. In fact contraceptive methods are hardly ever described in sex education programmes. But even if factual information about contraceptives is not provided, those who get education seem to attach more importance to knowledge about birth control.

2.12   Adequate and Poor

As the effects seem to be so slight, the question arises whether sex education in general is ineffective, or whether it depends on the type and amount of sex education. It is difficult to answer this question because the courses vary widely from school to school.

In the whole group 40 per cent had some sex education; 21 per cent had only one session, but 6 per cent had informal discussions and 13 per cent had a set course. Although the quality of these last two categories obviously varied, it was decided to classify them as 'adequate' and the others as 'poor'. So 17 per cent men and 24 per cent women had 'adequate' sex education, while 15 per cent men and 26 per cent women had 'poor' sex education. These arbitrary definitions seem to be in accord with the opinions of the men and women, because 36 per cent of those who received adequate sex education

found it helpful, whereas only 22 per cent who received poor
sex education said it was helpful.

These two definitions were used on many variables of
behaviour and attitudes to see if there were any differences.
Only a very few emerged. Whether they had adequate or
poor sex education made no difference to the number of girl/
boy friends they had, the amount of sex they had, the extent
of premarital sexual intercourse, promiscuity, knowledge
about sex, the kind of problems they experienced, their tolerance towards other people's sex activities or to the help they
intended to give their own children.

For example, Table A2/2 shows that there is hardly any
difference between the 73 who had adequate and the 76 who
had poor sex education in the number of partners they had
intercourse with in the last twelve months. Similarly Table
2/6 shows clearly that those receiving adequate sex education
did not feel better informed about sex than those with poor or
no sex education.

TABLE 2/6. Do you feel you know all you need to know about sex?
The answers of those with adequate sex education compared with
those who had poor or no sex education

Sex education	Men and women who felt they had adequate knowledge		
	Yes %	No and DK %	Total %
None	36	24	60
Poor	13	8	21
Adequate	11	8	19
Total %	60	40	100
No.	224	142	376

There were signs that the type of sex education they were
given did sometimes have an effect. For example, about 57
per cent of the whole group thought that the teacher was the
best person to give information about sex, but among those
who had received adequate sex education the figure rises to
70 per cent. Similarly 13 per cent of the whole group were in

favour of learning about sex from experience, but only a few (4 per cent) of those who had received adequate sex education held this view.

But when it comes to avoiding trouble, the type of sex education appears to be immaterial. Those who had received adequate sex education were not less likely to become pregnant before marriage, were not less likely to have had an abortion and were not less likely to have been infected by a venereal disease. But although it did not seem to help them to avoid trouble, they seemed to be more aware of it.

Those with adequate sex education were more likely to have heard about VD although they were not any better at describing the symptoms correctly. Furthermore those with adequate sex education were more likely to want to be informed about birth control; 27 out of 73 (37 per cent) with adequate sex education wished to be better informed compared with 19 out of 76 (25 per cent) with poor education (Table 2/7). But those with adequate sex education were not more likely to use contraceptives.

TABLE 2/7. Those who felt the need for more information on birth control: those with adequate sex education compared with those who had poor or no sex education

Sex education	Desire for more information		
	Yes	No	Total
None	56	171	227
Poor	19	57	76
Adequate	27	46	73
Total %	27	73	100
No.	102	274	376

So the division into poor and adequate sex education has produced only a few relatively unimportant statistical associations, but it has given us a clue as to a possible effect of sex education. Obviously there are many other powerful factors which are going to have an influence on the sexual behaviour of young people. Sex education appears to have some effect on attitudes and may help young people to be more aware of the problems, but the sort of sex education this group of twenty-five-year-old men and women received does not seem to have had much effect on their actual behaviour. It seems to have been enough to make them aware of the possibilities of change, but not enough to persuade them to do anything about it.

2.13   Reasons for Ineffectiveness

Before I started this research I had hoped to discover some of the effects of sex education. The conclusion must be either that the effects are very small, or that I have failed to find them because we did not ask the right questions.

In fact there is some evidence to suggest that education of all kinds is not the powerful force for social or individual change that we like to think it is. The Plowden report (1967) on primary schools emphasized the importance of the home and other influences outside the school on teaching effectiveness. This is consistent with the findings of Douglas's (1964) annual follow-up study of school children. Peaker (1971) studied some of the same children seen for the Plowden report and he estimates that the influence of teaching is about one third that of home circumstances. Little (1971) suggests that the difference between a good home and a bad one is far greater than the difference between good and bad teaching.

It seems likely that the young adults in this group would have forgotten much of what they learnt in school. How many of them would have been able to name the Plantagenet kings or known how many tons of coffee are exported from Brazil each year? Of course Plantagenet kings or Brazilian exports are not subjects that often exercise the mind and so the information fades away because it is not 'reinforced', as the psychologists say. But the information given about sex is not intended to be training for the mind (the usual excuse for giving school children irrelevant information) or even a subject to test the pupil's powers of recall at examination time. It is information that is intended to be remembered and used, not in the school setting but on some late Saturday evening a few years later.

The fact that education is less effective than the home is bad news for those who believe in sex education because the earlier research* showed clearly that those who are in most need of sex education are precisely those who are least likely to get it.

Apart from the lack of impact to be found in all education, there are other reasons why sex education might be particularly ineffective. One is because the teaching is not very good. Sex education can mean many things – anything from one forty-minute talk to an elaborate course on health education and biology; it can occur right across the age spectrum from primary school to A-level students. Most often it is a lecture given to a large class, half of whom think they know it all already. Outside opposition to sex education sometimes means that it is given by nervous teachers using over-cautious books and audio-visual aids. It is possible that really good sex education is much more effective than I was able to show in the previous section because the arbitrary division between adequate and poor did not really differentiate between good and bad.

In other countries where the school curriculum is decided by a central educational body, there is an opportunity to look for the effects of a more consistent level of sex education. In Sweden where sex instruction has been given to the majority of its school children for almost thirty years and where it has been compulsory in schools since 1956, the indicators of sexual maladjustments have shown a continuous rate of increase as in most other Western countries; the incidence of gonorrhoea is higher, especially among the young; more children are born out of wedlock; there are more legal abortions and more divorces. If these indicators are to be the only criteria, the claim that Swedish sex education has failed could be justified.

But these sexual maladjustments are on the increase in all modern industrial countries and most of them do not provide any kind of sex education in their schools. The increases in the rates of VD, illegitimacy, abortion and divorce are the

* *The Sexual Behaviour of Young People*, p. 249.

result of fundamental changes in the attitudes to sex which, at the same time, affects the attitudes to sex education itself. As sexual mores change, the demand is for more sex education, not less, because many people hope that this will slow down the increase of sexual problems, in the belief that knowledge about sex is more likely to restrain than increase social or moral maladjustments.

It is possible that the apparent lack of effect of even a long course of sex education may be because the measuring instruments available to social research are too blunt. Perhaps the effects of sex education are too subtle to be measured by these inexact devices. Changes in attitudes are much harder to detect than changes in behaviour. Rogers (1971) studied the effects of the BBC/TV sex education programmes for primary schools and found that they reduced emotional attitudes and misunderstandings about sex. The results in this chapter support the idea that sex education is more likely to change attitudes than behaviour.

If we can devise a course of sex education which helps to modify attitudes, this may be as much as we can hope for and may indeed be as much as we need. Attempts to change behaviour by means of sex education programmes usually look suspiciously like a set of instructions or a list of negative rules.

2.14   The Changing Sexual Scene

It is not enough to try to persuade young people to accept the existing moral code. Indeed any rigid static code of behaviour would soon be outdated. We live in a state of transition and this is not temporary. This situation of instability is going to continue for a long time.

There have already been vast changes in the last few years. As children reach puberty at an earlier age and extra schooling postpones the age of financial independence, attitudes to premarital sexual intercourse have changed, especially since contraceptives are more effective and more readily available. Compare the attitude to sex today with the ideas of only five, ten or fifteen years ago. So what is it going to be like for the children who are now in school; in five years when they are married; in ten years when they have a family; in fifteen years when they will be called old-fashioned by their own teenage children? Sex education, if it is to be any good, must help the pupils to adapt to new conditions, new ideas, different ethics, different values.

There are many signs that there will be other fundamental changes in our attitudes to sex in the near future. For example, the traditional attitude to marriage is changing. Many people now regard marriage as no more than an economic and social institution, whereas in the past it was regarded as a sacred bond at one end of the scale, and at the other end simply as a way of legitimizing an unexpected pregnancy.

At present we believe that the only satisfactory way of bringing up children is with both parents in the home, but in fact as many as 20 per cent of the population do not have this privilege, and perhaps we will adopt some of the ideals and beliefs of the Israeli kibbutzim or of the very interesting experimental communes recently set up in this country.

Already the state has taken over many of the duties which were performed by the head of the family in earlier times; we accept numerous free services and subsidies, and prohibitions on the ill-treatment and exploitation of children. The family unit is becoming weaker as we change from the large three-generation family to the smaller two-generation family.

The idea that women can only find fulfilment as wives and mothers is not so strong as it used to be. As we now have the technical means to abolish unplanned childbirth, we are moving away from the idea that sexual intercourse outside marriage is always sinful. Above all the looming problem of over-population will force us to change our sexual code in the near future.

It is the pupils, not the older generations, who are going to have to cope with this changing situation. We must educate for change. This does not mean we should neglect to give the basic facts, but we must also teach pupils how to use the facts, not merely give them a set of rules.

This is true of all education. The rapidity of changing technology and the advent of automation means that everyone now at school must re-train for a different job at least once in his working career. So there is little point in modern education if it trains a person for a particular job. It has a much deeper, more important task. The teacher's job is to help his pupils to acquire the capacity to adapt to, and cope with, these rapid changes. And just as this is true of all education, it is certainly true of sex education.

For all these reasons, our hope should be that sex education will have some effect on attitudes. It does not matter so much if it does not appear to have a direct influence on behaviour in the immediate future. What may be the solution for today in one situation may not be the solution for tomorrow in different circumstances.

The aim of sex education should be to prepare the pupils for the future so that they can adapt to new situations, new sexual ethics, and even new moral values.

2.15 Do We Need It?

The results of this research suggest that the effects of sex education on behaviour are very small and the effects on attitudes are fairly slight. One solution would be to give it all up and stop wasting time and money. But all changes in social policy have some effect and this is also true of a negative policy which seeks to ban or stop something. Those who advocate a ban on sex education will find there are new problems to solve, not all of them obvious.

Studies of children's sexual knowledge indicate that when information is not forthcoming, the child makes up his own explanations and fills the gaps in his knowledge with fantasy. For example, pregnancy is often thought to be connected with food intake, and birth is seen as the result of an operation. Many of the confusing myths about sex are developed from these childish theories and fantasies.

When the child grows up to adolescence or young adulthood, commercial enterprise sets out to fill the gap left by inadequate sex education. Nearly all the educational publishers have put out one or more sex education books. Hill and Lloyd-Jones (1970) studied forty-two of them and report: 'They are in general inaccurate, misleading (in some cases deliberately deceitful), and almost invariably contain insidious moralising of the worst kind. They are often badly written, and badly produced by publishers who know that any production of this kind is snapped up by parents and teachers, provided only that it avoids a too frank presentation of the physical, psychological and social facts.' Books are still in circulation which state that masturbation is harmful. Books published in the last ten years refer to semen as 'colourless and odourless', contain diagrams in which the urethra is labelled as the vagina, give the average age of puberty as fifteen, claim that those who have sexual intercourse without intending to marry each other are mentally ill, and declare that it is against the law to have intercourse before you are married. There are also some comic examples of unconscious humour. If you are worried about the child's masturbation, you should call for 'a skilled outsider who may be able to put his finger on the cause of the trouble fairly quickly' (Dawkins, 1964); Barnes (1966) writes, 'Girls often don't know what is coming until the last moment'; and he warns that a young man should beware of girls 'seeking to avoid the issue by manipulating his feelings'; while Hacker (1963) writes that at the onset of adolescence 'disturbing manifestations appear in connexion with the sexual apparatus'. Most of these books warn against the dangers of learning about sex from friends because their stories are sometimes inaccurate, misleading and even frightening. This is true, but many sex education books seem to suffer from the same faults.

As well as the books intended for young people, there are hundreds of sex manuals written for adults who feel they are not as well informed about sex as they should be. One famous one* which has sold three quarters of a million copies has been the subject of protests to the publishers on the grounds that it is full of misinformation and downright prejudice.

There are several periodicals catering for a similar market. The best known is *Forum*, which has a monthly sale of 200,000 copies and which contains good informative articles as well as other pages of titillation and sexual fantasies.

* Reuben, David, *Everything You Always Wanted To Know About Sex*, W. H. Allen and Pan, 1970.

There are also a large number of films which are masquerading as sex education but are really intended for the semi-pornographic cinemas. As well as the innumerable articles in periodicals that set out to help their readers to fill the gaps in their knowledge about sex, there is the commercial exploitation of sex by some of the national Sunday papers which almost every week contain salacious articles written as if they were protesting about the sexual activities which they so gleefully report. There is no doubt that the commercial exploitation of sex will increase if all attempts to give sex education in schools are abandoned.

The Longford Committee on Pornography (1972) complain that sex education is too explicit, but many books have confusing anatomical drawings. Dallas (1972) notes that sex educators are often biology teachers who are used to relating a diagram to its place in the human body, but children do not possess these skills. She reports: 'A large picture of a sperm revolted one class, as it looked more like a snake or a worm than anything which one would like to have in one's insides. Others have had to be convinced that their Fallopian tubes were not purple and did not have white tacking stitches running down them.'

Critics of sex education argue that sometimes it upsets a child, but we should ask why some children are so vulnerable that it becomes a traumatic experience to learn facts about our own bodies. Indeed it is argued, with justification, that sex education is better started at primary school because at that age children are curious but have not acquired guilt feeling about sex. Children who are so sensitive that they are upset by simple factual information are likely to come from homes where sex has always been regarded as naughty and from parents who have not had the benefit of sex education themselves.

Opponents of sex education would also have to face the fact that any restriction would be an unpopular decision. Public opinion polls invariably show a majority in favour of sex education; the recent study by Rogers showed 72 per cent in favour before the programmes were televised and 77 per cent in favour afterwards.

Recently there have been suggestions to the Minister of Education that parents should have the right to opt out for their children. At present the only subject which parents can stop their children from attending is religious education. In California there is a state law that requires schools giving sex education courses to notify parents and give them a chance to review the study materials used. This law has in fact crippled sex education in the state and many schools have given up trying to find programmes that will get the approval of all parents. Significantly California has one of the highest venereal disease rates in the United States and yet hardly any schools have been able to include information about the symptoms of VD in their health courses.

The strange thing is that the people who wish to eliminate sex education are also the people who object most strongly to the blue films, porno shops, strip clubs and other commercial excesses of sex. But the only antidote that has been suggested is more effective sex education. If more and better sex education is not going to make an impact on VD, illegitimacy and abortion statistics, what other solutions can be proposed? The situation at present is that most people have either had very little sex education or none at all. It seems unlikely that there will be less sexual maladjustments if there is even less sex education.

2.16　Motivation is Not a Problem

If we assume that what we are trying to teach about sex is worth learning, then the fact that at present sex education is relatively ineffective should make us decide to have more of it, not less. In particular we have to recognize that what we want to do is worth doing but we are not very good at doing it.

Nearly all the pupils in school would agree with this diagnosis. The teacher was most often chosen as the best person to give information about sex (as reported in section 2.6 of this chapter). This finding is confirmed by the attitude inventory which was given to most of the men and women at the end of the interview.* Only 9 per cent agreed with the statement

* The first 27 (7 per cent) people interviewed were not given the attitude inventory because the decision to use it was not made until later.

there is no need to teach about sex in schools because you can find out all you need to know for yourself; 80 per cent disagreed. On the other hand 78 per cent agreed that *it is important for a person who gives sex education to have had some first-hand experience of sex*; 12 per cent disagreed. And 89 per cent agreed with the statement *young people should be taught all about birth control*; only 3 per cent disagreed.

Most (80 per cent) of this group felt they could have been told more about sex. Of the 227 who received no sex education, 182 (80 per cent) felt they should have been told about sex. Of the 76 who received what was defined as poor sex education, 60 (79 per cent) were dissatisfied. Of the 73 who received adequate sex education, 59 (81 per cent) wanted to be told more. So even bad sex education does not seem to put them off and the sex education that was defined as adequate was not enough. Eight out of ten of them wanted more help from the school.

These findings make it clear that whatever the problems of providing effective sex education may be, the motivation of the pupils is not one of them. They want to learn and they need to learn.

In a detailed study of the curriculum carried out for the Nuffield Foundation in preparation for the raising of the school leaving age,* it became obvious that relevance was the all-important factor in any course for the less academic adolescent. This has been confirmed by dozens of teachers. If the pupils can see the relevance of what he is learning, then half the educational battle has been won. If the pupils can see that what they are learning will really be useful and will actually be used when they leave school, then they will listen and pay attention.

Every teacher will know that it is not always possible to put across this notion of relevance. Some people live only in the present and lack the capacity for what is called deferred gratification. But this is not true of sex education. Nearly all boys and girls desperately want to know about sex; they are confused by these strong emotions welling up inside them and

* *Society and the Young School Leaver,* Schools Council Working Paper No. 11.

they want to understand them and learn to control them.

This is an educationalist's dream. Much of the time teachers have to work out all sorts of schemes and gimmicks to retain the interest of their less academic pupils who simply do not want to know. Here they really do want to know and they need to know.

2.17   Reasons for Official Resistance

There is no law against giving sex education in Great Britain; most of the pupils and a majority of the parents want it, the subject has been discussed for many years and there are numerous courses which have been tried out in schools and reported upon in the educational press. So what holds up progress? Why do those who need this advice and help not get it? Many will say that we can advise and help, but we are not allowed to give it at the time when it is most needed. It is important to look at this resistance from the authorities, because the best sex education course in the world is quite useless if it is not acceptable to those who decide what shall be taught in the schools.

There are two main factors which hinder the development of effective sex education. The first is fear, especially fear of promiscuity. The second is the way the educational system works in this country.

There are a few people who think that sex education does more harm than good. Dr Eickhoff has said that sex education is the cause of illegitimacy, venereal disease, promiscuity, prostitution, smoking, drinking, drug taking and what she calls 'sexually symbolic crimes'. It may be thought that this is an extreme point of view, but Dr Eickhoff has been invited to write articles for the *Guardian* and TV producers ask her to provide what they call 'balance' on discussion programmes. She has said that 'some schools also give courses in perversions' and has described the sex act as 'the assault of one body on another accepting body and the passage of a body fluid from one to the other, an idea so revolting to the mind that a tremendous excitement is generated to blot out thought processes.' Dr Eickhoff is consultant child psychiatrist to the South Birmingham Hospital Management Committee.

Not many people hold such melodramatic views, but opinion polls show that about one fifth of the population is against sex education, although this opposition is diminishing. The main fear, sometimes declared but more often unspoken, is that sexual knowledge leads to sexual promiscuity.

This research provides no evidence that the people who received sex education were more likely to be promiscuous. Nor were they more likely to have an illegitimate child, an abortion or get VD. Unfortunately this research also shows that sex education did not prevent these sexual maladjustments and had very little effect at all on anyone for good or evil, but this is more a criticism of the quality of the sex education than an indication of its possible influence.

There is no research evidence to suggest that sex education acts as a catalyst for promiscuity. It would not be unreasonable to ask those who maintain there is a connection to produce the evidence. It would be possible to set up a good longitudinal research to find out if there is any relationship between effective sex education and unacceptable sexual behaviour (providing one can find the sex education that is effective and agree upon what is unacceptable).

The second factor is not so easily answered. In some countries the school curriculum is planned from a central body, as in Sweden or Austria. In others there are educational boards that supervise the curriculum for groups of schools, as in most European countries. In Great Britain the headmaster is quite autonomous and he decides what shall be taught in his school.

This is not always very reassuring. A recent attempt in this country to inquire about attitudes to sex education (Harris, 1969) produced some discouraging replies from headmasters such as: 'Those who are determined to behave like animals can doubtless find out the facts for themselves', and 'I am sick, sick of talk about sex. I'll have none of it in my school.' But, of course, such remarks are exceptional and it is estimated that the majority of secondary schools now make some attempt to give sex education mainly in biology or religious education under such headings as 'human biology', 'hygiene', 'learning to live' or 'the family'. But it is often too limited and too late. Harris found that 40 per cent made no mention of masturbation and 90 per cent gave no information about methods of contraception. The headmistress of a famous comprehensive school was thought to be rather progressive because she allowed contraceptive information to be given to her girls after they had reached the age of seventeen. But 60 per cent of her girls had left before that age and most of them will have no further contact with the educational system. Who is going to tell these girls, the very ones who need contraceptive advice, about birth control methods? This headmistress was directing her energies towards those who did not really need her help and ignoring those who did.

To be fair, the head is not so autonomous as it may appear. He ought not to displease the school governors, the local education committee, the parents or his staff. So the extent and type of sex education depends not only on the views of headmasters, teachers and educationalists, but also upon the public at large.

This is appropriate because the sex education programme of a school should not give the pupils material that will offend the moral or religious beliefs of the majority. Equally those parents with strong religious or moral views have no right to demand that only their views should prevail in sex education. More perversely, some parents press the headmaster to impose on their children standards of behaviour that they themselves do not adhere to.

In such a situation the school should give a correct presentation of the facts and a respectful interpretation of the various points of view. This does not mean that the teacher has to adopt a completely passive attitude and offer no moral guidelines of any kind. There remain many important moral issues where the teacher can make definite statements.

For example, a person should never force an unwilling partner to take part in sexual activities. The sexual behaviour of men and women should be judged by the same standards. Racial discrimination should not be part of a person's sexual values. It should be an absolute rule that sexual relations are discontinued when one is infected by a venereal disease. There is the duty to use contraceptives if the girl does not want a child or cannot look after a child. Everyone should try to develop a tolerant attitude towards those whose sexual drives are channelled in directions other than those most common.

This is the only feasible position for a teacher to take in a pluralistic and democratic society. Even so, some headmasters will resist the introduction of more effective sex education and some parents will protest against it. Furthermore, some education officers and heads will not have the courage to stand up against minority points of view. Inevitably some people will complain if their own viewpoint does not prevail. Such people should be content with the fact that their views are treated with respect in the sex education programme.

The tide is in favour of those who take a progressive and radical view, but it is still possible to move too fast and thus create a climate of moral outrage in which those who wish to restrict all sex education may make their voices heard. The very mention of the word sex produces emotional feelings of one sort or another. For nearly two thousand years there have been taboos forbidding conversation about sexual matters in most Western cultures. Even the description of simple anatomical details were thought to be immodest and distasteful. The sexual act was regarded as dirty and children had to be protected from unclean thoughts. All this is very recent history and it is a background which must be taken into consideration.

Wren-Lewis in *What Shall We tell the Children?* (Constable, 1971) warns against the mistake 'of believing that the exposure of fallacies in people's thinking or opinions automatically disposes of feelings or experiences they have hitherto associated with those thoughts or opinions'. It is not enough to show that a person's views on sex education are illogical or false; he has lived by these opinions and erected a set of values around them; he cannot suddenly abandon them. The general process of discussion and argument is the best method of public enlightenment in a free society and is the best way towards a balanced solution of a community problem.

However, we must recognize that sex education suffers from a particular disadvantage which is likely to slow down progress. Sex is one of the major facets of life wherein adults disapprove of youth behaviour and attempt to control it. Headmasters must keep the respect and support of these adults, whether they are local councillors, parents or the general public. Consequently sex education in most schools is more likely to be too slow than too fast, and more likely to be too timid than too frank. Yet the results of this research have shown that these young men and women are overwhelmingly in favour of more thorough sex education, given sooner. This is something we should remember when we criticize those who wish to push ahead too fast. We might be going too fast for the local authorities and religious leaders, but perhaps we are going too slowly for the pupils. And whom, we might ask, is the sex education for, the authorities or the pupils?

3. Venereal Diseases

3.1 Sexually Transmitted Diseases

The main venereal diseases are syphilis and gonorrhoea. In England in 1971 there were 1,606 cases (1,270 men and 336 women) of early infectious syphilis, and 55,914 (37,929 men and 17,985 women) of gonorrhoea. The best way to understand the extent of these contagious diseases is to state the number per 100,000 of the population. The rate for syphilis is 3 per 100,000 and for gonorrhoea it is 121 per 100,000. Those between the ages of eighteen and twenty-four are more likely to get gonorrhoea than other age groups as Table 3/1 shows.

TABLE 3/1. The extent of gonorrhoea in different age groups*

Age group	Men	Women	Rate per 100,000
Under 16	129	400	4·4
16–17 } 18–19 }	4,393	5,588	252·5 541·1
20–24 } 25+ }	33,407	11,997	527·5 94·3
All ages	37,929	17,985	121·3

* From *On the State of the Public Health:* The Annual Report of the Chief Medical Officer of the Department of Health and Social Security for the year 1971.

There are other infectious diseases which are spread almost exclusively through sexual contact. The most common of these is non-specific urethritis (NSU), so called because doctors are not agreed on the cause of this disease. It is difficult to identify NSU in women and records have not been kept until recently. There were 72,420 new cases of NSU in 1971 and this is a rate of 157 per 100,000 which is higher than the rate for gonorrhoea.

The numbers of new cases of the other sexually transmitted diseases are not high, but 69,260 people who were not infected visited the VD clinics during 1971 and this is a rate of 150 per 100,000. Over a quarter of a million either came direct or were referred to the clinics and this put a severe strain on the staff and facilities of these already overburdened clinics.

3.2   Possible Reasons for the Increase

The number of people suffering from one of the venereal diseases was high during the war and then after the war the figure fell sharply. The incidence of syphilis has remained under control, but as Figure 3/1 shows, the number of cases of gonorrhoea has been increasing since 1956 until it is now higher than it was during the war.

Various reasons are suggested for this rise in the number of new cases of gonorrhoea. The most common explanation is

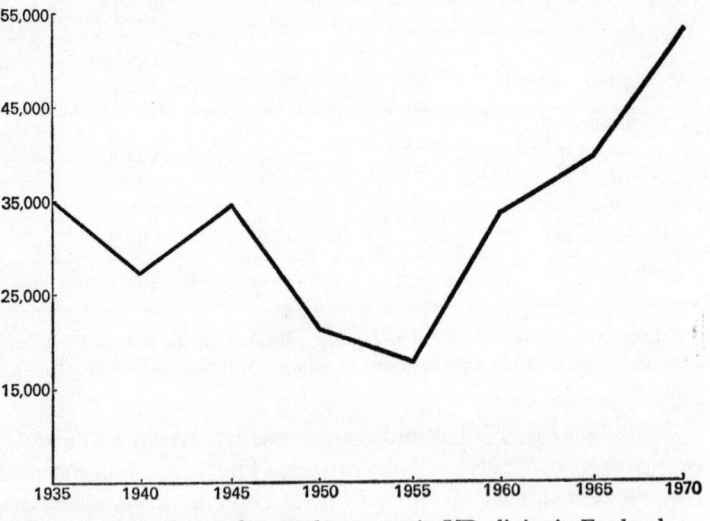

Figure 3/1. New cases of gonorrhoea seen in VD clinics in England and Wales

that young people are more promiscuous than they used to be, but there is very little research evidence for this. It is said that more women are having a greater number of partners and many of them are spreading gonorrhoea because they do not know they are infected. Cauthery and Cole (1971) estimate that about half of all infected women have no symptoms. In such cases the only way a woman finds out she has got gonorrhoea is when the man she has infected notices the symptoms. The time between the original infection and the moment when the woman attends the clinic is unlikely to be less than a week and may be a much longer period. Other people may be infected during this period.

There is also the possibility that the infected woman with no symptoms may not go to the clinic at all, either because her partner does not know her name or is unable to tell her that she has gonorrhoea for some other reason, such as embarrassment or fear; or she may be unwilling to go for treatment, even after she has been informed; this may be irresponsible but if there are no symptoms and if she hardly knows the man who has told her she is infected, it may not be difficult for a woman to convince herself that there must be some mistake.

For all these reasons one theory to explain the rise is that there is an unknown number of women with gonorrhoea who are not being treated and who are a continuing source of infection. Another explanation is that many couples now use the contraceptive pill instead of the condom, which acted as a barrier to the transmission of the venereal diseases. The increased geographical mobility of young people is also given as another reason for the rise; the available evidence suggests that people are more likely to contract VD away from their home town; it also means that any outbreak in one area can soon be spread throughout the country and the increased amount of foreign travel means that the infection may be brought in from other countries where the disease may be more common. Another explanation is the increase in the incidence of NSU which is similar to gonorrhoea and is often confused with it. It is also often said that the germs are becoming resistant to penicillin; this a problem which medical men meet when dealing with many kinds of diseases, but so far with increased dosage and the use of other antibiotics nearly all cases of gonorrhoea can be treated successfully.

Some people use the word epidemic when talking about the rise in the number of VD cases and others are more concerned with the moral state than the physical health of the nation. In fact medicine has had a notable success in the fight against the venereal diseases, which are not the dangerous menace they were a century ago. Seen from a medical point of view these diseases are no longer dangerous and, again in medical terms, they are comparatively easy to cure.

But the nature of the diseases, the way they are spread, the stigma that is attached to them, and the method of treatment all suggest that public education must be a major factor in any attempt to reduce the incidence of VD. It is, therefore, a social problem as well as a medical problem, and it is accepted that a widespread publicity campaign against VD is necessary.

In the past this campaign was hindered and limited by the law, which forbade all advertising of remedies. This was a law intended to stop the advertising of worthless commercial remedies for VD, but recent pressure from the Health Education Council resulted in the amendment of this law in 1970 so that publicity campaigns against the sexually transmitted diseases are now permitted if they get the approval of the Department of Health and posters can be put up where people can read them.

In an attempt to get information which would help in the planning of future campaigns, this research set out to discover how much was known about the venereal diseases and where this information was obtained. Those who had contracted VD, or who feared they had at some period in their lives, were asked several extra questions in an attempt to see if there was a special group that was particularly vulnerable. In addition all the men and women were questioned about their attitude to VD clinics to see if there was any reason why they might hesitate to seek medical advice.

3.3 Knowledge and Names

The first question was asked simply to ascertain whether any of them knew anything about VD. In fact 25 per cent of the men and 38 per cent of the women said they did not. In a sense this question was not intended to be much more than an opening gambit, signifying a change of subject, before going on to questions about symptoms, treatments and cures. As it happens a quarter of the men and a third of the women admitted their ignorance of the subject.

This is really quite surprising because over the last ten years the subject has received widespread publicity; in schools during sex education classes, from specific campaigns initiated by the Health Education Council, from TV programmes, from special articles in periodicals and regular reports in the press as the annual figures are announced, and not least from prominent people publicly wringing their hands about the so-called permissive society. Perhaps these answers should be interpreted as meaning that they do not know enough, rather than they do not know anything. This would be more encouraging. But others made it clear that they did not want to know anything about the venereal diseases; for example:

'I don't know and I don't want to know.'
'I've never thought about it. I don't think I want to.'

When they were asked to be more specific and name the diseases or illnesses associated with the sex organs, in fact 79 per cent of the men and 58 cent of the women mentioned gonorrhoea, or a slang name for that disease.

Almost as many (77 per cent men, 58 per cent women) were able to name syphilis, now a rare and declining disease.* As the Venereal Disease Act, 1917, recognizes only gonorrhoea, syphilis and soft chancre (a disease rarely seen in Britain but common in tropical countries), it could be argued that the publicity campaigns have had some effect. However, only 9 per cent of the men and 3 per cent of the women men-

---

* In 1951 there were 8,432 cases of syphilis compared with 1,606 in 1971.

3

tioned urethritis or NGU or NSU,* although the total number of cases of non-specific urethritis seen in VD clinics now exceeds those of gonorrhoea among men.

Another common infection not often named is pediculosis pubis, usually known as crabs. Only 6 per cent of the men and 1 per cent of the women appeared to know about this louse that lives on the pubic hairs and also infests hairs round the anus and even in the armpit. It may be thought that this is an unimportant bit of information, but unlike the other diseases it can be caught from lavatory seats, as well as during intercourse, genital apposition and mutual masturbation. For this reason it is more common than most people realize, and as it is hardly ever mentioned in sex education books it can cause much distress. Even in this group there was one case of a man who had a series of very hot baths when he discovered these lice on his pubic hairs and after he found this to be ineffective, because the hot water only served to hatch the eggs, he put garden DDT on the infected parts; another shaved off all his pubic hairs.

A few others (2 per cent) named other genital infections such as trichomonas and warts, and others (4 per cent) named imaginary conditions. Over a third of all the people who go to a VD clinic do not have an infection, but it is important that anyone in any doubt should be encouraged to seek medical advice.

The men were better informed about the venereal diseases than the women. They seemed to be more aware of the problem in a general way and were able to name more of the specific diseases. Nevertheless they were not well informed about NSU (a disease that does not seem to affect women) or about crab lice. Nearly half the women were unable to name either gonorrhoea or syphilis. No doubt some women would

* Cases of urethritis which are not identified as gonorrhoea are labelled non-gonococcal urethritis (NGU). Urethritis means inflammation of the urethra and this can be caused in many ways, not always by sexual intercourse. In 60 per cent of all cases of NGU, no germ can be found to account for the discharge and these cases are called non-specific urethritis. It is presumed that NSU is usually spread during sexual intercourse but it is difficult to be certain of this because the infective agent has not been identified.

claim that they did not require to know about these diseases. If they never kissed, cuddled, touched the genitals of or had intercourse with anyone but their husbands and if their husbands also avoided all these activities with other women or men, then it could be claimed quite rightly that the risk of contracting a venereal disease had been eliminated. There are, of course, many couples who can make this claim, but these circumstances are not so common that all information about VD can safely be disregarded.

3.4   The Symptoms

When they were asked to describe the symptoms of gonorrhoea and syphilis, the results were disappointing. Only 17 (8 per cent) men and 6 (4 per cent) women were able to describe the symptoms of both diseases absolutely correctly. Another 91 (42 per cent) men and 71 (45 per cent) women gave a fairly correct version of one or both of the diseases. But 51 (23 per cent) men and 19 (12 per cent) women gave replies that were quite incorrect, while another 60 (27 per cent) men and 61 (39 per cent) women were not able to give any reply (Table 3/2).

TABLE 3/2. The symptoms of the venereal diseases as described by 219 men and 157 women

Rating of the description	Men %	Women %
Quite correct	8	4
Fairly correct	42	45
Incorrect	23	12
DK or not answer	27	39
No. (100%)	219	157

So only 6 per cent of the group would have known for sure if they were infected and another 43 per cent might have been able to recognize the symptoms if they had contracted VD. But over half would not have known and this can only be regarded as unsatisfactory. Those who had received sex education were more aware than the others about the dangers of VD, but they were no better at recognizing the symptoms. The campaign against the venereal diseases seems to have made the majority aware of its existence, but has not provided them with the information required if the spread is to be halted.

Each person who gave a description of the symptoms, whether correct or not, was asked where he or she had obtained this information. Table 3/3 gives the results. The first three columns are the actual numbers who were able to name a definite source and the fourth column is a percentage showing how often each source was mentioned. Those who were unable to describe any symptoms are omitted from this table. The 23 people who gave quite correct replies named 33 sources, the 162 who were fairly correct named 177 sources

TABLE 3/3. The symptoms of the venereal diseases showing how the replies of both men and women were rated and the source of the information

Source of information	Quite correct No.	Fairly correct No.	Incorrect No.	Total %
Books, leaflets	12	60	20	25
Friends	6	46	23	20
TV	0	17	6	6
School	3	13	4	5
Press	0	16	5	6
Posters	1	7	2	3
Work	3	7	1	3
Parents	2	5	1	2
Experience	4	3	2	2
Doctor/clinic	2	3	0	1
DK	0	2	6	2
Total (No.)	33	179	70	75*
Total (%)	6	43	19	68*

* Some people named more than one source and 32 per cent could not describe any symptoms.

and the 70 who gave incorrect replies named 64 sources; 8 people could not remember how they found out about the symptoms.

Books were the most frequent source, but not a good one; 22 per cent were incorrect. This is not very surprising because Hill and Lloyd-Jones (1970) found that most of the books either did not mention VD at all or else it was brought in as a practical threat against premarital intercourse without giving information about symptoms.

Friends were the next most frequent source and this was the reason for the highest proportion of incorrect information; 31 per cent of all the information given by friends was incorrect and a third (36 per cent) of all the incorrect information was provided by friends. As in all forms of sex education, young people obtain the information from friends because it has not been provided by the school or by parents.

Only 20 obtained their information from school, most of it fairly correct. Another 8 people named their parents as the source, usually fairly correct. TV and the press both came high in the list but they did not seem to be able to get across the information in an accurate way: not one person relying on either of these two sources could describe the symptoms absolutely correctly. The reason is that evasions and timid approximations only confuse the child and in some cases the information is misinterpreted, with the result that mistaken ideas are developed and passed on to their friends.

Of course it is not the accuracy of the actual source which is being measured in Table 3/3, but the effect it has on those who receive the information and this is, after all, the important aspect. It is possible that most of the material printed in the press, books or leaflets is factually correct, but somehow the result of their efforts was to produce misunderstanding and ignorance in 25 cases.

Posters emphasize the dangers and sometimes give the address of a local clinic, but do not often describe the symptoms, so they are not a helpful source. Books, the press and TV must be more specific if they are to make a contribution towards solving this problem. Although a majority of schools now claim to give some kind of sex education, only 5 per cent in the whole group mentioned their school as a source of information.

It is not difficult to see how easily the venereal diseases can spread after considering some of the incidental figures that turn up in a research like this. For example, 17 people in this group who had experience of sexual intercourse with more than one person before the age of nineteen (when they were first interviewed) still did not know the symptoms of VD by the age of twenty-five. Of the 34 men whose girl friend had become pregnant only 6 were quite correct and 12 were wrong about the symptoms; of the 32 women who became pregnant before marriage, one was quite correct and 16 were incorrect. Of the 29 people who had an abortion, or whose girl friend had an abortion, 6 gave the symptoms quite correctly, 12 fairly correctly and 11 incorrectly.

But, if it is any consolation, those who had had an abortion were better informed than those who had not; 59 per cent of those who had experienced an abortion (or whose girl friend had undergone one) were at least fairly well informed, whereas 43 per cent of those who had not had this experience knew some of the symptoms. Those men whose girl friend became pregnant, and the women in this group who were pregnant before marriage (58 per cent) were better informed than the others (47 per cent) about the symptoms of VD.

Those with the most sexual experience were nearly always better informed. Those who had the most girl/boy friends were more likely to know about the symptoms of VD. Among those who had sexual experience before the age of nineteen, 54 per cent knew a little at least about the symptoms compared with 40 per cent among those who had not had any early sexual experience. Among those who had premarital sexual experience, 56 per cent had some information about the symptoms, compared with 35 per cent of those whose first experience of sexual intercourse was with their spouse, and compared with 23 per cent of those who had no experience of sexual intercourse by the age of twenty-five. Most significantly, among those who had experience of sexual intercourse with more than one person, 61 per cent knew something about the symptoms compared with 48 per cent among the others.

So it seems that at least some of this information is getting through to those who most need it. The pity is that so little of it is really accurate (6 per cent rated absolutely correct) and most of it is rather vague (43 per cent rated fairly correct). It is also true that among those with no useful information about the venereal diseases there are some sexually active men and women. It is possible that the 51 per cent who were poorly informed about VD suffer more worry and distress than the others, but it is hard to believe that this is the deliberate policy of those who use the threat of the venereal diseases to discourage premarital sexual intercourse.

A further analysis was carried out to see if there was a particular segment of the population who were unlikely to get this information. There seemed to be no association with background or personality; those who came from a broken home were not likely to be more ignorant; those who came from homes in which the parents were churchgoers were not better informed; those who had been in trouble with the police were neither better informed nor more ignorant.

The only differences that could be found were the factors usually noted in health education studies when important information reaches only a small segment of the population. Among the middle class 55 per cent knew the symptoms compared with 47 per cent among the working class; 58 per cent of those with O levels knew a little about the symptoms compared with 43 per cent who had not taken GCE; 56 per cent of those earning over £25 a week knew the symptoms compared with 47 per cent who earned less than this.

The situation, therefore, is that the well-educated middle class are better informed, as are the more sexually active, but these two groups are not necessarily the same people. The conclusion must be that there is a potential here that is not being realized. The sexually active find out for themselves because they are aware of the need as they feel more exposed to the dangers. The middle class find out for themselves because they are able to make better use of the educational resources. This is a clear indication that this information needs to be, and can be, made available; so far we are not responding to either their desire, or their capacity, to learn how to recognize the venereal diseases.

3.5　Incidence and Type of Disease

In this group 44 (20 per cent) of the men and 6 (4 per cent) of the women thought they had contracted a venereal disease at some time in their lives; 8 said this had happened more than once, and more than twice to 3 of them.

But it turned out to be surprisingly difficult to find out if they had really been infected. When they were asked what type of disease they had and what they did about it, there was some confusion and vagueness. This is partly because some of them did not seek medical advice and partly because the difference between gonorrhoea and other forms of urethritis is not clear to the general public, nor to some doctors as we found out later.

Of the 50 who thought they had contracted VD, it seems certain that 19 really were infected and 18 were not (including 2 who had crab lice). Table 3/4 is an attempt to account for these and the others.

TABLE 3/4. Those who thought they had contracted VD

Known result	Men No.	Women No.	Total %
Gonorrhoea	11	2	3
Syphilis	5	1	2
Other	5	0	1
Not known	8	0	2
Crab lice	2	0	1
Not infected	13	3	4
Totals (%)	20	4	13

This table shows that 13 had gonorrhoea (or possibly NSU) and 6 had syphilis (including two who also had gonorrhoea). Five others had been to a doctor, but it was not possible to be sure from their replies whether they had been infected or not; the most likely explanation is that they had contracted non-specific urethritis; some general practitioners like to reassure their patients by telling them that NSU is not a venereal disease (and according to the law they are correct). Another 8 men did nothing about it and they said the symptoms disappeared; it is possible that these men were never infected and equally possible that they are still harbouring the disease. Unlike some diseases (for example, the common cold), recovery from gonorrhoea does not occur without medical treatment. The remaining 18 had not contracted a venereal disease; 2 had crab lice and 16 were told at the clinic or by their doctor that they were not infected. So 5 per cent definitely were infected and 8 per cent may have been.

Among the 8 who thought they had been infected more than once, 4 had gonorrhoea at least twice, 2 had both syphilis and gonorrhoea, and 2 had twice feared they had contracted the disease but had not sought medical advice on either occasion. One of the unfortunate characteristics of the venereal diseases is that one attack does not confer immunity.

3.6 Those Most Likely to be Infected

It would obviously help future campaigns against VD if it were possible to isolate and identify particular segments of the population who are more liable to contract the disease. Because it was so difficult to be precise about the number who had really been infected, the analysis in this section includes all 50 who at one time or another thought they might have been infected. I have included the 16 who were told they did not have VD because from their replies it appears that even some of these had contracted non-gonococcal urethritis.

This group did not appear to be very different from the other 326 men and women as regards area, background or home circumstances. The recurring statistical correlation with VD was always the extent of sexual activity. But this most unoriginal finding requires some amplification. Quite obviously the more promiscuous an individual, the more likely he is to catch VD. But there also appears to be another group who are sexually very active from an early age, but who appear to be settled down and married by the age of twenty-five.

Over half those who thought they had contracted VD at some stage in their lives are now married; one of them is now separated, but of the 257 people in this group who are still married, 28 (11 per cent) at one time thought they had VD – 18 of them now have one or more children; one of them admits infidelity, and 2 (one man, one woman) claim they caught it from their spouses; but 25 said this happened before they married.

Of the 50 who thought they had contracted VD, 26 out of 123 (21 per cent) had experienced sexual intercourse by the age of eighteen, compared with 24 out of 227 (11 per cent) who had not. But considering only the 46 who had sexual experience with more than one person by the age of eighteen, 4 (9 per cent) later feared they were infected. These percentages are based on small figures, but it does seem as if the venereal diseases are more closely correlated with sexual activity than with promiscuity.

The correlations are not limited to activities that are sexual; it seemed to be the more active extrovert boy or girl who was more likely to be infected. Of the 161 who had only one or two jobs in their working career, 23 (14 per cent) feared they had VD; of the 84 who had four or more jobs, 14 (17 per cent) feared they had VD. Of the 91 who had been in trouble with the police, 20 (22 per cent) feared they had VD; of the 259 who had not been in trouble, 30 (12 per cent) feared they had VD. These and other correlations suggest that it is the outgoing characters who are more likely to be infected. For example, of the 106 who had been to a public bar within the previous twenty-four hours, 22 (21 per cent) feared they had VD compared with the 10 out of 123 (8 per cent) who had not been to a bar for over a week.

Although it appears that those most likely to get VD are the boys and girls who combine high sexual activity with other lively and hedonistic pursuits, some of them seem to quieten down and marry. Those who have not married, or who have not found a steady girl or boy friend, will continue to be active and have several sexual partners and, not surprisingly, they are the ones more likely to be infected.

The point to be learnt from this section, besides the obvious fact that the more sexual partners a person has the more likely he is to catch VD, is that among those who are infected when they are young there are some who will soon marry and have a family, and there are others, a minority, who will continue to seek out new sexual partners. There is no justification for the assumption that a young person who contracts a venereal disease will always be promiscuous, and considerable caution is required when using the VD rate as an indication of moral turpitude in individuals or society.

3.7 Contacts and Treatment

An attempt was made to find out the source of the infection and all those who thought they had VD were asked where they supposed they had caught the disease. It is always difficult to get this information at the clinic and our interviewers did not find it easy. Eight people said they did not know and a further five were so evasive that it is better not to put them in a definite category. The answers given by the 50 who thought they had VD and the 19 we know for sure were infected are given in Table 3/5.

TABLE 3/5. The source of infection according to the replies of 50 people who thought they had contracted venereal diseases

Source of infection	Those who thought they had VD		Those who were diagnosed for sure	
	M	W	M	W
Spouse	1	1	1	1
Girl/boy friend	4	2	3	1
Acquaintance	12	0	6	0
Stranger	6	1	3	1
Prostitute	2	0	0	0
Homosexual	1	0	1	0
Non-sexual	5	0	0	0
Other	2	0	0	0
DK	7	1	2	0
NK	4	1	0	0
Totals	44	6	16	3

The eight who suspected husbands, wives, boy or girl friends were likely to be involved also in emotional problems. The men often felt their infection was caught from an acquaintance or a stranger, but this is rarely the case with the women. It is not certain that the two suspected prostitutes were really carriers but the one man who named another man had syphilis. Five men thought they had been infected from lavatory seats or in some other non-sexual way, but it is unlikely that any of them really had VD. This table shows that the disease can also be caught even though the individual is part of an apparently stable relationship. It also reflects the great difficulty in getting this information and the 13 people who did not name a source might also be too embarrassed to admit that the disease was caught from someone they knew very well.

Those who thought that they had VD were also asked what they did about it and their replies are summarized in Table 3/6. Almost half went to a doctor not at a VD clinic and this suggests that those running the clinics have not succeeded in breaking down all the barriers against going there. Unfortunately other doctors do not always have the right equipment and are not so expert at recognizing urethritis, especially as they may be misled by the patients.

TABLE 3/6. The action taken by those who thought they had contracted venereal diseases

Action taken	Told infected	Told not infected	Other and DK	Not known	Total
Went to clinic	7	11	0	0	18
Went to GP	12	7	5	0	24
'Disappeared'	0	0	0	8	8
Totals	19	18	5	8	50

Even in the unlikely event that none of the eight who did nothing about it were not infected, it is worrying that one in six of those who thought they had VD did not seek medical treatment. All of them were men. The probable reason why there are no girls in this category is that the symptoms of

gonorrhoea are not always obvious and many girls only discover they have the disease after they have infected someone
else.

Only two people in this group had taken the precaution of
going to a clinic although they had no suspicions, but many
who had not been infected had clearly been at risk for several
years.

3.8   The Attitude to Clinics

Not only is it important that people can recognize the symptoms so that they know when they have got one of the venereal diseases, it is also important that they realize that they
are relatively simple diseases so that they will not be frightened to attend a clinic. Because of the efficiency of modern
treatment the venereal diseases can usually be cured without
difficulty. Penicillin is very effective in the treatment of
syphilis. From time to time rumours are heard suggesting
that the gonococcus (the germ which causes gonorrhoea) has
developed a tolerance towards penicillin; for example, there
was said to be an incurable strain spreading among American
troops called Vietnam Rose, but the American Army Sur-
geon General's office deny this. New antibiotics and new
schemes of administration have largely overcome the decreased sensitivity of the gonococcus, and gonorrhoea can
nearly always be cured quite successfully. Antibiotics are also
used in the treatment of NGU which is a milder, less dangerous disease, but relapses are more common than in gonorrhoea.

People in authority, including teachers, seem reluctant to
admit that VD can be cured fairly easily and I suppose this
stems from a fear that young people will not take the risk of
infection seriously. But this is a mistaken policy. If those who
are infected are going to be persuaded to attend a clinic
immediately, it is essential that they should not be held up
by doubts or fears. Some people are frightened to tell their
doctor about a growth in case it is cancer; this fear is more
understandable, though mistaken, because they may feel they
would rather not know about a disease that may be incurable.

But it would be quite wrong to encourage people to think this way about any disease which is highly infectious but relatively harmless like chicken pox, or german measles, or VD.

All the men and women, whether they had been infected or not, were asked if they knew how the venereal diseases were cured and what they would do if they were infected. The question was not intended to elicit a medically correct reply, but to show if the individual was aware of the existence of VD clinics and whether he would worry about having to go to one.

Many of them said they had no idea how it could be cured; 42 per cent of the men and 59 per cent of the women did not mention the VD clinic in their replies. On the other hand 19 (9 per cent) men and 3 (2 per cent) women gave replies that showed quite clearly that they would be frightened to go to a clinic. The preponderance of men may be the result of the well-established rumour that VD is cured by putting an instrument up the entrance of the penis.* Less than half (49 per cent men and 39 per cent women) said they would go to a VD clinic.

Therefore there is some doubt if 55 per cent of this group would go to a clinic at the first sign of VD. Of the 50 who thought they had contracted VD, 2 showed a definite fear of clinics, 17 did not mention clinics, and the remaining 31 said they would go to a clinic for treatment. This suggests that those who get one of the venereal diseases benefit from this experience in the sense that they would know what to do next time, but this is hardly a comforting thought.

The characteristics of the gonococcus make it unlikely that a vaccine for gonorrhoea will be developed in the next few years and, no matter what progress is made in medical science in the next decade, it remains certain that tens of thousands of people are going to get VD. Recent campaigns have made people more aware of this possibility, but it is clear that the new campaigns must encourage people to take the next step towards a clinic when they find that they have been infected.

More than half the group (56 per cent) did not know where their local VD clinic was situated. The women (60 per cent)

* For example, 'They scrape the penis to get the scabs out.'

seemed less likely to know than the men (53 per cent). As well as the 18 who had been there for treatment, 4 others said they had visited their local clinic; 8 of the men and 4 of the women found it an embarrassing place. Obviously the whole experience of contracting VD is embarrassing, but if over half of those who go to the clinic find the visit unpleasant, venereologists must ask themselves what else can be done to make the patient feel more at ease.

Everyone was asked: How would you find out where it is, supposing a friend of yours needed treatment? Most people (36 per cent) said they would ask their doctor. Almost everyone knows about the notices in public lavatories but only 12 per cent mentioned this; perhaps it is not really a very practical way of getting the information, because a person is hardly likely to visit his local convenience and take out a pencil and paper to note down the name of the local clinic.

There are 190 clinics in England but very few of them appear to list their telephone numbers or addresses in the local directories, so that the 6 per cent who said that they would look up the address in the telephone book may not succeed in getting their friend to a clinic. Another 7 per cent said they would ring up the Health Department, but one can easily imagine that in some town halls it might be difficult to be put through to the relevant extension.* The 4 per cent who said they would ring up the local hospital might experience similar difficulties. Two people said they would ring up the police.

It must be quite difficult to get the address of the local clinic and it may be necessary to make it easier for the anxious patient to find out. Many people said they would ask their doctor and the majority of those who thought they were infected went to their family doctor. There may be a case, therefore, for channelling more information through him, but this has considerable drawbacks. The evidence suggests that people are more likely to get VD when they are away from home and so away from their general practitioner. Furthermore there must be many who would not want their own

* One person rang his local town hall; when he said venereal disease, the operator asked, 'How do you spell that, sir?'

doctor to know that they had been infected, especially if their parents or spouses share the same doctor. This is particularly so now since a recent case, whatever its rights and wrongs, when a doctor betrayed the confidence of a girl to her parents. This was widely reported and has severely shaken the faith of the younger generations in the notion of the strict confidentiality of information entrusted to doctors.

3.9   Ideas from Informants

Most of the people who have the task of taking action against the spread of the venereal diseases have reached the age when, according to the statistics at any rate, they are not so likely to be involved in the problem. This research took the opportunity to solicit ideas from the age group said to be most at risk. Everyone, no matter what his or her personal experience, was asked for his or her own ideas on how to stop the spread of VD.

'Educate people to recognize the symptoms and impress upon them to use self-control when they've got it.'

'It's hard to say. I suppose regular check-ups at the doctors. It would be easier if it was limited to prostitutes.'

'After sex a couple should go to the doctor to check – catch it in the bud.'

'You can't tell people to stop doing something they've been doing for centuries. By the year 2000 it will be quite common, like the 'flu is now.'

'Brand everyone who has got it. Tattoo them on the backside.'

'You can catch it from a toilet seat and you can't stop that, can you?'

'In any case everyone I go with is spotless. I always make inquiries first.'

Quite a large number (19 per cent) had no ideas at all, but the other 304 men and women contributed 411 suggestions which have been classified into eight general categories.

Most (34 per cent) thought the best solution was more publicity and more public education. In fact in the last few years there has been a large amount of publicity so that most people now know about the dangers of VD, but this research suggests that the education has not been thorough enough and not of the right kind. Among those who suggested more education, 26 (7 per cent of the whole group) specifically mentioned that there should be less stigma attached to these diseases. This is a sensible suggestion, but one that places the health authorities in a dilemma because they must not appear to be condoning promiscuity. It may be of significance to some people that all but 3 of the 26 who made this suggestion were men.

The women were more likely to think that the best solution would be to put a stop to promiscuity; 23 per cent of the women and 13 per cent of the men made this suggestion. It is not easy to see how this can be done, as much depends on the form of restrictions envisaged and on the definition of promiscuity. It is of course a truism to say that if no one ever had sexual intercourse outside marriage, the venereal diseases would soon be brought under control. However, the men and women probably had a wider meaning of promiscuity in mind, but it is difficult to see how there can be legal restraints on this kind of behaviour.

In fact 6 per cent of the men and 5 per cent of the women did suggest stronger legal restraints on prostitution, but the evidence obtained at the clinics suggests that this is a minor factor in the spread of the diseases. Other researches (Hitchens and James, 1965) have also indicated that promiscuity and prostitution is less common among young people than in some older age groups. This research has shown that in only about half the cases of VD was promiscuity a factor.

Many informants (15 per cent men, 19 per cent women) thought more attention to cleanliness would halt the spread of the venereal diseases.

'Plenty of soap and water.'

'It's up to the schools to teach girls to keep themselves clean, as men pick it up from them.'

'Cleanliness is the only way.'

'By keeping to your own toilet, towel, flannel and things.'

'Make everyone bath in the morning and at night. I haven't the faintest idea really.'

These replies are an echo from the old idea that nice girls don't get VD. Although hygiene is to be encouraged for many good reasons, it is a great mistake to give credence to the theory that you will avoid VD if you have a good wash after intercourse. Prompt attention to personal hygiene soon after intercourse may indeed reduce the chances of infection, but the germ can survive soap and water, and it is harmful to use strong disinfectants.

A more practical suggestion is to use a condom, mentioned by 10 per cent men and 4 per cent women. But it would give a false sense of security to maintain that this is a definite safeguard. Although modern condoms rarely split or leak, they do sometimes slip off, particularly after a man has lost his erection. It is also true that the handling of the genitals of an infected partner followed by the handling of one's own can transmit gonorrhoea or syphilis. It is frequently said, especially by those who are against sexual experimentation by the young, that the present rise in the venereal diseases is caused because the condom is being abandoned in favour of the contraceptive pill. But this is not altogether correct because more condoms are being sold than ever before. Some people may be changing to the pill, but many more are using the condom whereas before they used no contraceptives at all.

Only 11 per cent of the men and 15 per cent of the women suggested immediate treatment for the infected, which is probably the main weapon against VD that we have at present. The fact that so few made this suggestion means that those planning campaigns to reduce the rise of the venereal diseases should put more emphasis on this aspect.

Another 7 per cent of the men and 10 per cent of the women suggested that people should submit to regular checkups to make sure they are not infected. During the war under Section 33B of the Defence Regulations, a woman named by two men as a source of infection could be compelled, under the threat of prosecution, to attend for treatment. Unfortunately this gave a few unprincipled men the chance to name an unpopular or uncooperative woman who would then be forced to submit to an examination. Another difficulty in any scheme of compulsory investigation is that there is not yet a simple and reliable diagnostic test for gonorrhoea in women. In any case it is difficult to think of any practical scheme which could ensure sufficiently frequent inspections. In a few foreign countries where prostitution is legally controlled, it has been found that a woman could spread an alarming amount of VD in between her semi-annual or quarterly inspections.

3.10 Future Campaigns

The difference between this chapter about the venereal diseases and most other monographs on the subject is that this research has set out to obtain the views of those who are thought to be most at risk, although in fact less than one in ten have been infected. Consequently it has been the social rather than the medical aspects of the problem that have been given more emphasis.

This research suggests that most people in this age group are aware of the dangers of VD, but that there is still considerable ignorance about the symptoms and some doubts as to whether an infected person would go to a clinic for help. Therefore any campaign setting out to increase public enlightenment on VD should put special emphasis on helping people to recognize the diseases and encouraging them to take action when they are infected.

It was found that 94 per cent were not fully informed about the symptoms. The 26 (7 per cent) people who had never experienced intercourse and the further 21 (6 per cent) whose experiences were very limited might complain that it is hardly necessary for them to know. But unless it can be assumed that they will have no further heterosexual or homosexual contacts, they will still be vulnerable. The same statement could be made about couples who do not intend to allow any infidelities to occur in their married life. These people are now twenty-five and as they grow older it becomes more and more unlikely that they will learn about the symptoms through any formal educational process; but it does not become any less likely that they may be incautious or unfortunate.

The best way to make sure infected people will go to a

clinic is to get them to understand that the venereal diseases can usually be cured and the treatment involves the patient in only a minimum of discomfort. In this research it was quite difficult to know exactly how many people had really been infected. This lack of precision in the results confirms that there is still a stigma attached to this disease and this can only mean that some people delay going to the clinic for medical help.

It has now become a fairly common rumour that there is a 'killer' strain of gonorrhoea which does not respond to treatment. This is an unhelpful attitude; all strains are treatable, although some are more resistant than others. At the other extreme it is said that the venereal diseases are no worse than having a cold, but this attitude is equally unhelpful because VD, unlike the common cold, will not simply go away without medical treatment.

The results of this research have brought to light some aspects that deserve attention when planning future campaigns.

Women are less well-informed than men. NSU is now a common disease but hardly known to the general public. Another unknown but relatively common affliction is infection by crab lice.

A future campaign should take into account that many people still go to a general practitioner in the first instance. In many cases the doctor will send these patients on to the clinic, but in others he will treat them himself. It is beyond the scope of this research to decide if this is desirable.

The evidence from this research suggests that much remains to be done to take some of the emotional steam out of discussions on VD. It is possible that some of the lurid pictures put out in past campaigns have resulted in more moral indignation, but not in fewer infections. Any future campaign must be free of prudery and should be careful not to lose credibility by exaggerating the dangers out of all proportion to their true significance.

Some of the figures given in the section on symptoms (3.4) show that a large number of people have taken a lot of chances and have not been infected. Inevitably any campaign has to combat the tendency to personalize this situation – the same tendency to be found in the cigarette smoker when he says, 'I've smoked twenty a day for forty years and I don't feel any the worse for it.' It was also shown that those who took the most risks had more knowledge – but not enough – about the symptoms.

It must also be a matter of some concern to those planning these campaigns to find that so many of the sources giving apparently correct information (such as TV, books and periodicals) can somehow produce so much misinformation. There may be a point where a prudish gloss over the real facts can produce more harm than good. It must also be time to wonder if those notices in public lavatories with their unsavoury connotations are the right way to assist public education. Instead, local authorities should establish telephone hot-lines to provide advice for worried callers on the symptoms of VD and where to go for treatment. This has already been done quite successfully in a few regions.

This research showed that the men and women learnt about VD from many different sources and no source was particularly dominant. This should be encouraging because it means that most people have obtained their information more or less by chance and the opportunity exists for filling the gap, whereas with the acquisition of early information about sex the task is to correct misinformation already acquired from friends. The controversy about the extent to which information on VD should be given in sex education has yet to be settled. Indeed it is pertinent to ask if the object is to make a serious effort to help those who might be infected or merely to reduce the risk of infection. And if it is decided to give realistic help, it is difficult to decide where the line should be drawn. For example, if it is accepted that the condom provides protection, it is logical that sex education should include instruction on the use of French letters.

Furthermore consideration should be given to the possibility of encouraging some people to attend clinics for regular inspections. Two people in this group visited a clinic although they had no symptoms and no reason to suppose they had contracted a venereal disease. At present the National Health

Service could not cope with many people arriving at clinics for regular check-ups, but there are probably some circumstances where regular inspections would provide a spectacular reduction in cases.

It has been suggested that it may be necessary to introduce an element of compulsion directed towards those groups most likely to get VD. This research indicates that those who are exceptionally active, sexually and in other ways, before the age of nineteen may be one of those groups. But it is extremely difficult to see how such a group can be identified, let alone compelled to attend a clinic. There are also serious objections to any such scheme from a civil liberties point of view.

Various attempts have been made to introduce an element of compulsion in prisons, hospitals and clinics. For many years all girls sent to Holloway were inspected. It is a legal requirement in some states in America for women applying for a marriage licence, or pregnant women, to undergo an inspection. In Chicago, health officials carry out routine checks among persons coming to the city hospitals for various reasons other than VD. In most countries where brothels are legal, some form of inspection is compulsory. Many of these schemes have produced remarkable results, but there are two serious disadvantages. The first is that it would take large resources to make the inspections frequent enough to prevent others being infected; and the second is that the test for gonorrhoea is complicated and uncertain. When syphilis was the main scourge, it might have been possible to put up a compelling argument in favour of compulsion. But now that gonorrhoea and NSU are the most frequent infections, the loss of civil liberties would not be justified by the probable effectiveness of compulsory inspection.

3.11   The Fear of Success

A study of medical history indicates that no infectious disease has ever been eradicated until a vaccine had been devised that would confer immunity on those who were given it. But research is expensive whereas exhortation is cheap.

Doctors believe it may be possible to develop a vaccine for

syphilis within the next decade if more money is made available for research. The outlook for the medical control of gonorrhoea is less hopeful and the lack of even basic knowledge about the transmission of the gonococcus suggests that a large amount of expensive fundamental research will be needed before we can expect a successful vaccine. The medical prospects may be discouraging, but in the end we shall probably find that it is easier to produce a vaccine than change the behaviour of people.

Meanwhile we must use the resources that are available and most clinics attempt to trace the source of the infection through their patients. But many patients are vague and unhelpful about their sexual partners and the task of tracking down the contacts can involve time-consuming detective work. As gonorrhoea has a short incubation period, other people may be infected before the contact is traced and the case worker sometimes finds herself in a race in which the spread of the disease works faster than she can.

Contact tracing has had some success, particularly among women who have no symptoms and do not even know they have got gonorrhoea. In 1970 contact action was tried in 31,539 cases and this brought in 10,259 people; indeed the Chief Medical Officer of Health states that half the new cases of women were brought in as a result of contact tracing. But some clinics have no investigators and most of them do not have the resources to employ sufficient case workers.

Recently the Department of Health made a large grant to the Family Planning Association to conduct and evaluate a concentrated birth control campaign in two areas. A similar scheme should be tried with contact tracing. It would be possible to devise an action research in which large resources are deployed in two relatively isolated areas in an attempt to trace all the sources of venereal infection. It is essential, however, that proper research methods are built into the scheme so that its real effectiveness can be evaluated.

Even if extra money were put into contact tracing and the Health Education Council was given the opportunity to conduct a nationwide campaign, there remains one outstanding difficulty, unique to this disease. That is the fear of success.

Many people have the feeling, sometimes undeclared, that the successful elimination of the venereal diseases would cause more harm than good because it would encourage promiscuity. Dr Comfort (1967) gives many quotations from the medical press which support the notion that efforts to stop the spread of venereal disease were unjustified because VD was regarded as a proper punishment for sexual irregularities.

No one would think of blaming a boy who goes to a party and unfortunately contracts hepatitis because he dances with a girl who is a carrier. But a boy who gets VD is held to blame. This is one of the few diseases (alcoholism is another) where we tend to blame the patient rather than the disease.

The fact is that the more sexual partners you have, the more likely you are to contract a venereal disease, just as the more miles you travel by car, the more likely you are to have an accident, for the same reason in both cases: it does not wholly depend upon your own care and responsibility, but also upon the care and responsibility of others and this is outside your control.

The more promiscuous you are, the more likely you are to get VD; but it does not follow from this that the less chance there is of getting VD, the more promiscuous people will be. One of the significant findings of this research is that over half the people in this group who had contracted VD are now married and have not been unfaithful, however many partners they may have had before they became infected. So clearly it is a mistake to think that all VD patients will be promiscuous.

People who argue that a rise in the total VD rates indicates that there is an increase in promiscuity forget that the number of new cases of syphilis has fallen; it would be as reasonable to use the decrease in syphilis to argue that there has been a decrease in promiscuity. In fact the reasons for the rise in the incidence of the venereal diseases are varied and complex; we do not understand all of them, but many have been noted in this chapter.

Improved methods of detection is one reason why the numbers are higher. Another reason is the increased mobility of people of all ages and social classes. The annual report of the Chief Medical Officer of Health notes that 15 per cent of all new cases of syphilis and 3·4 per cent of all new cases of gonorrhoea were contracted abroad. Those who think the VD statistics are a sign of the moral decline of the British should note that it is a world-wide problem and many countries have a higher rate than Great Britain. In this country the gonorrhoea rate is 121 per 100,000, but in America it is 308 per 100,000 and in Sweden it is 514 per 100,000.

Only in the People's Republic of China is the VD rate said to be falling rapidly. This was achieved by training thousands of para-medical workers to carry out the treatment and by conducting a massive propaganda campaign. 'Syphilis is a disease that was bequeathed to us by the rotten society we have thrown out,' the peasants were told over and over again on posters, at meetings and in talks over the radio. Of course VD is not the only social problem we can solve if we are prepared to accept a large reduction in personal freedom and send the more recalcitrant members of the community to special institutions for thought reform.

It is at least encouraging for our own campaigners that those who are most active sexually are those who are best informed. It suggests that there is a receptive audience where information is most likely to have the greatest impact and this is by no means always the case. My earlier research (and that of others) has shown that those most likely to be involved in unstable relationships were also those who were least likely to use any birth control method. But here we find that those most likely to spread VD are also those who are most anxious to get to know about it.

For once we have a reversal of the usual health education situation in which those who most need help are those who are most difficult to help. But it does mean that we must tell them what they want to know. Most people now know about the dangers of VD. The information they need now is (1), to know when they have got it – that is, to recognize the symptoms, and (2), to know what to do about it – that is, to visit the clinic.

4. Contraception

4.1 The Earlier Research

Seven years ago less than a third of this group had experience of sexual intercourse. Only two out of five of these experienced boys and one out of five of these experienced girls always used a contraceptive method. Nearly all the boys used a condom or withdrawal. All but a very few girls depended upon the man to take the precautions. Only one in twenty of the girls used a diaphragm, douche or a chemical method. None of them had used the contraceptive pill.

Almost all the girls had a very real fear of an unwanted pregnancy, but it was difficult for them to get female contracaptives as they were unmarried and the pill had only just begun to be used in this country. These girls left it to the boy to decide what form of birth control he would use, if any.

Since then there have been very great changes in the development of contraceptives used by the female, notably the pill and the coil. Later researches (Cartwright, 1970; Gorer, 1971) have shown that these contraceptive methods have become much more widely accepted, at first among married women, and more recently the pill has been made available to unmarried girls if they have courage enough to go and ask for it.

Surveys in America, Scandinavian countries and Great Britain have shown an overall increase in the number of people who now use a contraceptive method of some kind. The greatest increase has been among middle-class married couples and among people who previously had not used contraceptives for religious reasons. Despite this increase each year there are still over 74,000 illegitimate births, over 120,000 legal abortions (and an unknown number of criminal abortions) and over 90,000 brides are pregnant on their wedding day. It is obvious, therefore, that there are still a large number of people who do not use any form of birth control for one reason or another.

4.2   Knowledge and Information

There may be some people in this country who do not use any method of birth control because they do not know that it is possible to take precautions to avoid pregnancy, but if so they must be very few. When the men and women in this group were asked to name all the contraceptive methods they knew about without prompting from the interviewer, nearly all of them mentioned the pill (oral contraceptives) and the condom (sheath, protective, French letter). A large number also mentioned the cap (diaphragm) and, more surprisingly, the coil (loop, IUD). There is doubt in the minds of some people if the safe period (rhythm method) and withdrawal (coitus interruptus) can strictly be called contraceptive methods, even so about half of these informants did mention them. Chemicals (spermicidal creams, jellies and pastes) and suppositories (foaming tablets) appear to be less well known. About a quarter mentioned sterilization, but again this may be because not everyone thinks of it as a contraceptive method. Only 3 men and 1 woman were unable to name any type of birth control. These results (listed in Table A4/1) are similar to the findings of Cartwright (1970) who questioned a group of older married women.

It seems probable, therefore, that most people know that it is possible to take precautions against the birth of an unwanted child. When they were asked if they wanted more information about contraceptives, 69 per cent men and 79 per cent women said they did not need it. This can be regarded as quite a high number considering that contraception is a fairly complicated subject and the options are fairly wide. But only about a quarter, mostly men, felt they needed to know more (see Table 2/7 on page 46).

This time the group was not asked where they had obtained their information (as in Chapters 2 and 3) because it was likely that the different methods were acquired over a number of years; most of them probably found out about the condom during adolescence, but information about the coil must have been acquired much more recently; the earlier research showed that only a few knew about oral contraceptives when they were eighteen and none of them had taken the pill.

It was more pertinent, therefore, to ask if they had discussed birth control with anyone. Most of them had talked about it to at least one person. Although friends are nearly always the main source of information (or misinformation) on sexual matters, their influence is nothing like so dominant on contraception as it is with other things. But 64 per cent of those who were married discussed it with their wife or husband, and 72 per cent of those who said they were going steady discussed it with their girl friend or boy friend. Although many people do seem to discuss contraceptives with their spouse or regular sexual partner, over a quarter of the couples in this group have not done so; it would be better if even those who decide they did not like contraceptives at least discussed it with their partners.

Over half (55 per cent) of the women had discussed contraceptives with professional people, either their doctor (38 per cent) or at a clinic (15 per cent) or with other social workers (2 per cent). Only a few men (9 per cent) had sought advice from professional people. It is a subject that is much more likely to be discussed by women, although more men than women actually take precautions.* Only 10 per cent of the women said they had not discussed birth control with anyone compared with 25 per cent of the men. More women than men discussed it with friends (40 per cent compared with 25 per cent) and with parents (53 per cent compared with 3 per cent). Only a few of either sex discussed contraceptives with a clergyman (2 per cent women, 1 per cent men) or with a teacher (1 per cent women, 1 per cent men).

The women, and to a lesser extent the men, seem to be fairly well informed about the various contraceptive techniques. It is worth noting that this information has been

* The condom and withdrawal are probably still used more often than all the contraceptives used by women.

acquired quite recently. At the age of eighteen it was found*
that 'the teenagers' understanding of birth control was often
sketchy, even among those who claimed to have some knowledge of the subject'. They had learnt little or nothing about
contraceptives from school, nor from their parents except in
a very few cases. But nearly all boys are fertile and girls are
capable of conception before the age of eighteen and over a
quarter of them had experienced sexual intercourse by that
age.

4.3 Obtaining Advice

Although three quarters of the group said they did not need
more information about contraceptives, all of them were
asked where they would go if they wanted advice. Most of
them, men as well as women, would go to a doctor (51 per
cent women, 42 per cent men) or a clinic (36 per cent women,
31 per cent men).† The number of men who said they would
seek advice from a clinic is surprisingly large when compared
with the number of men who actually attend family planning
clinics. They probably mean that they would send their wives
to the clinic to get the advice.

No other source of advice was mentioned with any frequency. Only 1 per cent said they would go to parents.
Another 1 per cent said they would go to their clergyman,
but it is becoming clear that the church is no longer an
important influence on contraceptive practices even though
13 per cent of this group were Catholic. Hardly anyone said
they would go to friends, the most usual source of information about sex. But 16 per cent did not know where to go for
advice on contraceptives; about a quarter of these were also
the people who said they felt the need for more information,
so there is a small group here (only 4 per cent) who want help
and do not know where to get it.

These answers make it clear that most women and many
men see contraceptives as part of a medical situation. The

* Schofield, *The Sexual Behaviour of Young People*, p. 106.
† About half of those who named a clinic specifically mentioned a
FPA clinic.

users of contraceptives should not be encouraged to think of themselves as patients, as this means only a doctor can solve their problems. It is also a situation that may flatter the doctor's competence; Ward (1969) inquired among general practitioners in Sheffield and found that only 32 per cent had received undergraduate or postgraduate instruction in contraceptive techniques, although 93 per cent advised their patients directly on birth control.

At present most general practitioners will give advice on family planning if they are asked, but many of them, according to Cartwright (1968, 1972), are reluctant to initiate a discussion about birth control for social as opposed to strictly medical reasons. All the contraceptives used by women can only be obtained in a formal clinical atmosphere. The doctor's consulting room and the busy clinic are not the ideal places for a diffident person to ask embarrassing questions. This must mean that there are some cases where information about the importance of adequate contraception is not received because the woman is not at ease and the man is not there.

4.4   The Extent of Use

In this group there were 19 (9 per cent) men and 33 (21 per cent) women who were having sexual intercourse, but had never used any kind of contraceptive method in their whole lives. In addition a further 26 (12 per cent) men and 6 (4 per cent) women said they had hardly ever used any contraceptive method, and this includes douche, withdrawal and the safe period among the possible methods.

The men who used contraceptives started much earlier than the women. Only one woman had used a contraceptive before the age of seventeen, but 16 per cent of the men had done so; by the age of twenty, 19 per cent of the women and 38 per cent of the men had started. The graph (Figure 4/1) shows the age when the men and women had their first experience of sexual intercourse and the age when they started to use contraceptives.

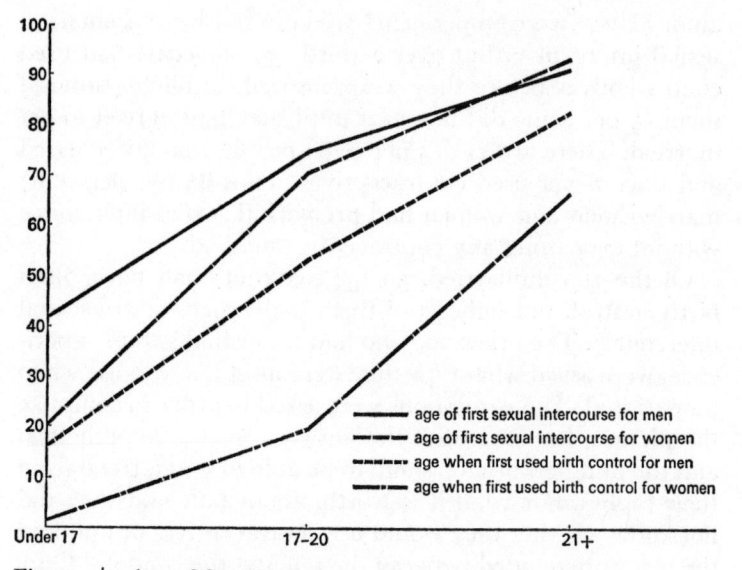

age of first sexual intercourse for men
age of first sexual intercourse for women
age when first used birth control for men
age when first used birth control for women

Under 17   17-20   21+

Figure 4/1. Age of first intercourse compared with the age when contraception was first used

For men the number starting to use contraceptives keeps pace with the number who are experiencing sexual intercourse and gradually the gap narrows from 26 per cent at seventeen to 11 per cent at twenty-one. But for women the regular increase in those experiencing intercourse for the first time is not matched by an increase in those using birth control. The gap between the two lines between seventeen and twenty-one represents a large danger area where inexperienced girls are risking an unwanted pregnancy at an age when most girls are very fertile.

This situation reflects the ease with which a young unmarried man can get a condom at a shop or by mail order, compared with the considerable difficulties, psychological as well as practical, which a girl has to overcome before she can obtain the pill.

Those who were married were asked if they used contraceptives before or after marriage. Many (45 per cent of those married) said they did not start until after they were married;

among these were 29 per cent* who did not have premarital sexual intercourse. But over a third (39 per cent) had used contraceptives before they were married, although some of them (5 per cent) did not start until they had agreed to get married. There are 41 (15 per cent) people who are married and have never used contraceptives. Thus 84 (31 per cent) married men and women had premarital sexual intercourse without ever using any contraceptive method.

Of the 109 unmarried, 59 (54 per cent) had never used birth control, but only 33 of them had experience of sexual intercourse. The other 26, who had never had sexual experience, were asked what type they were most likely to use when they started. These questions were asked in order to complete the picture, but in reality the answers are too hypothetical and the numbers are too small to be able to spot a trend from their replies. For what it is worth, about half said they did not know whether they would use contraceptives or not, and the rest were divided between the pill and the condom. Only one said he did not intend to use any method, but some of the others were a bit vague and said they would think about it when the time came. Unfortunately the time comes unexpectedly in many cases and finds the young people unprepared.

Over the whole group it was found that 24 per cent were sexually experienced but had hardly ever or never used any kind of contraceptive method, not even the simplest type such as withdrawal or suppositories. All the discussion, propaganda and talk about birth control has passed by these people. On the other hand 21 per cent claimed that they had always used a contraceptive of one kind or another (except when they were planning to have a child). This leaves nearly half (48 per cent) the group who have used contraceptives intermittently but not regularly. This is the group that can be persuaded that contraception is important and necessary.

Table 4/1 compares the answers to the two questions on the regularity of use. The figures on the left-hand side are the

* All the percentages in this paragraph are based on 267, the number of men and women in the group who have been married. Percentages for the whole group are given in Table A4/2.

replies to the question asking if they have *ever* used any form of birth control. The figures on the right notes the number of people who use some form of birth control *now*. All forms of contraceptive practice were counted from the most to the least effective.

TABLE 4/1. Extent to which contraceptives have ever been used in the past and are used now

Have you ever used some form of birth control?			How often?	Do you use some form of birth control now?		
Men %	Women %	Total %		Men %	Women %	Total %
22	21	21	Always	54	62	58
50	44	48	Sometimes	15	5	10
21	29	24	Hardly ever or never	23	27	25
8	6	7	NA	8	6	7
219	157	376	No. (100%)	219	157	376

This table shows that there is a hard core of people who do not wish to use contraceptives. The number who once used them and do not now is quite small; only 2 per cent of either sex have lapsed. The number of regular users has increased from 21 per cent to 58 per cent.

4.5 The Various Methods

Table 4/1 shows that over half (58 per cent) the group now use contraception regularly and over two in three (68 per cent) use it at least sometimes. There remain 52 (23 per cent) men and 43 (27 per cent) women who hardly ever or never use it. It is surprising to find how many of them are married; 54 of the 267 (20 per cent) who were married do not now use a contraceptive method; some of these people say they will start to use birth control when they have completed their family.

Among the 109 unmarried, 26 (24 per cent*) have not had sexual intercourse, 50 (46 per cent) use a contraceptive

* Percentages based on 109 unmarried.

method of one kind or another, and 33 (30 per cent) never do this. So about one in three of the unmarried do not use contraceptives compared with one in five of those who are married.

Table 4/2 shows the contraceptive method of the 263 users at the time the question was asked. It includes those who use contraception only occasionally as well as those who always use it.*

TABLE 4/2. Methods of birth control and the extent of use

| Method used | Extent of use | | | | |
	Always %	Occasionally %	Never %	Total %	Total No.
Pill	31	1	—	32	120
Condom	17	8	—	25	96
Coil	3	0	—	3	12
Cap	3	1	—	4	12
Withdrawal	2	1	—	3	11
Safe period	1	1	—	2	8
Vasectomy	1	0	—	1	2
Chemical	0	0	—	0	2
None	—	—	23	23	87
N/A	—	—	7	7	26
Total %	58	12	30	100	—
Total No.	216	47	113	—	376

This table shows eight possible contraceptive methods and there are others. This is a wide distribution spread over a small sample and it should not be used as a representative picture of the extent to which different contraceptive methods are used. But it does reveal some interesting information about the regularity of use.

The pill seems to be used regularly and only a few people said they took it occasionally. A few students take it when they are in college but do not continue when they are at home during the vacation. Although some women find that they

* In Table 4/1 those who said they 'hardly ever' used contraception have been put with those who never use it. In Table 4/2 these people have been added to those who said they 'sometimes' used contraception.

have to give up the coil for medical reasons, obviously the intra uterine device is not a method that one can use occasionally. The same might be said of vasectomy.

In contrast the condom, withdrawal and the safe period appear to be used spasmodically by some people. Of the 115 people using these three methods, 39 (40 per cent) do not use them always. It is surprising to find the safe period in this list, but the explanation seems to be that some of the women use it as a rough guide but are prepared to make exceptions. It is easier to understand that the condom and withdrawal are subject to the vagaries of time and mood. Incidentally the effectiveness of the condom has been undervalued for many years because it is so difficult to conduct trials which take into account that it is often used irregularly.

Among the unmarried only 10 were using the pill. Most of them (29) relied on the condom if they used anything at all; 5 used withdrawal, 3 used the safe period, 2 used the cap and 1 used a spermicidal cream; 33 used nothing at all.

The most popular method with the 267 married men and women was the pill; 110 (41 per cent) of them used this, 96 (36 per cent) used the condom and 12 (4 per cent) used the coil. In this group there were 2 men and 9 women of twenty-five who had three or more children; 3 used the pill, 3 used the condom, 2 used withdrawal and 3 did not use anything.

Gorer (1971) conducted a survey which attempted to find the distribution of the various contraceptive methods. As far as can be judged by studying two of his age groups (21–4 and 25–34) and comparing them with this group of twenty-five-year old men and women, less of his sample take the pill and more of them do not use birth control at all. Otherwise the proportions are similar except that he seems to have had more people who did not wish to answer this question. The reason for the difference may be that middle-class men and women are over-represented in our group, but even when Gorer sub-divides by social class, his AB (middle class) group are less likely to use the pill compared with the people interviewed in this research.

A more likely explanation is that Gorer's interviews were carried out at a time when there had been several scare stories about the dangers of oral contraceptives. This may have persuaded several people to stop (or not to start) using the pill. As more information became available, it was realized that these dangers had been exaggerated and more people are now using the pill.

The number of people now using some form of contraception presents a more satisfactory picture than I would have expected when I started this research. When these same people were boys and girls of eighteen, those with sexual experience were much less likely to use contraceptives; less than a third always used them and almost a half had never used any form of birth control. But although the figures reported in this section show that some progress has been made, there are still 134 men and women (38 per cent of those who have had sexual intercourse) who are still not convinced about the importance of adequate birth control.

4.6   Supply and Demand

Although many more people are now using contraceptives, it is surprisingly difficult for some people to get them. There is a flourishing trade in contraceptive appliances of all kinds, some of them of dubious value, but retail outlets have always been limited* and advertisements soliciting mail orders are often arbitrarily banned by publishers, not under any law but simply because they 'might give offence'. The London Passenger Transport Board, the Independent Broadcasting Authority and many other public authorities have always refused advertisements by the Family Planning Association.

Out of the 232 local health authorities in England, Scotland and Wales, only 15 provided advice and free supplies to all in 1972; another 146 provided a limited service, usually restricted to residents living in the area and only if they needed contraceptives for strictly medical reasons. This situation will improve when family planning becomes part of the National Health Service in 1974.

* Most local authorities prohibit the sale of contraceptives through vending machines in public places.

The men and women were asked where they obtained their contraceptives and of course their replies were quite different because the men are likely to buy only condoms (although one wrote to the Health Education Council for a supply of withdrawals). Most of them get their supplies from a chemist, and the barber still seems to do a good trade in contraceptives; these two retail outlets accounted for two thirds of the men who used the condom. There is some doubt if this will continue to be the best method of retail distribution. The small independent chemists are disappearing and the big chains are becoming more like gift stores staffed mainly by young girls; many men would be too embarrassed to ask for a packet of Durex in these smart shops. The modish hair stylist establishments now frequented by trendy young men feel that it would spoil their image to keep a stock of condoms.

About a tenth of those who use condoms seem to get them from agents or friends, and this may be an indication of their reluctance to get their supplies from ordinary shops. Rather fewer (about 7 per cent of those who use condoms) get their supplies from mail order houses and this may be because many popular magazines will not accept advertisements from these firms.

A few women bought caps and condoms from chemists, but the overwhelming majority went to the doctor for their contraceptives. Only about one in five of the women went to a clinic. Many towns still do not have family planning clinics and in others they are too far away from the centre and the main bus routes. Even so, it does seem that the straightforward supply of contraceptives is adding an unnecessary burden to the daily tasks of the already over-worked general practitioner.

Unfortunately it is a burden that most doctors are unwilling to relinquish. Of course the doctor makes money from selling contraceptives, a fact usually glossed over during discussions on this subject. It is difficult to estimate how much* and it would obviously vary from practice to practice. The

* Because most doctors have regarded this as a perquisite and have not declared it for tax purposes.

income is not so small that it deserves to be dismissed as unimportant, but the reasons given for retaining the doctor's hold on the source of supply are usually said to be medical, not financial.

Most of the knowledge and work involved in contraception is technically very simple and can be done by nurses or paramedical staff. Only a small amount of training is necessary for them to learn how to fit the cap or the coil. Peel and Potts in their *Textbook of Contraceptive Practice* (Cambridge University Press, 1969) write that: 'The prescription of the Pill is generally limited to medical practitioners, but this is more for administrative and legal convenience than for medically defensible reasons.' Casper Brook, Director of the Family Planning Association, has said that the apparatus of prescription should be scrapped and the pill should be sold over the counter.

It is possible to make out a case for medical advice before a woman starts taking the pill, because there are many types to choose from and one may be more suitable than another. But this does not mean that every woman need take up the doctor's time for repeat subscriptions once she has found a brand that suits her. It is sometimes said that the pill is a particularly dangerous drug (see section 4.7) which requires the doctor to be very careful before prescribing oral contraceptives, but Cartwright (1970) found that very few doctors conduct an examination when prescribing the pill.

The real reasons for preventing the pill and the coil from becoming more easily available are more political than medical. The greatest hindrance is the fear that more contraceptives leads to more promiscuity. The same fear is dominant when attempts are made to increase the number of the retail outlets for condoms and other contraceptives. It has been argued that the best way to sell condoms and caps is in a supermarket (not one of the recently opened sex supermarkets because many people would hesitate to enter the doors of these places), where the customer can simply pick up the brand he or she wants without having to ask for it. Advocates of birth control also hope that displays of contraceptives will lead to a certain amount of impulse buying. But any suggestion that contraceptives should be put on display is resisted, although there is no law against it.

Vending machines in public places have the same advantages as self-service stores with the additional advantage that contraceptives can also be obtained in the evening when the shops are closed and at the hours when there is more likely to be a demand for them. To those who argue that this is pandering to the demands of the thoughtless and improvident, it is fair to point out that these are probably not the sort of people who should be encouraged to produce illegitimate children.

The authorities and others who fear that the moral state of the nation will decline if contraceptives become available too easily tend to forget that there is one very popular form of contraception that does not require a retail outlet. Furthermore it costs nothing. But withdrawal is not a very effective form of birth control and if the other types are difficult to get, the number of unwanted pregnancies and the demand for abortions will increase.

The previous section showed that a hard core of men and women refused to use contraceptives for reasons strongly held though often mistaken. As well as these, there is another group who use birth control only occasionally or rarely and it is likely that they would become more regular users if contraceptives were more readily available. This is particularly true of the unmarried who are not having regular intercourse.

Although there have been some notable victories, in particular the establishment of the Brook Centres and the decision of the FPA in 1969 to allow their clinics to give advice to the unmarried, there are still many areas of Great Britain where a single girl cannot get supplies of contraceptives because she does not want to go to her family doctor and there is no clinic nearby which will supply her. It is often particularly difficult for a girl who goes out to work, for many clinics are only open for short periods at inconvenient times. Cartwright found that 38 per cent of the visitors to clinics had to wait an hour or longer.

Even some of the clinics supplying the unmarried have adopted a patronizing and forbidding attitude. Their clients have to go through a long interview, which goes beyond acquiring the necessary medical information, and are required to answer personal questions about their private life. In some areas the idea has spread (with some justification it is sad to report) that it will be much easier to get a supply of pills if you say you are engaged and just about to get married. It would be quite beyond the nerve of most girls to go to a clinic and tell the inquisitor that she had not got a regular chap but she feels it would be a sensible precaution to take the pill as she does occasionally have intercourse. From time to time various clinics produce statistics to show that most of their unmarried clients have regular boy friends (Lambert, 1971; McCorice and Hall, 1972). But it would be a great pity if the more feckless girls are discouraged from going to the clinic. It would seem to be far more important to prevent an unplanned pregnancy in an irresponsible girl than in someone who is engaged to be married.

People who oppose clinics that supply unmarried girls forget that the condom has been available to unmarried couples for many years and that the clinic is not doing anything new except giving the girl, instead of the man, the right to make the choice.

As sexual intercourse within marriage is socially accepted, it is not too difficult to make preparations and have contraceptives available. But premarital intercourse is often discouraged and when it does take place it may be unpremeditated and clandestine. These unmarried men and women may be theoretically aware of the risk they are taking, but sexual desire can override their awareness of the possible consequences and unless contraceptives can be obtained easily and without delay, birth control is unlikely to be used. Unfortunately the consequences of an unwanted pregnancy are far more serious for the unmarried than for the married.

4.7   Fears about the Pill

'I won't use it. I'm frightened I'd die.'

'It can cause harm to women, especially if she comes off it. It might cause deformity in the child.'

'It's not been tested enough. It needs more research.'

'I wouldn't take them myself because it's not advisable unless you're a hundred per cent fit. I had a chest complaint and the doctor asked if I was on the pill. That made me think a bit.'

'I didn't like Sheila using the pill. She's a perfect person. Why spoil it?'

'I'm quite frightened. Well, you hear so many things about it, don't you?'

Almost as many people have heard about the dangers of the pill as know about the pill itself. The advantages receive much less publicity although they are appreciated by the million and a half women who take it. There are many useful side effects including a sense of well-being,* freedom from the fear of pregnancy which often results in an increase in sexual pleasure, regular periods, the relief of premenstrual tension, the abolition of dysmenorrhea† in a large number of cases, reduced menstrual loss, the relief of acne‡ and less greasy hair.

The motives of people who exaggerate the dangers of the pill are mixed. Sometimes it is part of a campaign against all contraceptives. Sometimes it is because any unimportant remark on sexual behaviour receives more publicity than a similar comment on any other subject. Occasionally it is the older generation unconsciously expressing their jealousy about the facilities now open to the young when previously the sexual adventurer had to take greater risks. Most often it is deplored as just one more facet of the permissive society.

Most drugs produce side effects and the contraceptive pill is no exception, so there are genuine reasons for fear. Some of

* One doctor compared the 'alert, jolly and bright-eyed woman calling for her repeat prescription of oral contraceptive' with the 'anxious, sullen-faced drab who, perhaps as little as six months previously, had . . . asked in hopeless tones, as an aside from her myriad complaints, for information on the pill'.

† Dysmenorrhea is a severe pain over the lower abdomen at the onset of bleeding.

‡ Although some may consider this is a superficial advantage, a clear skin is of immense importance to adolescent girls at a time when appearance, acceptance and dating may be their main concern.

these side effects are pharmacogenic (i.e. caused by the chemicals in the pill) and others are psychogenic (i.e. caused by emotional upsets associated with taking the pill). It is not always easy to distinguish between the two.

Some of the disadvantages thought to be due to the actual ingredients in the pill are tenderness of the breasts before the period, gaining weight, headaches and depression; in addition the pill very slightly increases the chances of a serious illness, in particular thrombo-embolism.*

But many people now believe that the side effects are more often the result of the emotional state of the woman. There have been so many stories about the unpleasant effects of the pill in the press and woman's magazines that it can be an unnerving experience for a woman to start taking the pill. She will positively expect to experience side effects. In such cases it is the horror stories rather than the hormones that are the real source of the trouble.

Others start to take the pill to show they are willing, but are so apprehensive that they really wish to stop. Such women may complain excessively hoping their husbands, friends or doctors will take the responsibility of ordering them to stop. It also worries others that the pill is taken by mouth and that it is an unnatural interference with her whole body instead of being restricted to the genitals as in the case of other contraceptives.

Other women suffer from more deep-rooted unconscious emotional disturbances caused by shame and guilt about sex. The pill makes sex too easy because it affords safe protection and makes intercourse possible all the time and at any time. A woman with inhibiting guilt feelings will blame every incidental pain or illness on the pill.

All these emotional upsets can produce real psychological effects which may result in disturbances in the body. They are not caused by the ingredients of the pill, but by unconscious anticipation of possible side effects. This creates a self-fulfilling prophecy. The popular mythology emphasizes the

---

* This is a blood clot usually in a vein which may be carried to the lung causing a blockage there.

harmful effects of the pill and this causes women to be fearful before they start to take it.

Whatever the motives, the exaggeration of these dangers has frightened many people and persuaded them to give up taking the pill. In this group 29 (8 per cent) had changed from the pill to some other contraceptive.* In addition there is an unknown number who might have chosen to take the pill if they had not been put off by the mythology that is associated with it.

On the other hand 97 (26 per cent) had changed from some other contraceptive method to the pill. This is an encouraging figure but it should be remembered that oral contraceptives were not available to most of these young people when they first had intercourse, especially if they were not married at the time. It is interesting to note that among these 97, as many as 68 (18 per cent of the whole group) changed from the condom to the pill, and yet the sales of condoms in this country have not decreased which suggests that these are being sold to people who previously used withdrawal or no birth control method.

Among the remaining 70 per cent who use contraception, 15 per cent made various other changes not involving the pill, and 21 per cent have not changed from their original choice. Therefore the changes made by the men and women in this group suggest that a few people have been discouraged from using the pill, but the majority seem to be progressing from the less effective birth control methods to the more reliable techniques.

Nevertheless the fear is widespread and firmly planted in the minds of a large number of people, especially among the less well-educated groups. Gorer (1971) gives several examples of the folklore which so often surrounds sexual activities; one woman thought the pill was addictive; a man thought it made women frigid and a woman thought it made them aggressive; more than one person said it produced deformed babies; Peel and Potts (1969) also noted the confusion between oral contraceptives and thalidomide. One woman in

* This does not include a few more who stopped using the pill at the height of the scare but have now started taking it again.

this group suspected the pill was not working properly because she did not feel any side effects.

When they were asked specifically if they had any fears about the pill, only a third (38 per cent) of the group said definitely that they had no worries and a further 14 per cent gave non-committal replies. This leaves nearly half (48 per cent) who expressed some kind of concern. It is likely that the proportion would be even higher in an older age group.

The same proportion of men and women expressed fears, but there was some difference in the types of fear. The men were more likely to make a specific reference to thrombosis or blood clots (6 per cent women, 11 per cent men). The women were more likely to mention changes in appearance; 5 per cent women but only 1 per cent men said that it caused an increase in weight, and 27 per cent women compared with 21 per cent men mentioned other trivial (but annoying) side effects.

Another 6 per cent women and 11 per cent men made the valid point that the pill had only been taken for about ten years so it was impossible to be sure that some harmful long-term effect would not be discovered. This is true, of course, but the same reservation would have to be made about practically all the recent advances made in bio-chemistry and to a great many other things as well, such as the latest cosmetic creams, food additives and the residue of pesticides in food. It would be absurd to ban all new chemical discoveries because we are unable to provide certain proof that they were harmless. Even if we can show that a particular substance is harmful upon occasions, we still have to weigh the advantages against the drawbacks. The suspicions aroused by oral contraceptives have meant that no other preparations have ever been subjected to such rigorous and intensive investigation.

A significant 4 per cent said that they were unable to name any particular harmful effects but they had been told about acquaintances who had become ill after taking the pill. Gorer (1971) also found that many of the objections to the pill were based on vague ideas and unsubstantiated rumours. He and other workers found, as we did, that some women replied:

'My husband won't let me take it.' When the husband refuses to allow his wife to take the pill, there may be other more compelling reasons for this prohibition. There is no doubt that some men object to losing the initiative and wish to retain the power to decide whether birth control is to be used or not. (This is referred to in more detail in section 4.9.)

Much has been written on the health risks of oral contraceptives and this is not the right place to deal with the medical effects.* But there are certain social and demographic facts that should not be ignored.

The chances of death as a result of taking the pill are much smaller than many other activities which are not considered dangerous. There are many more people drowned while swimming for pleasure than there are fatalities from the pill. There are more accidents in the home which result in death than from the pill. For every million women aged 25–34 in England and Wales, 35 die in road accidents, 62 from suicide, and 13 from oral contraceptives.

It is impossible to get a true measure of the danger of oral contraceptives unless the mortality rate is compared with the mortality of those who do not use it. Peel and Potts (1969) compared the life chances of different groups of women and calculated that among a million women, 23 would be expected to die from taking the pill, 125 from abortion and 2,600 from maternity risks if they made no attempt to control their fertility rate. They conclude: 'The woman who begins taking oral contraceptives has a greater likelihood of being alive one year later than has her sister who chooses to have a baby or to use some less effective method of contraception.' Coroners and other doctors make speeches about the dangers of using the pill when they could equally well make remarks about the dangers of not using it.

4.8   Reasons for Rejection

Fear of the pill is not the only reason for not using contraception; perhaps it is not even the main reason. In this group 134

* This is discussed thoroughly in Peel and Potts, *Textbook of Contraceptive Practice*, pp. 101–27.

people did not use contraceptives on every occasion when they had sexual intercourse, but questions asking why do not often produce helpful replies. It is probably unreasonable to expect rational thought on such an emotive problem. Furthermore some of the group had only limited experience of sexual intercourse and it is not altogether surprising that they did not have contraceptives at the isolated moments when intercourse occurred. For example, 9 (5 per cent) of the girls had intercourse on less than twelve occasions in the last twelve months and it is unlikely that they would want to take the pill in these circumstances.

When they were eighteen those who did not always use birth control were asked why they did not do so. And about half of them seemed to have very little interest in making use of any contraceptive method at all. At that time I suggested that these boys and girls would be 'slow to profit from instruction in the use of contraceptives'. Answers to the same question seven years later indicate that this remark may have been too severe.

Among the 134 (36 per cent) who do not always use contraceptives, now that they are twenty-five, 25 (7 per cent) said they did not do so because they wanted another addition to the family and in a further 21 (6 per cent) cases the wife was already pregnant. Of course it is possible that the second group did not want to have a pregnancy at this time and a more careful spacing of the family would have been advantageous, but I felt it was too indelicate to ask our informants about this. So over a third of those who do not regularly use birth control gave an acceptable reason in the sense that it was a conscious choice and not the result of apathy or irresponsibility. It is worth noting that many researches do not take this reason into account when they report the large number of people who do not take precautions against producing an unwanted child. In any group of young married couples there must always be a large number who are not using contraception because they are planning to increase their family.

It was possible to put only 48 of the remaining 88 (out of 134) into meaningful categories; 21 (6 per cent) said they did not like to use contraceptives, 15 (4 per cent) claimed that they were 'not necessary', 7 (2 per cent) said it was not their concern, and only 5 (1 per cent) gave religious reasons; 40 (11 per cent) either said they didn't know, suggested it was no business of the interviewer's, or gave vague replies that could not be classified.

If it is thought that these replies are in the main unsatisfactory, it should not be forgotten that not even the experts agree on an objective evaluation of the reliability and use-effectiveness of the major contraceptive techniques. In fact there is something to be learnt from these results even if the replies of the men and women are sometimes confused and irrational.

It is clear that many people do not hold strong opinions and do not produce convincing arguments for rejecting the regular use of contraceptives. For example, religious reasons are given only rarely. 'It's not something you think about until you go to bed'; 'It's difficult to get the wife to discuss these things'; 'It's a good idea but I haven't got around to doing anything about it.' All these expressions of inertia present the birth control campaigners with an opportunity to change the attitudes of these people.

No one mentioned the cost of contraceptives and it is rarely considered when people think about the reasons for rejecting birth control. When the price of the pill, the condom or any of the others is calculated on an annual basis, it is true that the cost is fairly small, though not negligible. The £9 spent a year on condoms is money that could be spent on something else which might give more immediate pleasure. It is always extremely difficult to get people to pay now in order to save later. The cost of the pill over the year may be small, but it is not always easy for a woman to find the cash, especially if the doctor is charging a fee. The initial financial outlay for the coil, and even more for vasectomy, may have been a real obstacle for some, and it may have been the reason why others put off going to the doctor for the time being. It is not being over-dramatic to suggest those extra days at risk may be the cause of an unwanted pregnancy or an abortion. The cost of contraceptives may not have been the main reason for rejection, but it is unfortunate that the less effective contraceptives (caps, creams, jellies, suppositories) are less expensive and the least effective cost nothing at all.

4.9   *The Mythology*

'It is like having a bath with your socks on.'
'If God had intended it, it would have grown on you.'
'It's like eating toffees with the paper still on.'
'It just sort of messes it all up. It's inconvenient.'

These are some of the remarks made about contraceptives. Quite apart from the flippant remarks, however, if using contraception does spoil the pleasure of sexual intercourse, this is an important criticism and should be taken seriously. All those with sexual experience were asked if they found contraceptives spoilt or added to sexual pleasure and I have analysed the replies in some detail in Table 4/3.

More than twice as many people felt their particular birth control method spoilt (36 per cent) rather than added (15 per cent) to their sexual pleasure; but 25 per cent said it made no difference and 17 per cent could not answer (not including a further 7 per cent who were not asked the question because they had not had sexual intercourse).

There were considerable differences between the men and the women. Nearly half (47 per cent) the group of men felt contraception spoilt their enjoyment compared with only a fifth (20 per cent) of the women. Almost the same number of women (21 per cent) said it made sexual intercourse more enjoyable, but not many men (11 per cent) agreed with this. Similarly a third (33 per cent) of the women said it made no difference compared with less than one in five (18 per cent) of the men.

Withdrawal and the safe period, two of the least reliable methods, turned out to be the least popular. Of the 11 who used withdrawal, 9 disliked it; and 7 of the 8 who used the safe period said it spoilt their pleasure.

Not only were the least reliable the least popular, but vasectomy, without doubt the most effective, turned out to be the most popular. One man and the husband of one woman had undergone this minor operation, and both of

TABLE 4/3. Do you feel contraception spoils or adds to sexual pleasure: the replies of 284 (76 per cent)* men and women analysed by the birth control method used

	MEN				WOMEN				Total	
	Add	No difference	Spoil	Total	Add	No difference	Spoil	Total	No.	%
Pill	21	14	30	65	31	22	2	55	120	32
Condom	0	18	49	67	0	17	12	29	96	25
Coil	2	3	1	6	1	5	0	6	12	3
Cap	1	3	2	6	0	5	1	6	12	3
Withdrawal	0	1	5	6	0	1	4	5	11	3
Safe period	0	0	3	3	0	1	4	5	8	2
Chemical	0	1	0	1	1	0	0	1	2	1
Vasectomy	1	0	0	1	0	1	0	1	2	1
None	0	0	12	12	0	0	9	9	21	6
Total (No.)	25	40	102	167	33	52	32	117	284	—
Total (%)	11	18	47	76	21	33	20	75	—	76

* 66 (17 per cent) men and women could not answer because they had not used contraception and 26 (7 per cent) men and women were not asked the question because they had no experience of sexual intercourse.

them insisted that their sexual pleasure had increased after vasectomy. As the physical sexual act is not affected in any way, they must mean that without the fear of an unexpected pregnancy, they can feel more relaxed and enjoy more freedom in sexual expression.

But of course it is the condom that is the butt of all the jokes and to a certain extent it lived up to its bad reputation. Of the 96 users, 61 (64 per cent) said it spoilt their sexual enjoyment; most of them (49 out of 67 – 73 per cent) were men; indeed more women said it made no difference than said it spoilt their enjoyment. No one said it added to their pleasure. In fact it is well known that the condom can be helpful for men who suffer from premature ejaculation, a not uncommon complaint, but we did not ask about this and it is not the sort of information a man is likely to volunteer during an interview.

Among the 120 using the pill, 52 (43 per cent) felt it added to their sexual enjoyment and 32 (27 per cent) said it spoilt it. Almost as many men thought it spoilt their sex (30) as thought it added to it or made no difference (35). Almost all the women felt that it either added to their enjoyment or made no difference.

There is no shortage of stories about the women who got headaches, felt depressed or had other irritating side effects after taking the pill. Wherever these women may be, very few of them are to be found among this group. Only 2 of the 55 (4 per cent) women taking the pill felt that it spoilt their sexual pleasure. Perhaps the explanation is that although many women do get these trivial but irritating side effects when they start, for most women who persevere there is a pill that is found to be suitable after the initial effects have been overcome.

Perhaps the most surprising result is that 30 of the 65 (46 per cent) men whose sexual partners are taking the pill say that it spoils their enjoyment of sexual intercourse. It does not affect the sexual act except that it is believed to increase libido in some cases and decrease it in others; consequently some wives may be more demanding, while others may become less interested in sex. It may be because the man's fears about the dangers of oral contraceptives are greater than hers. Gorer (1971) has noted that it is often the husband who decides that his wife should not take the pill.

But the most likely explanation for this attitude is that the man regards the pill as a threat to his dominant role. The man is usually the initiator of sexual intercourse (in his opinion, at any rate) and he fears that he will lose this initiative if it is the woman who is in control of contraception. Many people still think that birth control is the man's business. A quarter of all the men in this group said that it was the man's responsibility (see section 4.12). This explanation is consistent with the two suggested reasons given in the previous paragraph. It might be very embarrassing for a man after several years of marriage and a regular pattern of sexual activity if the woman suddenly starts to make more demands. A woman can allow sexual intercourse to take place even if she is not in the mood for it, but a man may not be able to get an erection. A husband may resent not having complete control of the birth control situation because not only may he want to forbid his wife to take the pill, but also he may not know when she has not taken it. It is not difficult to envisage a situation where the husband does not want another child for financial or other reasons, but the wife who wants another baby forgets, perhaps unconsciously, to take her pills.

There was only one person who felt that the coil spoilt sexual enjoyment and this was a man. The loss of male dominance may also be the explanation for this. Among the other 12 users, 3 said it added to their pleasure and 8 said it made no difference.

There were 66 people who do not use any birth control method and were unable to say whether contraception added to or spoilt their sexual enjoyment. Not all those who reject contraceptives were quite so reticent. In fact 21 of those who do not use contraception said it spoilt their enjoyment and 15 of these had never used contraceptives.

The views of those who have never tried it and the large number of fanciful remarks about the condom suggest that an elaborate mythology still surrounds the true facts of birth control. The attitude of some people can be summed up in the feeling that somehow it is not natural. For others it is just not a subject for discussion. For others it is 'chicken' to use contraceptives, epitomized in the remark, 'If you take away the risk, you take away half the fun.' For others it is unmanly and for many, as the results of this research indicate, it is an intolerable loss to the man's dominance and dignity.

There are two important conclusions to be noted. The first is made abundantly clear from the last part of this section: more time and money should be spent on persuading the man that contraception is acceptable, propitious and neccesary. In Formosa the girls found contraceptive pills more useful as beads for their necklaces and it was not until men were convinced that progress was made.*

The second conclusion is that the problem is not as formidable as it appears at first sight. In this section the negative attitude to contraception has been discussed, but Table 4/3 indicates that over half (53 per cent) believe that contraceptives either add to their sexual pleasure or make no difference to it. It most be some encouragement to find that the ineffective methods are the least popular. This at least raises the hope that those who use withdrawal and the safe period can be persuaded to change if contraceptives can be obtained without trouble and expense.

This has been demonstrated by the undoubted success of the domiciliary services. A two-year survey of a FPA scheme showed that the birth rate per 1,000 among the families visited had dropped from 72·8 to 6·3. But this is a very expensive way of providing contraceptives, said to cost from £10 to £15 per head.

The plan proposed by the Birth Control Campaign (1972) has suggested that it is necessary to mount an advertising and publicity campaign on a similar scale to that undertaken by the Milk Marketing Board, costing over £2,000,000 a year. It is beyond the scope of this study to suggest details or attempt to cost educational campaigns on family planning.

* Men with large families were paid a reward if they agreed to vasectomy, but success was more often achieved by persuading the fathers that begetting a few healthy sons was better than many weak and starving children.

But these results do suggest that pound for pound, the money spent on such campaigns is likely to be more effective than, for example, publicity campaigns against smoking or VD, or encouraging the wearing of safety belts.

4.10   Identifying the Non-User

If there is to be a campaign to persuade more people to make use of effective contraceptives, it is important to know something about the people we are trying to influence. The results of this research suggest that a large number who have been irregular users now make a point of always using contraceptives. This suggests that the remaining irregular users may be persuaded to use contraceptives more frequently. Quite apart from any campaign some of these irregular users may be influenced by the new popular interest in ecology and the increasing awareness of the problem of over-population.

But there remains a fairly large group who do not use contraception and never have used it. Furthermore the present attitude of these people is that they do not ever intend to use contraceptives. If these people were middle-aged, we would expect them to be more inflexible in their attitudes; we might have to accept that their views could not be changed and that we could only wait until they reached the age when they were no longer fertile. But here we are describing a group of twenty-five year old men and women, one quarter of whom do not intend to use contraception. These women and the wives of these men can expect to be fertile for about another twenty years.

We must try to find out more about this group. In Table 4/4 I have compared the two ends of the scale. The first column refers to those who now always use a contraceptive method (of one kind or another); the second column refers to those who never use contraception; the third column is the total for the whole group. If the first column is higher than the third column, then those in that particular category are more likely to use birth control; if the second column is higher than the third column, then those in that particular category are less likely to use birth control. For example, in the first comparison 20 per cent of those who came from a broken home never used contraceptives compared with 17 per cent in the whole group, and 87 per cent of those who came from a home with two parents always used contraception compared with 83 per cent in the whole group. Thus it is fair to deduce that those from a broken home are less likely to use contraception than those who were brought up in a home where there were two parents. The various factors being compared cover home background, education, present situation and sexual behaviour.

TABLE 4/4. Those who always use contraception compared with those who never use contraception

	Always %	Never %	Total %	
Parental background				
Broken home	13	20	17	Those from a broken
Two-parent home	87	80	83	home are less likely to use contraception.
Parents' church attendance				
At least once a month	27	37	27	Those brought up in
Less than once a month	73	63	73	religious homes are less likely to use contraception.
Father's social class				
Middle class	31	27	30	Those from working-
Working class	69	73	70	class homes are less likely to use contraception.
Type of school				
Secondary modern	48	59	50	Those from secondary
Grammar or private	40	29	38	modern schools are less
Others	12	12	12	likely to use contraception.
GCE O levels				
None	56	74	54	Those who did not get
One or more	44	26	46	O levels are less likely to use contraception.
GCE A levels				
None	79	83	82	Those who did not get
One or more	21	17	18	A levels are less likely to use contraception.

	Always %	Never %	Total %	
Age left school				
15	46	64	49	Those who left school
16–17	37	25	35	earlier are less likely to
18+	17	11	15	use contraception.
Socio-economic class				
Middle class	32	20	29	Those who are now
Non-manual	28	25	28	manual workers are
Manual	36	48	39	less likely to use
Not known	4	7	4	contraception.
Wages (men only)				
Under £20	22	37	32	Men who are paid low
£20–£25	30	22	26	wages are less likely to
£25+	46	39	40	use contraception.
Not known	2	2	2	
Church attendance				
Never	69	67	69	Those who regularly
Less than once a week	22	15	19	go to church are less
Every week	9	18	12	likely to use contra-ception.
Visits to public houses				
Never or very rare	33	38	33	Those who never or
More than 3 days ago	40	32	39	rarely go to bars are
Less than 3 days ago	27	29	28	less likely to use con-traception.
Experience of sexual intercourse before eighteen				
No experience	69	73	72	Those who have not
Sexual intercourse	31	27	28	early experience of sexual intercourse are less likely to use contraception.
Premarital pregnancy of self or partner				
Not pregnant	81	76	82	Those who have had
Once	16	17	14	experience of premari-tal pregnancy are less
More than once	3	7	4	likely to use contra-ception.
No. (100%)	216	87	350	

Table 4/4 only includes those factors where there is a marked difference between those who use birth control regularly and those who never use it. Before commenting on these results, it is worth noting some of the factors that might have been expected to be in the table. For example the unsettling effect of being brought up in a situation where the parents move home is often thought to be a poor prognosis, but there was no difference regarding the use of contraceptives among those who came from stable homes and those who changed their homes often when young. The number of different jobs is often said to be an indication of poor adjustment, but those who had been employed in many jobs were neither more nor less likely to use contraception. Those who had been in trouble with the police or who had a court record were not less likely to use contraception.

It was even more surprising to find that those who were promiscuous were neither more nor less likely to use birth control. This was also true of those who had been infected by VD; although those who used a condom were less likely to get VD, over the whole group those infected were neither more nor less likely to use contraception.

The picture of the non-user of contraceptives that emerges from Table 4/4 is rather more complex than might have been expected. It is true that the deprived people from poor backgrounds with inadequate education appear here as they do in every health education problem. It is also true and not very surprising that those who do not use contraceptives are more likely to be involved in an unwanted pregnancy. But there are facets in this tabular description of the non-user that deserve special attention.

It can be seen in Table 4/4 that those from religious homes and those who are now churchgoers are less likely to use birth control. But an analysis of denomination does not support this association, apart from the Roman Catholics. Many of those who said they were Church of England, Non-Conformist or Jewish did use contraceptives, but more often than not these were the ones who did not attend their denominational church or synagogue. In other words, churchgoers are less likely to use contraception, but among non-churchgoers those who profess some religous affiliation are more likely to use birth control than those who disclaim any religious interests.

All those who gave religious reasons for not using contraception were Roman Catholics but this accounts for only 6 per cent of those who never used any birth control method. Among the 50 Roman Catholics in this group, 5 (10 per cent) never used birth control, 11 (22 per cent) used the safe period and 34 (68 per cent) used some other method.

The association between drinking and birth control is rather misleading. Although Table 4/4 showed, surprisingly, that those who rarely go to bars are less likely to use contraception, the same table indicates that among those who often go there is also a tendency not to use birth control. It seems to be the people in the middle group who go for an occasional drink who are more likely to be the regular user of contraception.

Another surprising result is that those who have had early experience of sexual intercourse are more likely to use contraceptives. A further analysis of this association reveals that there is a tendency among those with inceptive experience* at the age of eighteen to become regular users of contraception. It is also those who had very little or no sexual experience as teenagers who were less likely to use contraception when they did start sexual intercourse at a later age.

It is also interesting to note that early promiscuity is not a significant factor. There is no difference between those who had intercourse with several different partners, or with only one sexual partner; both of these groups were more likely to become regular users of contraception compared with the others.

The women who had a premarital pregnancy and the men whose girl friends had become pregnant were less likely to have used contraception. This is hardly surprising. A further analysis of these figures shows that some of them had an unwanted pregnancy more than once and still do not use any contraceptive method. A second illegitimate pregnancy, like a second abortion, suggests a failure in medical welfare.

* Inceptive is defined as extensive sexual intimacies which fall short of intercourse (from pages 41 and 55 of *The Sexual Behaviour of Young People*).

From the factors tested in this research the typical non-user of contraceptives comes from a working-class broken home where the remaining parent goes to church; she (or he) went to a secondary modern school, left at fifteen and did not take GCE; she is now a manual worker and not well paid; she goes to church and hardly ever drinks alcohol; she did not have sexual intercourse as a teenager but was pregnant before she married.

Of course this description must not be taken too literally. There will be some who never use contraceptives and yet do not conform to this pattern. Furthermore the picture is sure to be incomplete and there must be other factors that this research was not designed to identify.

Nevertheless there are many clues here to help those who wish to increase the use of contraceptives. It is not quite the usual picture of the men and women from deprived homes who are usually the last to benefit from medical or social progress. The religious factor complicates the picture. The various factors suggest that these people would tend to be placed towards the introverted end of a social attitude scale.

These people are not likely to be impressed by arguments from environmentalists, conservationists, demographers or ecologists. They are not likely to see posters in the town hall or advertisements in the *Guardian*. They may be influenced by a quiet word from a social worker or the example of a neighbour. They are more likely to be convinced of the acceptability of birth control when it becomes official government policy. They are more likely to use contraceptives if they can be obtained easily as well as inexpensively.

4.11   *The Gap between First Intercourse and Contraception*

It is tempting to say that things are not so bad as had been feared. The proportion who always use contraceptives is higher than in the past. There are signs that the irregular users can be persuaded to use contraception more often. Even among those who have never used any contraceptive method, there are some who say they will start to use birth control when their family is completed.

But the age of this particular group is significant. They have grown up and married in a decade when new contraceptive techniques have received much publicity. There will be older couples who are fertile, but who will be reluctant to make changes in the most intimate part of their lives. It is even more important to note that many of these men and women who are now using contraceptives at the age of twenty-five have only recently become regular users of contraceptives. Some of them have had to learn through bitter experience.

In this group of 350* men and women, there have been 85 cases of premarital pregnancies among 66 people; 18 per cent of the girls and 11 per cent of the sexual partners of the men had one pregnancy, while 3 per cent of the girls and 5 per cent of the partners of the putative fathers had more than one pregnancy before marriage. Taking into account only the last pregnancy of the 66 people concerned, 5 had self-induced miscarriages† and 24 had legal or criminal abortions, so in 29 cases it did not result in a live birth. In the remaining cases, 28 married the father or mother, 1 married someone else, 2 arranged for an adoption and 4 of the unmarried women kept their children.‡

It is very significant that 46 per cent of those who went through the experience of a premarital pregnancy now use contraceptives and 19 of the 29 (66 per cent) who had an abortion now always use birth control. So the extent of contraceptive use now is quite different from the situation five or six years ago when most of these young people were unmarried and starting their sexual activities. It is in this gap of about five years between the first experience of sexual intercourse and the regular use of contraceptives that much of the harm is done. Two out of three girls marrying under the age of twenty are pregnant and 22 per cent of all births under twenty are illegitimate. An unwanted pregnancy can cause considerable difficulties to a married couple, especially

* Not counting the 26 who have not had sexual intercourse.

† Spontaneous abortions were not included.

‡ In two cases the putative father did not know what the unmarried mother had done with the child.

among those who are poor and already have a large family. But the greatest distress for both mother and child occurs when an immature schoolgirl or student becomes pregnant. The girl who accepts the notion of premarital sexual intercourse is more likely to take precautions. It is often the girl with high moral principles who gets into trouble. These are also the girls who think that the solution to this lapse is to marry the father of their child. But these forced marriages are often unstable and a large number of them end up in divorce.

The conclusion must be that the extent of contraceptive use at the age of twenty-five presents an over-optimistic picture of the true situation. The gap between the age when a young person becomes fertile and when they start to use contraceptives is the cause of many personal tragedies, some of them irreparable.

4.12   Whose Responsibility?

One of the main reasons for the gap between the first experience of intercourse and the regular use of contraceptives is that many people are reluctant to talk about birth control at any time and especially during the preliminaries of love-making. One of the advantages of oral contraceptives is that it is easier to talk about the pill than about the intimacies of other contraceptive methods.

This chapter has shown that there has been much less discussion among friends about birth control than about other sexual matters. This reluctance is partly caused by embarrassment and partly by ignorance. The solution in either case is to introduce the subject in all sex education programmes in schools so that boys and girls become familiar with the words as they learn about the various methods. In this way the subject can be discussed and the most suitable method chosen.

At present many women are not given a free choice because they are not sufficiently well informed to question the man's decisions. In a study amongst women who had had an abortion (Morton-Williams and Hindell, 1972), it was found that men, whether husbands or lovers, often had a marked influence on a woman's contraceptive behaviour, for example, by encouraging her to take chances, by lulling her into a false sense of security or by expressing prejudices against a particular method (mainly the pill) which deterred the woman from using it. In section 4.9 of this chapter it was noted that many men feel threatened if they are not allowed to assume the dominant role.

We asked all the informants whether the man or the woman should be responsible for birth control decisions. Three quarters of the group gave fairly definite replies:

39 per cent (40 per cent men, 37 per cent women) thought it should be a joint decision.

21 per cent (25 per cent men, 14 per cent women) thought it was the man's responsibility.

6 per cent (10 per cent men, 24 per cent women) thought it was the woman's responsibility.

The majority think it should be a joint decision and this implies that the subject must be discussed. But a quarter of the men thought it was up to the man to decide, perhaps without consulting his partner; similarly about a quarter of the women felt it was better for them to take on the responsibility. As contraceptives used by females are more reliable than those used by men, the least satisfactory situation is when the man takes charge. But it should be pointed out that when the condom is used with competence, it has a low failure rate. The potential danger is that the man may be careless, drunk or out of supplies, and for these or other reasons, he may decide to take a chance. Morton-Williams and Hindell (1972) report that several of the women interviewed had become pregnant as a result of relying on the man to use some method of contraception which he had failed to use, or had used inefficiently.

We asked all the married informants who did not take responsibility for birth control themselves if they insisted that their spouse took precautions. Less than half (42 per cent) said they did. So there are still a considerable number of people who feel it is not their business, or who do not like to bring up the subject of contraception at all. Among the unmarried this attitude is even more prevalent and some of the unmarried girls said that a question about contraceptives would spoil the romantic mood of the moment.

4.13   Distribution

Another reason which limits the use of contraceptives is that it is still not easy to get supplies of the pill (as noted in section 4.6). There are still a few local authorities that are supplying no facilities and most of them supply only a limited service. It is estimated that of the 8 million potentially fertile women, $1\frac{3}{4}$ million receive contraceptives from their doctors and $\frac{3}{4}$ million get them from hospitals, health visitors and clinics. The reorganization of the National Health Service will remove responsibility for family planning from the 232 local health authorities in Great Britain after April 1974. On that date contraceptives will be provided at the standard NHS prescription charge of 20p. Those with adequate reasons will be exempt from this charge. This is a great advance on the existing situation, but it will still require special efforts to improve the way contraceptives are distributed. There are only a few clinics in the less privileged areas where they are most needed. Some are very crowded and others are open at inconvenient times. Even after April 1974 there will be doctors who will refuse to prescribe contraceptives to girls who are not married.

Some single girls fear that when they go to the clinic they will meet a hard-faced spinster who will give her a moral lecture. This fear is unjustified although a very few girls in this group did complain about off-hand treatment. It is easy to understand that the clinics try to appease their critics by emphasizing that most of the unmarried girls who come for contraceptives are, if not actually engaged to be married, at least involved in a 'mature and lasting relationship with one partner'. From the client's point of view, if she says she is in love, there are smiles all round and much less embarrassment. But it is possible that this attitude is forcing some young people into premature commitments which they are not ready to undertake.

The reports from the Brook clinics and the FPA both indicate that nearly all those who come are already sexually experienced. But this is really a cause for concern because it means that there is a period when nearly all girls are taking risks without taking precautions at a period of their lives when an unwanted pregnancy will have lamentable consequences.

The accusation that clinics will encourage promiscuity has made their administrators over-cautious, with the result that the sexually adventurous are too fearful or too embarrassed to seek contraceptive advice. Promiscuity is often misunderstood and misinterpreted both as a word and as a form of behaviour. But it is beyond argument that promiscuous sexual activity without contraceptive precautions is reckless behaviour. Imprudent girls need help and it is sad that they are not finding their way to the clinics.

Another factor which hinders the spread of contraceptive use is the fear of the pill. A section (4.7) has already been devoted to this. The Office of Health Economics (1972) has included a graph in their report *Family Planning in Great Britain* showing how the sales of oral contraceptives have increased over the last six years. But the graph is not a smooth upward curve; there are sudden dips in the curve and each one of these can be attributed to publicity given to the health hazards of the pill. Some of these warnings were justified, some were not. Each one caused a fall in the number of users and almost certainly an increase in the number of unwanted pregnancies.

The Government has decided to increase the budget for family planning to some £30 million per year. It would cost only a further £3 million a year to provide a completely free service. The NHS prescription charge is small, but it may still deter some people in the lower income brackets, the people who are least likely to use contraceptives. The choice is more likely to be between the cost of the pills and more housekeeping money, or a packet of condoms and a packet of cigarettes.

It is rather unfortunate that one firm has over 90 per cent of the market in condoms. LRC International which manufacture Durex and nearly all other brands sold in this country have annual sales of about £5 million. The Government has instructed the Monopolies Commission to investigate this situation to see how far it acts against the public interest and it is probably true that condoms would cost less if there was more competition. The price of contraceptives may seem small, especially when thought of in unit costs, but when advertisers spend thousands of pounds to announce two pence off a washing powder, it is a mistake to assume that the financial implications are unimportant.

Closely allied to the difficulty of obtaining contraceptives is the medical orientation that surrounds their distribution for the female. Many people, especially doctors, will maintain that this is necessary. The coil appears to give rise to tiresome side effects for one woman in four. The pill is a powerful drug and all such drugs can be dangerous, even though it is not so dangerous as some other drugs in common use.

But when the problem is so acute and so urgent, it is right to ask if distribution must depend on such a small number of medical men and women who are already over-worked. John Peel has referred to the 'closed shop of contraceptive techniques' and others have suggested that most of the techniques involved in contraception are simple and can be performed by non-medical staff.

Doctors are not well known for their enlightened attitudes to sex. In 1868 the *British Medical Journal* was objecting to the idea 'of assigning to medical men the intimated function of teaching females how to indulge their passions and limit their families'. Things have changed since then, but medical opinion still produces an occasional moralistic or alarmist warning. In 1963 the Assistant Secretary of the British Medical Association declared: 'As a doctor I can tell you that extra- and premarital intercourse is medically dangerous, morally degrading and nationally destructive.'

To the young the image of the typical family doctor today is of an over-worked, rather puritanical soul with old-fashioned ideas about sex and without the time or inclination to learn about the results of modern sex research. The well publicized case in which a doctor told the parents of a girl that she had asked for oral contraceptives was not resolved in a way that would give confidence to other young people. The kindly doctor who has visited the small girl in her home when she had measles or chicken pox is not likely to be the person in whom she can confide without embarrassment when she wants to obtain contraceptives.

Some women who prefer the anonymity of a hospital or clinic ask the prescribing doctor not to communicate with her own practitioner. Other women find it difficult to discuss contraception with a man and the great majority of general practitioners are male. Cartwright and Waite (1972) found that the advice given about birth control by general practitioners was limited; in many cases they were doing little more than responding to the patient's request for the pill. Only one in three would raise the subject of contraception unless there were special health problems.

The results of this research indicate that there are strong physical and psychological hindrances to the wide distribution of contraceptives, ranging from the girl in the chemist's shop who unknowingly inhibits the shy young man, to the doctor who is reluctant to talk about birth control to the girl he has known since the day of her birth. For many it is an intimate and embarrassing subject; they can easily be persuaded to put it off for another day. It is important that everything is done to prevent them from putting it off until it becomes a larger, more serious problem.

4.14 Publicity and Education

There remains an element in birth control that should never be forgotten. It always involves behaviour of the most intimate kind. People have a right to privacy. No matter how urgent the problem or tragic the circumstances, the solution should never be at the expense of a person's civil liberties. It follows that the only possible form of persuasion must come through publicity and education. It is an important part of the democratic process that changes are preceded by informed discussion. It is one of the fortunate by-products of publicity and education that it becomes easier to talk about the subject as the methods and words become more familiar; for this

5

reason, 'coil' is preferable to IUD, and the manufacturers should be discouraged from propagating in their timid advertisements euphemisms like 'protective' when they mean 'condom'.

There should be a change of emphasis in the publicity campaigns. The results of this research suggest that people are aware of the advantages of contraception, even if they do not make use of it soon enough or often enough. There are also indications that there should be less emphasis on the medical connotations and more emphasis on the part played by the man; this suggests a new evaluation of the centuries-old male methods and, more importantly, a better understanding of the man's attitude to the female methods. Professional advice is usually restricted to female methods of birth control, but Peel (1970) has shown that advice offered to men by social workers can lead to a surprising reduction in pregnancies. After all the conventional expectation is that the male is the dominant partner and important decisions are left to him. Some women felt that as it was the man who was demanding sex, it was his responsibility. Hence the age-old cry: 'It was his idea, so I thought he was doing something about it.'

Indeed the condom is still the preferred method. In the apt words of the medical director of the International Planned Parenthood Federation: 'Barbers help plan more families than all the doctor services (including the FPA) put together' (Potts, Darwin Lecture).

Publicity depends upon media, money and motivation. As we have only a small amount of experience in this field, more research is needed into the results to be obtained from press, television, radio, posters and other media. Publicity is expensive but the social costing carried out by several reputable bodies (and mentioned in the next section of this chapter) clearly demonstrates that it is money well spent. We also need more sociological and psychological research to give us a better understanding of individual motivation. It is never the whole story, nor a satisfactory explanation, to say that people are apathetic when it is in their own best interests to take action.

4.15   Eight Basic Steps

Many people now agree that universal contraception is self-evidently desirable. The results described in this chapter indicate that there are eight major areas where progress can be made:

1   narrow the gap between first intercourse and first use of a birth control method
2   put more emphasis on the man's part
3   improve the distribution and availability of contraceptives
4   reconsider the doctor's role
5   provide a free service
6   publicize the financial benefits to the community
7   undertake more sociological research
8   integrate the birth control service with a new population policy.

The greatest damage and the most unhappiness is caused by the gap between first intercourse and the age when contraception is used regularly. This gap can be closed by better sex education and by making it easier for young unmarried girls to obtain contraceptives.

The attitudes of the man to birth control and his fears about loss of prestige have been under-emphasized in the past. Future propaganda must take more account of the male point of view. Furthermore the condom is a fairly reliable method and even withdrawal, which used to be thought of as undesirable because it produced psychological and physiological tensions, is less criticized than it used to be.

It is important that all contraceptives are more readily available. This means increasing the number and types of retail outlets, changing local laws which prohibit vending machines, relaxing the unofficial censorship on advertising contraception, and perhaps finding other ways of distributing oral contraceptives.

It is necessary to take a new look at the role of the doctor, not as the adviser, but as the supplier of contraceptives. It will be difficult to persuade the medical authorities that the suggestions made in this chapter are intended to bring about an increase in the availability of contraceptives but not to restrict the activities of doctors in any way. On the contrary, the professional education of medical students should provide adequate knowledge of contraception and sterilization, and general practitioners should be encouraged to go on special courses. Only about 4,000 of the 23,000 general practitioners have received formal training in family limitation.

The retail cost of contraceptives needs closer study. Years of research requiring large capital investment may account for the high cost of some oral contraceptives, but other simple devices are sold at unnecessarily inflated prices. A watch should be kept on the dominant position of the leading manufacturer of condoms. Patents controlling the sale and distribution of coils and other devices should be discouraged, and even disallowed when the improvement has not been the result of long research or large investment.

In fact it has often been shown (Brook, 1968) that the prevention of unwanted pregnancies would save the country considerable sums in medical care, welfare services and other expenditure. The financial savings to the community have been calculated in a recent report (Laing, 1972) which identified the potential savings as being equal to the difference between the unwanted child's consumption of health and welfare resources, and the average consumption among all children. Not all these costs could be measured; for example, there were no reliable statistics on differences in delinquency costs. But it could be demonstrated that the prevention of the birth of unwanted children would save a considerable amount of public expenditure in supplementary benefits, child care facilities, sickness benefits and temporary accommodation for the homeless. The potential benefits if contraception could prevent the birth of all unwanted children would be in excess of £250,000,000 per annum.

Although there has been impressive progress in medical knowledge, the contribution that can be made by the social sciences is only just beginning to be appreciated. Radical alterations in society will bring about changes in attitudes to contraception. The idea that a woman can only find fulfilment as a wife and mother has rightly been challenged by Women's Liberation movements. The occupational career of the wife may be as important as the husband's. In these circumstances family planning becomes an important factor in the domestic arrangements of married couples. Furthermore changes in the sex code and the results of modern sex research will have far-reaching effects. It is now accepted that the female sexual response can be as strong and as rapid as the male's, once sexual inhibitions have disappeared. Sociological and psychological research will help us to understand these changes. Different ethics and different values will start a demand for more reliable and more acceptable contraceptive techniques.

Finally the increase in the population has made this problem more urgent. Not long ago it was hopefully assumed that a comprehensive birth control service would solve the problem of over-population. Unfortunately we now know that even a world-wide use of contraceptives will not defuse the population bomb. The slogan 'every child a wanted child' represents a socially desirable goal, but the chief cause of over-population is that people want too many children. But effective birth control is an essential first step and indeed the *sine qua non* of any programme to retard the growth of over-population.

5. Premarital Pregnancies

5.1 The Incidence in This Research

The previous chapter indicated that much can be done to help women avoid an unwanted pregnancy. But even if all the steps in the programme are implemented, there will still be a number of unwanted pregnancies in the foreseeable future. In the near future it is the premarital pregnancies that will cause the most distress. This is a problem that requires swift action in the short term and a fundamental change of attitude in the long term.

All the married women in this group were asked if they had become pregnant before their wedding, and the married men were asked if they had ever been responsible for a girl's pregnancy before they had got married. The unmarried women and men were asked a similar question. This is a very personal question; even in an interview like this where rapport and confidentiality were given the highest priority, it is possible that some of them wished to avoid talking about what must have been a distressing episode for most of them. Even so 32 (20 per cent) women and 34 (16 per cent) men said they had been involved in a premarital pregnancy.

It had happened more than once to 14 (4 per cent) of them. Among these 66 women and men, there were 85 premarital pregnancies; to 10 of them it had happened twice, to 3 of them it had happened three times, and 1 said it had happened four times.* Although the parents of a girl who

* Throughout this chapter the cases of premarital pregnancy and (later) of abortions are sometimes totalled together. There were 66 premarital pregnancies, 34 of which involved the men. This, of course, refers to premarital pregnancies experienced by the girl friends of the men, not to 34 supernatural phenomena.

'gets into trouble' still tend to regard this as a shameful and dreadful event, it can hardly be regarded as unusual and appears to be the experience of at least one in five of all the families in the land.

They were asked if they had been using any contraceptive method during the period when the pregnancy occurred. This question referred only to the last premarital pregnancy in those cases where there had been more than one.

In 52 of the 66 cases (79 per cent) no contraceptive method was used. This re-emphasizes the point made in Chapter 4 that birth control is less likely to be used in premarital sexual intercourse because it is often unpremeditated and also because it is more difficult for an unmarried girl to obtain contraceptives. Only 14 of the 66 (21 per cent) claimed that their premarital pregnancy was due to contraceptive failure. This includes the less effective contraceptive techniques as well as the pill, and allowance must also be made for a tendency to use contraceptive failure as an excuse when an unwanted pregnancy occurs. In Lambert's (1971) survey of 3,000 unwanted pregnancies 19 per cent used contraception. This figure is probably closer to reality. It is beyond dispute that many more premarital pregnancies can be avoided if more people can be persuaded to use contraceptives, but these figures are a warning that this alone will not solve the problem. The least effective contraceptive methods are the easiest to obtain, and even when the more effective techniques are made more readily available, there will always be some who are careless.

5.2 *The Consequences*

The 66 people were asked what happened after they had discovered about the premarital pregnancies. Table 5/1 refers only to the last occasion and so there are 19 other cases of pregnancies in this group which are not accounted for in this section.

The table shows that the 66 pregnancies resulted in 37 live births. In most cases (28) the father and mother married. Since then 3 of these 28 (11 per cent) marriages have broken up, which is a higher rate than in the whole group where 10 of the 257 (4 per cent) married informants have divorced or separated. Although pressure to marry is often put upon the couple, a forced marriage is often a poor solution to the problem of a premarital pregnancy.

TABLE 5/1. The results of 66 cases of premarital pregnancies

Result of premarital pregnancy	Men	Women	Total
Married father or mother	11	17	28
Married someone else	0	1	1
Kept the child	3	1	4
Adopted	1	1	2
Not known	2	0	2
Induced abortion	13	11	24
Self-induced abortion	4	1	5
Total	34	32	66

One woman kept her child and married someone who was not the putative father. This marriage also ended in divorce. Another 4 people kept the child and none of these are married. People who advise girls to keep their illegitimate children often fail to warn the unmarried mother that her chances of marriage and family life are considerably diminished if she takes this advice.

Only two of the children were adopted. In one case the mother has now married and has no contact with the child. In the other case the child is being brought up by the grandparent.* In the remaining two cases the men concerned do not know what has happened to the child as they have lost touch with the girl they had made pregnant.

It is often assumed that an increase in the illegitimacy rates indicates an increase in the incidence of premarital intercourse. A rise in the number of illegitimate births in the future will reflect the weakening of the pressures upon the girl to marry the putative father and the strengthening of the woman's right to make a choice.

* None of the children were taken into residential or foster care.

5.3   The People At Risk

The men and women who are most likely to be involved in a premarital pregnancy are those who take the most risks. This straightforward relationship can be shown in several ways. Table 5/2 selects two examples that demonstrate the mathematical association between the number of occasions a person has sexual intercourse and the likelihood of a premarital pregnancy.

Of those who had their first experience of sexual intercourse before the age of seventeen, 28 per cent had a premarital pregnancy; this applied to 19 per cent whose first experience was between eighteen and twenty-one; and 3 per cent of those whose first sexual intercourse was after the age of twenty-one had a premarital pregnancy. So the earlier they start, the more likely they are to be involved in a premarital pregnancy.

TABLE 5/2. Those who have been involved in one or more premarital pregnancies compared with duration and frequency of sexual experience

| | Premarital pregnancies | | | Total |
	None	1	2+	
Age of first experience of sexual intercourse				
14–17	88	24	11	123
18–21	122	26	3	151
Over 21	71	2	0	73
NK or NA	29	0	0	29
Shortest time known partner before sexual intercourse				
Within a week	78	24	10	112
Week to a year	94	23	4	121
Over a year	95	5	0	100
NK or NA	43	0	0	43
Totals	310	52	14	376

The informants were asked what was the shortest time they had known someone before having sexual intercourse. About a quarter (27 per cent) of the group had known their partners for over a year, but about a third (30 per cent) had sexual intercourse within a week. The longer the interval between first meeting and first intercourse, the less likely they were to be involved in a premarital pregnancy. In fact 30 per cent of those who had sex within a week or less were involved; this applied to 22 per cent of those within a year; while only 5 per cent of those who said it was over a year before the friendship led to sexual intercourse were involved in a premarital pregnancy.

Those who use contraceptives are, of course, less likely to have a premarital pregnancy, but birth control appears to have only a small influence on this overall picture. This is because the number of people who are using effective contraceptive techniques during their premarital sexual adventures is too small to make a significant impact on the simple mathematical relationships between the extent of sexual intercourse and the chances of a premarital pregnancy.

Some of those who have a premarital pregnancy are not quick to learn from the experience. Only 3 per cent of those who now have only one partner had two or more premarital pregnancies, but it happened more than once to 13 per cent of those who had several partners last year. None of those who had sex with their spouse only before they were married had more than one premarital pregnancy; but 4 per cent of those whose first partner was a steady relationship and 13 per cent of those whose first partner was an acquaintance or pick-up had two or more premarital pregnancies. This is a very unsatisfactory situation. It suggests that those who are promiscuous find it much more difficult to get advice and help, and consequently they are less likely to avoid a second premarital pregnancy.

Given the present situation in the provision of contraceptives for unmarried women, the association between the number of premarital pregnancies and the frequency of sexual intercourse is only to be expected; even the relationship of promiscuity to a second premarital pregnancy is not altogether surprising. But it is surprising that there is a clear association between middle-class men and women, and the chances of a premarital pregnancy. In fact, 24 out of 110 (22 per cent) middle class (as estimated by occupational status) compared with 40 out of 250 (16 per cent) working class were involved in a premarital pregnancy (see Table 5/3).

TABLE 5/3. Those who have been involved in one or more premarital pregnancies compared with social class.

| Social class | Premarital pregnancies | | | |
	None	1	2+	Total
Middle class	86	19	5	110
Non-manual	88	13	3	104
Manual	122	19	5	146
NK	14	1	1	16
Totals	310	52	14	376

This is confirmed by an analysis of the wages of both men and women. For example, 33 per cent of the men earning over £30 a week compared with 9 per cent of the men earning under £30 a week had made a girl pregnant before marriage. In Chapter 4 it was found that the middle class were more likely to use contraceptives and it appears inconsistent that they are also more likely to be involved in a premarital pregnancy. The explanation is that the middle-class tendency to use contraceptives refers to the present time (at the age of twenty-five), but there is a very large gap between first intercourse and first use of birth control. In fact a girl of any social class is unlikely to use a contraceptive during the first weeks of sexual experimentation.

The extra premarital pregnancies among the middle class are probably accounted for by increased sexual frequencies. We know from the earlier research that there is very little difference between middle- and working-class boys at the age of eighteen, but that the sexual frequencies of middle-class girls are significantly higher. It seems likely that the sexual frequencies of both boys and girls in the middle class increase more rapidly than among the working class. We have no figures for the ages between eighteen and twenty-five, but all the circumstantial evidence would favour a more rapid increase in middle-class frequencies. They have more facilities (cars, separate rooms, living away from home); they adopt a more permissive attitude; the girls are more likely to assert their sexual independence; they marry later and so there are more years of premarital experience. By the age of twenty-five the sexual frequencies of the married working class have caught up, but it seems probable that in the pre-marital period the middle class are much more active and this would account for the greater proportion of pregnancies despite the increasing use of contraceptives.

The social class difference is confirmed by a comparison of the well educated with the others. Although 51 of the 319 (16 per cent) who left school at seventeen or earlier were involved in premarital pregnancies, this happened to no less than a quarter, 15 out of 57 (26 per cent) who left school at eighteen or older. This is a striking proportion and illustrates the risks to which the student population is exposed.

It is still more important to see what happens as a result of these pregnancies. Table 5/4 shows that 34 of those who left school at fifteen were involved in a premarital pregnancy; of these 34, 21 (62 per cent) had a forced marriage with the bride pregnant on the wedding day. This compares with the 32 who left school at sixteen or over and who were involved in a premarital pregnancy; only 7 of these 32 (22 per cent) had a forced marriage. On the other hand only 3 of the 34 (9 per cent) who left school at fifteen had an induced abortion compared with 21 of the 32 (66 per cent) who left school at sixteen or later. So the well educated are much more likely to get an abortion and the poorly educated are more likely to be persuaded to do 'the right thing', that is to 'give the child a name'.

The figures for unmarried mothers are low in this group, but the tendency seems to be for the working-class girl to keep the child. The unmarried mother who decides to eschew marriage and defy convention is not represented in this group; although she undoubtedly exists, the number is probably quite small despite the publicity. All the working-class unmarried mothers in this group were having a hard time, either having to find fees for a day nursery or living on subsistence. There is still a strong tendency to keep the child either as an un-married mother or by arranging a hurried marriage in the lower socio-economic groups; in this study 76 per cent (26 out of 34) of working-class families compared with 12 per cent (4 out of 32) of the more fortunate families decided against adoption or abortion.

5.4   Terminations and Miscarriages

Table 5/4 shows that in this group there were 24 induced abortions and 5 self-induced miscarriages.* All of these 29 terminations occurred outside marriage and between one and seven years ago. So they occurred before and after the 1967 Abortion Act which did not really become fully operational until the latter part of 1968.

TABLE 5/4. The result of 66 premarital pregnancies compared with the age of leaving school

Result of pregnancy	Age left school			Total
	15	16–17	18+	
Married putative parent	21	4	3	28
Married someone else	1	0	0	1
Kept child	4	0	0	4
Adopted	1	1	0	2
Induced abortion	3	10	11	24
Self-induced abortion	3	1	1	5
NK	1	1	0	2
NA	152	116	42	310
Total	186	133	57	376

At least 44 per cent of the premarital pregnancies did not result in a live birth; 12 (8 per cent of the whole group) women and the sex partners of 17 (8 per cent) men had an abortion. In addition the interviewers strongly suspected that another 2 women and 4 men were involved in an abortion, but they were not pressed on this point, and so they are not counted in the reckoning in this section. It is extremely difficult to obtain accurate information on the number of abortions, especially as some of the cases reported in this group

* Spontaneous miscarriages are not included in this section.

were illegal operations. Some researches indicate that, even when abortion is legal, women tend to report fewer than the actual number of abortions they have had. The question the men were asked was: Has a girl friend of yours ever had an abortion at the time you were going out with her? This limitation was imposed on the question to the men because we wanted to know something about the circumstances, but it means that a possible abortion before the girl met the man would not be reported. This reinforces the suggestion that the 29 (8 per cent) abortions reported here is an underestimate. Yet it is not a small figure. If 8 per cent of the female population aged eighteen to twenty-five have an abortion, this will require facilities for over 200,000 terminations.

Only 4 of the 29 (14 per cent) were done on the National Health. Another 10 (34 per cent) were done privately under the 1967 Act. But 8 (28 per cent) terminations were performed by doctors acting illegally. Before the law was changed many operations were carried out on those who could afford to pay a large fee and even today some doctors will dispense with the formalities required by the 1967 Act if the situation is urgent and the fee is sufficient.

A further 2 (7 per cent) abortions were carried out by non-medical personnel, the so-called back-street abortionists. Finally 5 (17 per cent) abortions are classified as self-induced because they were thought to be the result of various self-medications suggested by friends and relatives. There is an extensive folklore about the best way to abort, such as hot baths, gin, quinine and other doubtful remedies. Nearly always it involves administering some kind of poison to the body which will cause the foetus to be expelled. These activities are not illegal but are the cause of much illness and distress, often requiring admission to hospital.

Therefore in this group 48 per cent of the abortions were legal, 34 per cent were illegal and 17 per cent were self-induced. It is unlikely that the same proportions would be found today. It is generally assumed that as it becomes easier to obtain legal abortions, the number of illegal abortions will decrease. This theory is supported by the reduction of London Emergency Bed Service abortion figures, and by the widespread belief among clinicians that a substantial reduction has occurred among unskilled abortions reaching NHS hospitals. It was impossible to date each of the terminations reported in this research, but it cannot be assumed that none of the illegal and self-induced abortions occurred after 1968.

Although there was only one case in this group, most of the abortions since the passing of the Act have been carried out on married women. Many married women can get an abortion under the non-medical clauses of the Act because they already have several children and do not wish to enlarge their family. A single woman would find it more difficult to get a legal abortion on the National Health except for specific medical reasons. In this group 24 said the putative father was a steady boy friend and 5 said it had been a more casual relationship.* Even allowing for the understandable tendency for informants to make out that it was a steady relationship when in some cases it might have been of quite a short duration, it is noticeable how few were the result of casual affairs. Carelessness or irresponsible behaviour are not thought to be sufficient reasons under the Act for obtaining an abortion. But it is the child of a promiscuous affair that is more likely to be unwanted and unloved.

When they were asked why they decided to have an abortion at that particular time, the replies were not always easy to classify. Many expressed vehement opposition to the idea of giving birth to an illegitimate child without being able to give an explicit reason.

'I'd rather have died.'

'I told the doctor I'd commit suicide.'

'I couldn't stand the thought of bringing an innocent child into this sort of mess.'

Only two (one of them married) replies seemed to be for strictly medical reasons as defined in the Act. The others would be classified more generally as social reasons, although some mentioned more specific considerations; 2 said there

* Readers are reminded of the footnote in the first section of this chapter on p. 134. The total number of abortions includes terminations to the sexual partners of 17 men as well as to 12 women in this group.

was strong parental involvement and the girls were sent away from home for the abortion, so that the neighbours would not find out; 8 specifically said that it was unfair to brand a child with the stigma of illegitimacy; 2 said financial considerations were uppermost in their decision; the remaining 15 gave reasons that simply indicated that the child would be unwanted.

It is middle-class couples who are more likely to seek and obtain an abortion. The reason is that they do not feel emotionally or financially ready for marriage, or because they are not sure they want to marry the other person concerned, or that a child at that stage would seriously interfere with academic or occupational prospects.

The situation at the time of the interview was that 12 of the 29 are now married. A termination is not such a handicap to getting married as an illegitimate child. Of all those who had a premarital pregnancy, 29 married before the child was born, 12 married after an abortion, and 1 married after the child had been adopted. Among those who remained single, 17 had an abortion, 4 became unmarried mothers, and 1 arranged for an adoption. In two cases the result is unknown.

Everyone in the group was asked if they knew how to get an abortion. About half (48 per cent) said they did know what to do, 22 per cent were unsure of the attitude of their general practitioner and would hesitate to broach the subject, while 30 per cent said they had no idea how to set about getting an abortion. According to some of the reports in this research, there are still doctors who urge the girl to get married, even though they have never met the father and are quite unable to judge whether it would be suitable for the couple to get married.

The results of this research probably underestimate the number of abortions carried out on young people under the age of twenty-five and probably overestimate the number of illegal operations now being performed. A National Opinion Poll survey estimated that three quarters of all abortions in 1966 had been illegal. It is not possible to estimate the extent of illegal abortions since the 1967 Act but the numbers must be much smaller.

Abortion is an inevitable last resort even when contraceptives become more readily available. Indeed abortion is a form of birth control. None of the informants had ever thought of it in this way and few had imagined that they would be involved in an abortion before their unwanted pregnancy. But it seems likely that there will always be a certain type of person who will be careless about taking precautions although they are unable or unwilling to bring up a child.

5.5 Aborting and Abortionists

In section 5.3 it was found that premarital pregnancies were more likely to occur among people who had sexual intercourse more frequently and so were more often at risk. It is unsurprising that the same people were more likely to seek a termination. There was very little difference in the sexual activities between those who had a premarital live birth and between those who had an abortion. Nor could I detect any difference in the sex activities of those who had a legal operation and those who had an illegal abortion.

But the middle-class girls were more likely to have a private legal termination, and were also more likely to have an illegal abortion performed by a medical man. The working-class girls were more likely to have a non-medical illegal operation and were also more likely to have a self-induced abortion.

Clearly the deciding factor is the cost. Most private legal terminations are still very expensive and illegal operations even more so. The patient is expected to compensate the doctor for the risks he takes by performing an illegal operation. During the first three years after the 1967 Act it was much easier to get an abortion in the private sector than under the National Health Service. This was because there was a shortage of beds in NHS hospitals and a shortage of consultants willing to perform the operation. There are also cases in which the consultant gynaecologist has pointed out to the patient that, although she had grounds for an abortion, she did not live in the area of his hospital; this means that he could not carry out the operation under the National Health, but he could do it if she paid him.

Although cost was the reason why many working-class women did not go to the private sector, in fact they were not more likely to get an abortion on the National Health Service. Middle-class women had an equal chance of getting a NHS termination.

So middle-class women are more likely to have a premarital pregnancy and still more likely to have an abortion. This may be because they have a different attitude to sex, shot-gun marriages and abortion. But it is also because the procedures and facilities provided under the 1967 Act are so complex that only working-class women of unusual determination can find their way to someone who will help them. They also find it more difficult to persuade a doctor to carry out the operation.*

5.6   The Cost of an Abortion

It is generally estimated that an abortion can be performed for under £50 and this includes a bed in a private nursing home. The Pregnancy Advisory Services charge about £60 and this covers the cost of free abortions for women who cannot afford to pay.

The price charged in the private sector seems to be between £100 and £120. The cost to foreign girls is usually much more, sometimes as much as £200. In 1971 about 58 per cent of all the abortions notified were carried out in the private sector. About a third of these were under the auspices of the non-profit-making charities, notably the two Pregnancy Advisory Services. This leaves about 45,000 operations carried out by doctors privately, but does not include the considerable number that were not notified to the authorities as they should have been under the 1967 Act.

About 11 per cent of all operations in 1971 were performed

* One consultant has said publicly that he is prepared to help out 'sensible' students who have been 'unlucky', but he is horrified by 'dolly birds' who are likely 'to demand a discharge before the week-end because there is a party on Saturday night'.

on women not normally resident in England. At a conservative estimate this means that 5,000 operations at £150 each were performed on girls from abroad in 1971, which adds up to £¾ million of foreign currency and must put these doctors in line for the Queen's Award for Exports.

In addition they must have made a profit of over £2 million on the home market. In the *Release Progress Report* (d'Agapeyeff, 1972) it was stated that during a period of twelve weeks one doctor received £12,065 from girls referred to him (plus the fees paid by seventeen other girls who were sent to him but did not tell Release how much they had paid him).

The 1967 Abortion Act has provided an opportunity for private entrepreneurs to exploit human distress and has created a free market in medicine. It can be claimed that the private abortionists are carrying out tasks that the National Health Service was unable to perform in the early years of the new Act and has at least reduced the number of back-street abortions which were the cause of much physical injury that often ended up by filling beds in NHS hospitals, but the large fees and high profit margins demanded by the doctors expose them to the charge of exploitation.

Some doctors who used to do illegal operations are now making even more money performing abortions under the new Act. The situation is caused by the large number of women who need an abortion urgently and cannot shop around until they find someone to do the operation at a reasonable price. The main hope is that improvements in medical technology will allow an abortion to be carried out very cheaply without tying up scarce beds in NHS hospitals. But it is important that the National Health Service should quickly take up the vacuum aspiration technique and not leave the medical entrepreneurs to exploit this method by charging high prices to patients who do not have the time or the opportunity to look around for the least expensive operator.

5.7   The Fear of Premarital Pregnancy

This chapter has been considering the plight of those who
have been involved in a premarital pregnancy and the
smaller number of those who have been involved in an
abortion. What is less often taken into account is the fear of
a premarital pregnancy that affects very many single women
and many men. Many married couples also fear a possible
pregnancy.

Excluding those who have no experience of sexual intercourse, 52 per cent of the women had thought that they were
pregnant when they were not, and 45 per cent of the men had
thought that they had made a girl pregnant but it turned out
to be a false alarm. This proportion also excludes the 85
occasions when their fears of a premarital pregnancy proved
to be well founded.

For some people the possibility is not an isolated experience. For about one in five of those in this group, this is a
recurring fear. Of course many of them could not give an
accurate answer when asked how often these fears had
occurred, but we added up their estimates. In this group of
350 people (again excluding those who had not had sexual
intercourse), there were at least 470 cases when they were
troubled by this possibility. This figure does not mean very
much in itself, but it does suggest quite strongly that this fear
is interfering with the sexual pleasure of many people on
many occasions and inevitably causes one or both sexual
partners to feel ill at ease and unrelaxed during intercourse.

It is a surprise, therefore, to find that only a few people in
this group have used the facilities offered by the commercial
pregnancy-testing agencies, now widely advertised. In fact
only 38 (10 per cent) informants in this group had ever used
one and as many as 26 (7 per cent) said they were not satisfied with the services provided.

Many of the agencies do not make it clear that the results
of the test cannot be guaranteed to be 100 per cent accurate
and there are other disadvantages. But most of those who
complained were vague about their dissatisfaction and could
not give specific reasons beyond a feeling that they did not

feel absolutely sure even after receiving a negative result.* But it is only fair to report that there was no case in this research when a pregnancy-testing agency gave a negative result when the girl was in fact pregnant.

It is not always easy for a doctor to diagnose pregnancy in the first six weeks, so pregnancy-testing using urine samples is a useful guide. These tests are accurate in about 97 per cent of all cases. This may seem a high success rate to a statistician, but is not sure enough for a woman who has missed two periods. By this time (i.e. eight weeks after the last period) physical examination would be the best way to determine the presence or absence of pregnancy.

As there is such a widespread fear of pregnancy and so much uncertainty, there is no doubt that an efficient pregnancy-testing service would be of value. It is a pity that the situation has been allowed to develop in such a haphazard way with many fly-by-night agencies using different methods of uncertain efficiency. So far the medical profession has been less than helpful. More intensive research is needed so that the best methods can be identified. As the technique is simple and can be applied quite easily, the local chemists could be encouraged to provide the service if the doctors and hospitals are reluctant to do it themselves.

We asked the unmarried women what they would do if they found they were going to have a child before they were married, and the unmarried men what they would do if their girl friend was pregnant. The 23 single informants who had already been involved in a premarital pregnancy were not asked this question. The remaining 86 people replied as follows:

Most of the men (48 per cent) said they would marry the pregnant girl, but only a few women (19 per cent) said they would marry the father.

Most of the women (57 per cent) said they would keep the child, but only a few men (5 per cent) said they would wish to do so.

Few of the men or women (3 per cent) suggested an adoption.

---

* For example: 'You can't be certain because sometimes the frogs leap the wrong way.'

One in five of the men (18 per cent) and women (19 per cent) said they would seek an abortion.

Social class has some influence. The middle class were more likely to try to arrange an abortion; the working-class men were likely to suggest marriage and the working-class women were likely to want to keep the child.

The selfish answer for the men would be that the mother should keep the child, but to their credit only a few suggested this. However about a quarter (26 per cent) of all the men were unable to answer the question because they had not given the possibility much thought. None of the women failed to give an answer; for a girl premarital pregnancy is a real fear.

The urge to keep the child is strong among the single women just as the forced marriage is among the single men. Neither would seem to be an ideal solution to the problem.

5.8   Negative Attitudes to Premarital Pregnancies

The problems discussed in this chapter are the concern of a large number of people. It is not something that happens only to a small minority. There are over 214,000 premarital conceptions each year* – that is, over 570 a day. If one adds to this total the very large number of cases when a single girl fears that she may be pregnant, it is clear that this problem is the cause of much distress.

Unfortunately it is not true that all pregnancies can be prevented by making everyone aware of birth control and by making contraceptives freely available. But more information and a better distribution would certainly reduce the number of premarital pregnancies, and more important still, it would provide help where it is most needed.

From society's point of view, the premarital pregnancies which we would most want to prevent are those that happen to girls who are unable or unwilling to give the child love and

* Every year 90,000 brides give birth within eight months of marriage (240 a day); 74,000 illegitimate children are born a year (197 a day); 50,000 single girls have a legal abortion (133 a day); plus an unknown number of illegal and self-induced abortions.

a good home background. But it would be a serious infringement of civil liberties if we tried to make laws about this, attempting to make a legal definition of a good mother or a poor mother. Such an attitude would go far beyond the prerogative of the state to interfere in the private life of the individual.

But, fortunately, those who are unlikely to make good mothers are also those who most want to avoid a premarital pregnancy. Many married couples who find they are to have another addition to the family are prepared to accept the situation even though the pregnancy is unwanted. A couple who intend to marry, or are at least considering it, may have to bring forward the wedding day as the result of an unwanted pregnancy; the forced marriage is by no means an ideal solution, but many people (perhaps too many) accept this situation. But a girl who does not even like or know the man she happens to have had intercourse with would be more anxious to avoid a premarital pregnancy.

We are so determined to discourge sex without love that we inadvertently make it more likely that the result of such incidents is unnecessarily distressing. It might be better if we recognized that every day hundreds of people have intercourse because they are sexually attracted to each other, and for this reason alone; they are not in love and they do not want to live together for the rest of their lives. We cannot help these people to avoid unwanted pregnancies until we accept that this type of sexual activity is not unusual. Some people are ready to help 'the nice girl who has slipped up' but will not lend a hand to 'the bad girl who has got no more than she deserved'. But from the point of view of society and the unfortunate unwanted child, it is the so-called 'bad girl' who most needs our help.

In section 4.11 it was found that there was a large gap between the time of the first intercourse and the first use of contraception. Obviously we should do our best to narrow that gap. But even when contraceptives are freely available, there will always be a gap of a few weeks, unless it is going to be official policy to encourage a girl to use contraceptives before her first experience of sexual intercourse.

This research has shown that a forced marriage is still the most likely consequence of a premarital pregnancy for a working-class girl. This is partly caused by the lack of facilities, but is also the result of attitudes to premarital pregnancies, particularly among the men.

It is a moot point whether a child is worse off brought up in a home in which the mother and father are unsuited to each other and unhappy together, or in a home where there is no father. If the child's future is the main concern, there must be many cases where adoption is a better solution, especially as there are many childless couples longing to bring up a family. All psychological knowledge emphasizes the importance of a happy and secure home background for the future development of the child and this is more likely to be provided by adoptive parents than by an unhappy household or (although there are exceptions) by a one-parent home. But at present adoption is the least popular solution to the problem of a premarital pregnancy.

A recent report from the National Children's Bureau (Seglow, 1972) provides powerful support for those who believe adoption is the best solution when the parents cannot, or will not, provide a secure home background. The authors studied a group of seven-year-old children and tested them for educational achievement and emotional stability. They compared these results with a group of children of the same age growing up in two-parent homes, and another group who were illegitimate* but had remained with their natural mother. A simplified tabulation of the results is shown in Table 5/5. This shows that the adopted children by the age of seven were doing as well as the rest of the children in the sample, and dramatically better than the illegitimate children who stayed with their mothers.

This research has also shown that among those who did not get married after a premarital pregnancy, a surprisingly high proportion (38 per cent) became pregnant for a second time. This is extraordinary, especially as a woman is more motivated to accept advice about contraceptives after one premarital pregnancy. All these negative attitudes to the pre-

* 90 per cent of the adopted group were also illegitimate.

TABLE 5/5. The achievements of seven-year-old children from adopted, two-parent and mother-only homes using tests of oral ability, level of creativity, reading, arithmetic and emotional stability

Home background	Above average*	Below average*
	%	%
Adopted	33	16
Two-parent	23	28
Mother alone	10	45

* From figures given in SEGLOW, KELLMER-PRINGLE and WEDGE, *Growing up Adopted*, National Foundation for Educational Research, 1972.

vention of unwanted pregnancies are not an excuse for delaying the improvement of the supply of free contraceptives. But it should remind us that the most important aspect is to make birth control more acceptable to those who do not think it is agreeable or important. Inevitably this is a more complex problem requiring understanding, education and time.

5.9   Abortion as an Adjunct to Contraception

The use of induced abortion as a *substitute* for contraception is rarely justified, except possibly the menstrual regulation method (described later in this section) and there is some doubt if this method is really an abortion. Nevertheless abortion will remain a necessary adjunct of contraceptive practice. Although it is possible to imagine the perfect 100 per cent reliable contraceptive, it is less easy to imagine the perfect 100 per cent reliable human being.

At the present time not all methods of contraception are completely reliable and even the most effective methods are subject to mistakes and forgetfulness by the user. A recent study (Potts, *Jnl. of Gynaecology*) showed that if 100 couples rely on a 95 per cent effective contraceptive such as the cap or condom after reaching their desired family size, over 80 of them would have more children during the remaining twelve to fifteen years of fertile marriage. Even if more reliable methods like the pill or the coil are used, 30 out of 100 couples would have more children than planned.

It will still be necessary in the future to provide a second line of defence against an unwanted pregnancy. As population problems become more important, and as public awareness of the importance of birth control increases, induced abortions will become more, not less, important. In countries where family planning is accepted, many couples are strongly motivated against the birth of unwanted children, even if they have not been successful in sustaining contraceptive practice. In such circumstances the abortion rate will go up before it goes down. It is reasonable to suppose that eventually the rate of abortion will be reduced as contraceptives become more available, but it is utopian to suppose that abortions will cease to be needed. A rational birth control policy involves not only free access to contraceptives, but also to abortion as a last resort.

Experience in many other countries has clearly shown that women will seek criminal abortions when it is not possible to obtain legal terminations. Estimates on the number of illegal abortions vary from one out of every five pregnancies to half of all pregnancies. A survey in Turkey in 1970 showed that there were 24 abortions for every 100 live births. In Tehran it is estimated that there is at least one abortion for every five live births (Dalsace, 1970). In a recent publicity campaign for a reform of the law in France, many well-known personalities declared that they had had an illegal abortion.

After criminal abortions many women require treatment to remove the material left in the uterus which can cause infection and haemorrhage. Many of them suffer complications and need medical care. In many countries these women take up badly-needed hospital beds and emergency blood supplies. This was once the case in this country and to the extent that obstacles are put in the way of the woman who seeks an abortion, it is still true.

Apart from the people who had undergone a termination, there were 133 (35 per cent) men and women in this research group who knew people who had had an abortion; 67 of the 133 (50 per cent) were illegal. This is hearsay evidence and much of it applies to the circumstances before the 1967 Act was working properly; even so, it is a warning of what to expect if it becomes more difficult to obtain an abortion in this country. As long as the requests of some women for a termination are refused, there will be opportunities for the criminal abortionists. Even in 1970 there were 11 deaths directly attributed to illegal abortions.

The strongest criticism of the law as it operates at present is that the woman who is legally entitled to an operation is subject to unnecessary delays either because she cannot find a cooperative doctor or because she is unable to understand the procedure. The longer the delay, the more difficult the operation becomes. If the abortion is performed in the first twelve weeks of pregnancy, the risk of complication is less than having a baby. A study done in the United States showed that about 6 per cent of pregnancies terminated at seven to eleven weeks of gestation resulted in complications, nearly all of them minor, while about 23 per cent of the seventeen-week pregnancies terminated had complications (Callahan, 1970).

The world survey of abortion in the *International Planned Parenthood News* of March 1972 makes this point: 'Statistics from countries allowing abortions on request, and where most abortions are performed during the first few months of pregnancy, show a very low death rate. For example, in Hungary, where abortion, except for strictly medical indications, is illegal after 12 weeks, from 1964–67 only nine women died among the 739,000 who underwent legal abortions (a mortality rate of 1·2 per 100,000). The mortality rate is much higher in countries where the process of granting abortions on medico-social grounds may take several weeks, and consequently a large number of abortions are performed after 12 weeks of gestation. For example, in Sweden and Denmark the mortality rate was 40 per 100,000 during the last decade.' The mortality rate in England and Wales in 1970 for legal abortions was 12 per 100,000.

When the comfort and health and, in some cases, life of the individual depends upon a quick decision to operate, it is strange that the law seems to put so many delaying encumbrances in the way of a woman who wants an abortion. It is even more strange that so many doctors exaggerate the psychological effects of an abortion when these are often caused by the delays which in turn increase the physical effects.

The medical establishment has always insisted that a woman who has an abortion is very likely to suffer serious guilt feelings. As recently as 1966, the Royal College of Obstetricians and Gynaecologists expressed this view: 'There are few women, no matter how desperate they may be to find themselves with an unwanted pregnancy, who do not have regrets at losing it. This fundamental reaction, governed by maternal instinct, is mollified if the woman realises that abortion was essential to her life and health, but if the indication for the termination of pregnancy was flimsy and fleeting she may suffer from a sense of guilt for the rest of her life.'

If women do suffer guilt feelings or even serious psychological effects, we should look for the cause. Who has implanted these guilt feelings? The writers of the NOP report (1966) found it strange that those women who had undergone illegal abortions had rather pleasanter memories about it than those who had legal abortions. It is not really so strange when one remembers the censorious attitude of the medical profession in those (not so far-off) days.

In fact careful studies of women who have had an abortion cast doubt upon the whole theory that they have serious guilt feelings about abortions (Baird, 1965; Clark, 1968; Pare and Raven, 1970; Morton-Williams and Hindell, 1972).

The situation is gradually changing. Sclare (1971) analysed the long-term psychological effects on thirty-two women. He concluded that an abortion had a favourable outcome in most cases. He wrote that his study had changed his views: 'I have swung from being an old fuddy-duddy Calvinist to being quite permissive.' There will be more far-reaching changes in the near future.

Many of these problems will be solved when the vacuum aspiration treatment is available to everyone. This method removes the material safely and with the minimum chance of spreading the infection or increasing the blood loss. It also eliminates other hazards such as perforation of the womb or over-stretching the cervix. It needs no anaesthetic because it gives so little physical shock. In America it is used on an out-patient basis because the woman can go home so soon after the operation.

The Royal College of Obstetricians and Gynaecologists has claimed that the 1967 Act has placed intolerable burdens on doctors, but they have not welcomed this new method, which would not only lessen their task but would diminish the role of the gynaecologist. In fact there is some evidence to support the accusation that doctors are putting their moral views above the interests of their patients by operating the Act in such a ponderous manner. In 1970 more than 12,000 women had abortions by abdominal hysterectomy which is a major operation; yet 4,184 of these were carried out on women less than thirteen weeks pregnant; it seems probable that some other less risky method could have been used in these cases.

A development of the vacuum aspiration method is menstrual regulation. MR, as it is sometimes termed, may be described as the removal by vacuum aspiration of a suspected fertilized ovum, before or shortly after the onset of menstruation. There need be no delay because the operation is quick and, in the majority of cases, diagnosis is unnecessary. MR has been used in New York and California on 15,000 healthy women who came to an out-patient clinic within ten days of missing their first period. A study of the results has shown that the technique is virtually without complications (Davis, 1972).

The vacuum aspiration method can be used well before an unwanted conception can possibly be confirmed or denied. Consequently it becomes a semantic point whether or not it is an abortion because neither the doctor nor the woman can know if she was pregnant or whether she was just late with her period. This raises ethical considerations. Is it abortion or late contraception? The law as it stands takes no account of this situation.

5.10   The Right to Choose

The last part of the previous section indicates that new medical technology will make most of the arguments about abortion irrelevant and this will be greeted with some relief by many people. But it is still a matter of concern that abortion and some kinds of contraceptives are available to some but not to others. The results of this research show that there are big social class differences. Even more important, it has become clear that the girl who is least able to look after a child is also the girl who is most likely to have an unwanted pregnancy.

The right to a free choice can only exist when the pregnant girl is presented with the full range of possibilities. The risks and advantages of abortion should be explained to her. The possibility of adoption should be discussed.

Although the number of adoptions have doubled in the last ten years (from 14,668 to 26,049), it is still small compared with the number of abortions carried out on single girls (50,000) and the number of mothers who decide to keep their illegitimate child (45,000). There are still many people in homes for unmarried mothers who frown on the idea of adoption. Yet most adopted children are illegitimate and the report from the National Children's Bureau (noted in section 5.8) concludes that this is the best solution to the problem of a premarital pregnancy if the child's interests are paramount. Social class did not alone account for the differences between the adopted children and the others. It is true that many adoptive parents were middle-class, but the Bureau's research showed that adopted children living in working-class homes did much better in some tests than other children from the same social class background. The authors comment that 'working class adoptions have been among the most successful'.

The myth of the blood tie has been exaggerated. A secure happy home is more important. As Dr Pringle* says, 'A good mother is one who has the time, the means, and the will – not

* Dr Kellmer Pringle is the Director of the National Children's Bureau.

the blood.' This is certainly the case at present, but it need not be. Much can, and should, be done to improve the lot of the unmarried mother. At present both economic conditions and social attitudes weigh heavily against the mother who wants to bring up her child on her own. This is another factor which restricts the freedom of choice open to the girl involved in a premarital pregnancy.

Obviously moral and ethical considerations are important and must be considered. One advocate has suggested that the best birth control method of all is a glass of cold water – not before, not after, but instead of. This suggestion presents the average man and woman with a choice, but it is only one of many. Every kind of moral exhortation is permissible if it is intended to persuade a person to select from a range of free choices.

The objection to the present situation is that everyone does not have a free choice. When everyone has an equal opportunity to choose abortion, adoption or motherhood, then there will be time to consider moral and ethical problems.

6. Sexual Intercourse

6.1 The First Experience

Since the publication of the report on the sexual behaviour of young people, the incidence of sexual intercourse in the various age groups has often been quoted and there have been attempts to guess how far this has changed in the years that have followed. It is possible to make too much of this. The proportion of people who first experience sexual intercourse at a particular age is, of itself, a subordinate consideration and should only be a cause for concern if it leads to related problems such as illegitimacy, abortion or venereal diseases.

It is important, however, that those who wish to contribute towards solving these problems should attempt to understand current sexual customs and conventions. This will, of course, include the extent of premarital sexual intercourse but must also take into consideration other factors less easy to quantify, such as early experimentation, courting and inceptive activities, present-day fashions, movements like Women's Liberation, and overall sexual attitudes which vary from superficial opinions to deep-down irrational bigotry.

It is with these reservations in mind that the first part of this chapter examines the incidence and frequency of sexual intercourse among the younger generations. The earlier research based on a large representative sample gave some idea of this up to the age of eighteen. It was found that more teenage boys than girls had experience of sexual intercourse. Sexual intercourse before fourteen was rare, but by the age of sixteen, 14 per cent of the boys and 5 per cent of the girls were experienced. By eighteen, 34 per cent of the boys and 17 per cent of the girls were sexually experienced.

The first experience of sexual intercourse was usually with someone who was already experienced; the first partner was often older and in the case of the girls was quite often an adult. It was usually with a friend and more often than not took place in the parental home of the beginner or the partner. The first experience was often unpremeditated and unplanned, and a majority said they did not enjoy it.

Although more boys than girls had intercourse, when incidence and frequency were taken together, the total sexual outlet was found to be similar. Fewer girls had intercourse, but those who were experienced did it more often. Girls were slower to agree to intercourse, but once they had agreed they were more active sexually.

The second research tends to confirm these findings. The actual behaviour was similar to that reported in the first research, although attitudes to premarital sexual intercourse have changed considerably; these twenty-five year old men and women more readily admitted to early sexual adventures and some of them even appeared apologetic about starting out so late.

As they reached adulthood the girls continued to catch up the boys and by the age of twenty-one 75 per cent of the men and 71 per cent of the girls had experienced sexual intercourse. At the time of the interview more girls (94 per cent) than men (92 per cent) were sexually experienced. Of course most of them are married by the age of twenty-five, but 189 of the 267 (71 per cent) who were married had sexual intercourse before their wedding day.

In some cases the age of first intercourse is closely linked with the age of marriage. In addition to the 21 per cent (29 per cent of those married) who did not have sexual intercourse until after they were married, another 19 per cent (27 per cent of those married) only had intercourse with the person they later married. So 40 per cent of the group (over half those married) had either had no experience on their wedding day, or had only had experience with their spouse-to-be.

Among the unmarried men, 65 out of 82 (79 per cent) had experience of sexual intercourse, and this applied to 18 of the

27 (67 per cent) unmarried women. So taking into consideration the whole group, whether they married later or not,
about three quarters (72 per cent) had premarital sexual
intercourse, 21 per cent waited until they were married and
7 per cent had no experience.

Among the 200 (53 per cent) who had sexual intercourse
with someone who neither was nor would be their spouse, 129
(34 per cent) described their first partner as a steady. The
remaining 71 (19 per cent) started with an acquaintance, a
pick-up or a prostitute. The conclusion must be that sexual
intercourse before marriage is quite common and acceptable
among young people, although it does not appear to start
quite as early as some people think or fear. When these young
people do seek sexual experience, in the majority of cases it is
with someone they know very well, and it is often with someone they love and will marry.

6.2   The Reaction to the First Experience

It seems unlikely that many girls were persuaded to have
intercourse much against their will. We asked everyone,
except those whose first experience was with their spouse (12
per cent men, 33 per cent women) and those with no experience (8 per cent men, 6 per cent women), whether they felt
they had been willing participants in their first experience of
sexual intercourse. The majority (79 per cent men, 53 per
cent women) said they had been willing; eleven girls (7 per
cent) and three men (1 per cent) felt they had been persuaded
against their better judgement, and two girls (1 per cent) said
they had been forced into it against their will. Although the
first experience is often unpremeditated and rarely the consequence of mutual discussion or planning, there is no evidence
to suggest that many men are taking advantage of unsuspect-
ing girls, or vice versa.

The results of the second research confirmed the views
given in the first report that the first experience of sexual
intercourse was not always a great success. Only 43 per cent
(46 per cent men, 35 per cent women) said they enjoyed it;
18 per cent said they were disappointed; 13 per cent said they

felt ashamed or fearful after it was all over and 8 per cent (mostly girls) said they really disliked it. The others either did not have any strong feelings (11 per cent) or had not had sexual intercourse (7 per cent).

'It was not what I imagined. I didn't know what to expect, but all the same it was not what I'd imagined.'

'I don't think you really like it to start with. It grows on you as you get better at it.'

'I was very upset and frightened.'

'A lot of fuss about nothing.'

'Proud, more than anything else. A new step forward.'

'A funny feeling; a sense of guilt; against my upbringing.'

'An inside sort of nervousness, but I was pleased too at having achieved something.'

There was no indication that those whose first experience was within marriage liked it any more than those who had premarital experience. This does not provide any support to those who insist that sexual intercourse is rarely satisfying unless both partners are married and in love.

Indeed these results seem to suggest that those who start early are more likely to enjoy their first experience of sexual intercourse. Among those whose first experience was before the age of eighteen, 51 per cent said they had enjoyed it. Among those whose first experience was after the age of twenty-one, 36 per cent said they had liked it. One possible interpretation of this surprising difference is that those who have guilt feelings about sex, or who are afraid for one reason or another, find it more difficult to adjust to sexual intercourse when eventually they start. Whatever may be the explanation, these results do seem to contradict the suggestion, often made, that those who have early sexual experiences find them unpleasant and this may put them off sex for a long period.

The sad fact is that a large number do not actively enjoy their first experience of sexual intercourse, no matter how young or old they may be. About half of those who started early and about two thirds of those who started later appear to have had a negative reaction to their first experience. The reason in many cases must be because false attitudes and misinformation have not prepared the inexperienced. The combination of bad sex education which avoids telling them what to expect, and romantic stories in magazines and cinemas which lead them to expect too much, is probably the chief cause of their disappointment. This would apply whether the first experience is early and premarital, or later and within marriage.

6.3　Second and Subsequent Experiences

Although the first experience of sexual intercourse was rarely a success, it did not stop many people from trying again fairly soon. Indeed two thirds of the group (59 per cent women, 74 per cent men) said they wanted to do it again soon after the first experience. The disillusioned ones were a minority, but not a small one; several girls (13 per cent) and a few boys (4 per cent) said they definitely did not want to do it again, and a larger number (21 per cent women, 13 per cent men) implied that they were not very enthusiastic before the second experience. In fact, of course, nearly all of them did continue to have sexual intercourse, but this does not discount the general impression that the first experience was neither as pleasurable nor as satisfying as it might have been.

Table 6/1 shows how much time elapsed between the first

TABLE 6/1. The interval between the first and second experiences of sexual intercourse

Interval	Men %	Women %	Total %
One day	11	27	18
Up to a week	22	25	23
Up to 2 weeks	10	7	9
2–4 weeks	8	12	10
1–6 months	15	11	13
Longer	20	6	14
No more sex	1	1	1
DK or NK	5	6	5
No S.I.	8	6	7
No. (100%)	219	157	376

and second experience of intercourse. At one end of the scale one man and one woman (1 per cent) did not go on to have a second experience and over a quarter (27 per cent) did not repeat the experience within the first month. Sexual intercourse is not, as some would suppose, an irresistible impulse to which one soon becomes addicted.

At the other end of the table, 18 per cent decided to have a second experience within twenty-four hours of the first, by the end of the week 41 per cent had tried again, and half the group had their second experience within a fortnight. It is refreshing to report that not everyone finds sexual intercourse such a problem.

The earlier report on teenage sexual behaviour found that the girls started later than the boys, and were more reluctant at first, but once they had crossed this barrier, they were not more inhibited than the boys. Over a quarter of the women (27 per cent compared with 11 per cent of the men) had their second experience within twenty-four hours of their first, and over half (52 per cent women compared with 33 per cent men) within a week. The men are often younger when they start, and they may be impelled by curiosity or mistaken ideas about manliness. But some of them do not feel the urge to repeat the experience after they have satisfied their curiosity or proved something to themselves. It was over a month before a third of the men had their second experience (35 per cent compared with 17 per cent of the women) and it was over six months for one in five of the men (20 per cent compared with 6 per cent of the women).

The informants were also asked if they had sexual intercourse with the first partner more than once. Many men (64 per cent) and even more women (87 per cent) repeated the experience with the same person. The relationship continued for some time in many cases, for 47 per cent of the men and 82 per cent of the women had sexual intercourse with their first partner on more than five occasions. These percentages include the 78 people who had their first experience of sexual intercourse after they were married. But even when these are excluded, as well as those who have not had sexual intercourse at all, 44 per cent of the men and 79 per cent of the women continued to have premarital intercourse with the same person over quite a long period.

On the other hand 34 per cent of the men and 14 per cent of the women had a different partner. These figures, shown in Table 6/2, indicate that some men and a few women start off their sexual experience as an experiment or for reasons of curiosity. But for many men and most women the first act of intercourse is an extension of a strong loving relationship that continues to develop after the first experience.

TABLE 6/2. The number of men and women who repeated their first experience of sexual intercourse with the same partner shown as a percentage of the whole group and as a percentage of those who had premarital experience

Second and subsequent partners	Men %	Women %	Total %	Men %	Women %	Total %
Same partner, over 5 times	47	82	61	44	79	56
Same partner, up to 5 times	17	5	12	22	7	17
Second partner, different	28	7	20	34	14	27
No sexual intercourse	8	6	7	—	—	—
No. (100%)	219	157	376	176*	96*	272*

* Excludes 78 whose first experience was with their spouse and 26 who had no experience of sexual intercourse.

6.4   Premarital Sex

Although one in five (21 per cent) did not have sexual intercourse before they married, and 7 per cent have never had this experience, the first section of this chapter makes it clear that premarital sexual intercourse is now the normal pattern both for men (80 per cent) and for women (61 per cent). All of them were asked: Was it planned beforehand or did it just seem to follow naturally from what you were doing? In a large number of cases (60 per cent of the whole group) it was unplanned. The others were divided between those cases (6 per cent) where the incident was the result of mutual planning, and the other cases (6 per cent) where one of the partners had made arrangements but the other was taken by surprise.

The location of the first intercourse also suggests that it was often an unplanned and in some cases an uncomfortable experience. For some informants the first experience was out in the countryside (6 per cent), in a car (4 per cent), in a disused building or down a back street (2 per cent), in a park (4 per cent), in a holiday hotel or chalet (3 per cent), at someone else's flat or digs (8 per cent), at a party (2 per cent) or a brothel (1 per cent).* Only 39 per cent had their first experience of premarital intercourse in their own home or their partner's home. The others first had intercourse on their honeymoon (21 per cent) or have not had this experience (7 per cent).

The fact that premarital sexual intercourse continues to be unplanned and unpremeditated raises problems for those who are concerned about the rate of illegitimacies and brides who are pregnant on their wedding day. It means that few girls are likely to take any precautions before their first experience. In fact family planning clinics report that nearly all their clients are sexually experienced before they come to the clinic (Lambert, 1971). This may be the clinic's answer to the accusation that they are encouraging sexual laxity, but it does also mean that many young girls are taking risks at a time when an unwanted pregnancy would have most unfortunate consequences. On the other hand any attempt to prepare these girls before they have had their first experience is likely to be misconstrued.

This presents the Family Planning Association and the Government with an awkward dilemma. Obviously the authorities and the general public are going to look askance at any suggestion that appears to be encouraging premarital sexual intercourse. But if the real concern is to prevent the individual misery and the social cost caused by unplanned pregnancies in young girls, then the aim of the

* 3 per cent said they could not remember where the first experience took place.

clinics should be to close the gap between the first experience of premarital sexual intercourse and the first use of contraceptive precautions. If the gap is to be closed completely, then the girls should visit the clinic before their first experience, not afterwards.

Those who had premarital sexual intercourse were compared with those who waited until after their wedding day before they had their first experience. It was found that the better educated were more likely to have premarital experience. For example 70 per cent of those who left school before the age of sixteen had premarital intercourse compared with 77 per cent of those who stayed on until seventeen or later; 23 per cent of those who left school at fifteen waited until they were married, but only 14 per cent of those who left when they were seventeen or older had their first experience of sexual intercourse after they were married. (These percentages are taken from Table A6/1.)

This tendency is confirmed by considering the 68 in this group who got one or more A levels. In Table A6/2 it can be seen that 53 of them (78 per cent) had premarital experience compared with 219 out of 308 (71 per cent) who did not take this exam. Incidentally this table also shows that there is another group among the better educated who do not have sexual intercourse at all; 13 per cent of those with A levels compared with 5 per cent of the others have never had intercourse.

It might be expected that social class (as estimated by the occupation of the father) would show the same tendency, and to a certain extent it does. But there is very little difference between the proportion who had premarital intercourse in the middle class (76 per cent) and among manual workers (75 per cent). The big difference is among the non-manual workers, only 67 per cent of whom had premarital sexual intercourse. It was also found that 16 per cent of the middle class, 20 per cent of the manual workers and 23 per cent of the non-manual workers waited until after their wedding before they had intercourse. (See Table A6/3.)

The higher paid were also more likely to have premarital intercourse. Among those being paid less than £20 per week,

69 per cent had premarital experience, 16 per cent waited, and 15 per cent had no experience. Among those being paid over £30 per week, 82 per cent had premarital experience, 16 per cent waited and 2 per cent had no experience. This suggests that there may be a connection between premarital sexual experience and the money to provide facilities, such as a flat, a hotel room or a car, but it is also in line with the tendency of the better educated to have more sexual experience before marriage.

These results also reveal that there is a small group of well educated but not well paid people who at the age of twenty-five have had no experience of sexual intercourse. Working-class people are less likely to have premarital experience than those in the middle class, but manual workers marry earlier and so nearly all of them (96 per cent) have sexual experience by the age of twenty-five.

Religion seems to have some influence on sexual behaviour before marriage. Among the churchgoers, 59 per cent had premarital experience compared with 75 per cent of those who did not go to church (chapel or synagogue); 29 per cent of the churchgoers waited until after marriage compared with 19 per cent; 12 per cent of the churchgoers had no experience compared with 6 per cent. Roman Catholics were least likely to have premarital experience; 60 per cent compared with 68 per cent Non-Conformists, 71 per cent Church of England, 82 per cent Jews and 84 per cent of those who professed to have no denomination. So churchgoing and religious denomination do seem to have some inhibitory effect upon young people before they are married.

6.5 Frequency

All those with sexual experience were asked how often they had had intercourse in the last twelve months. The married men and women had very similar frequencies, as would be expected, but taking the group as a whole, girls tended to have sexual intercourse more often. Altogether 60 per cent (70 per cent women, 53 per cent men) reported intercourse more than fifty times in the last year, and nearly three quarters (73 per cent) of the group (80 per cent women, 68 per cent men) averaged more than once a fortnight. On the other hand 10 per cent (6 per cent women, 11 per cent men) had intercourse less than twelve times in the year and some of these (1 per cent women, 4 per cent men) had not had sexual intercourse within the last year, and this does not include those (6 per cent women, 8 per cent men) who did not have any experience of sexual intercourse. (A further 4 per cent women and 5 per cent men could not estimate the number of times they had had sexual intercourse in the last year.)

As Table 6/3 shows, most of the high frequencies occur within marriage. All the 257 married men and women had sexual intercourse within the last year (usually but not always with their spouses, as will be noted in section 6.8), and 203 (79 per cent) had intercourse over once a week. There is no regular pattern among the few divorced or separated in this group, although it is notable that all but one of them had at least one experience in the year.

TABLE 6/3. The frequency of sexual intercourse in the last year among married and unmarried men and women

Marital status	Frequency of sexual intercourse							
	Never	None	1–4	5–24	25–50	50+	DK	Total
Married	0	0	0	13	30	203	11	257
Sep. or divorced	0	1	2	2	1	3	1	10
Living together	0	0	0	0	1	4	0	5
Steady	7	3	6	8	13	12	3	52
No steady	19	6	3	13	5	4	2	52
Total	26	10	11	36	50	226	17	376

About a quarter (28 per cent) of those with steady boy or girl friends had high frequencies. When those living together are excluded, not many unmarried informants were having intercourse more than once a week (15 per cent unmarried compared with 79 per cent married). One reason why pre-marital intercourse is much less frequent than intercourse within marriage is that unmarried people have to find a place that is comfortable and private; in contrast four of the five who are unmarried but living together had sexual intercourse at least once a week.

Similarly low frequencies were much rarer among the married; only 13 of the 257 married (5 per cent) had intercourse less than once a fortnight compared with 14 out of 57 (25 per cent) of those with steadies, and 16 out of 52 (31 per cent) of those without regular partners. Among those who had not had sexual intercourse in the last year, including those who had never had this experience, 1 was divorced and 10 had steady partners (i.e. 17 per cent of all those with steadies). There were 35 people (9 per cent of the whole group) who had not had sexual intercourse in the last year, including 19 (5 per cent) who had no steady partner and had never had intercourse.

So the married have far more sex than the others, but many of the unmarried do have sexual experience; 76 per cent of the unmarried have at least one experience and more than half of those with steady partners have frequent pre-marital sexual intercourse. But only 39 out of the 109 (36 per cent) are having sexual intercourse more than once a fortnight and 44 of the unmarried (40 per cent) had very little or no sex in the last year.

Some people may wonder if those with low sexual frequencies are homosexual and Table A6/4 analyses these frequencies with those who admit to having some experience of homosexual activities. The numbers are small, but the table indicates that youthful homosexual acts do not necessarily mean that a young person will grow up to be exclusively homosexual. It may be that 4 out of 36 (11 per cent) who had no heterosexual experiences in the last year have homosexual tendencies. But it should be noted that 31 out of 36 (86 per cent) with a record of past homosexual interests now have fairly regular heterosexual intercourse, over half of them more than once a week.

6.6   Sexual Enjoyment

Although many thought the first experience was disappointing, the majority continued to have sexual intercourse and

by the age of twenty-five nearly all the experienced informants found it enjoyable. In reply to the general question
asking if they found sex enjoyable, 88 per cent (95 per cent of
those with experience) said they did; 47 per cent expressed
unqualified appreciation and 41 per cent had some reservations. A further 5 per cent said they definitely did not enjoy it.

Table A6/5 shows that the few who did not enjoy sexual
activities were more likely to be unmarried. Only 2 per cent
of the married found sex unenjoyable compared with 10 per
cent of those with steady partners and 15 per cent of those
with no regular partners. This certainly reinforces the claim
in the Longford Report (1972) and elsewhere that sexual
intercourse is more pleasurable when it takes place within
marriage, or at least between a man and a woman who are in
love. But these results do not support the assumption in the
Longford Report* that sexual pleasure is only obtainable in
the marital situation.

In fact 89 per cent of all the unmarried said that they
enjoyed their sexual activities and even among those who did
not have a regular sexual partner, 85 per cent found it enjoyable. These are large proportions and it makes no sense to
imply that those who have premarital sexual intercourse are
bound to be disappointed. It may be more furtive, uncomfortable and inconvenient, but clearly it is not unenjoyable
for most people.

The next question was: Would you say you were having
enough, too much or too little? It may be thought that this
was inviting flippant remarks from the men ('You can never
have too much') or coy answers from the women ('I'm
managing quite well, thank you'), but in fact the question
came quite late in the interview, long after the serious tone of
the inquiry had been established, and all but 3 per cent gave
sensible replies. The question was also put to the 17 (8 per
cent) men and 9 (6 per cent) women who had never experienced sexual intercourse.

* The Longford Committee quote with approval: 'Sex only works
properly if the person you are having it with is someone you care so
deeply about that you will stay around to raise the children who may
come. Anyone who doesn't know that doesn't know about sex.'

As well as those who said they were not getting enough (23 per cent) and a few others who said they were getting too much (3 per cent), a further division of the mid-way position became necessary. There were those (15 per cent) who gave ebullient replies which indicated that things were working out very well ('Neither too much, nor too little – just right.'). These were classified under the phrase 'just right'. Then there was a large number (57 per cent) who made rather less enthusiastic remarks which suggested that all in all things were satisfactory. These have been classified under the word 'enough'.

There is not much difference between the number of men and women who said they had enough (59 per cent men, 53 per cent women). But many more women (23 per cent) than men (10 per cent) felt their sexual life was just right. Although more men (25 per cent) than women (20 per cent) said they were getting too little sex, it is interesting to note that the converse does not apply, for as many men (3 per cent) as women (2 per cent) felt they were having too much sex. It is also significant that one in five of all the women in the group felt that they were not getting enough sex.

Most of the married (84 per cent) seemed to be content with the situation but 13 per cent did say they were getting too little sex. Over a quarter of those with steady partners (29 per cent) felt they had too few opportunities for sexual intercourse. On the other hand 14 of the 52 (i.e. 27 per cent) of those who had no regular partner (half of whom had never had sexual intercourse) said they were satisfied with their circumstances. So the overall impression is that most people are reasonably content with their sex lives without being very enthusiastic, but there is a considerable minority, including some married men and women, who say they are dissatisfied.

The informants were also asked if there were occasions when they intenbed to have sexual intercourse but were unable to get aroused sexually. This had happened to about a third (36 per cent) of all those in the group and there was not a striking difference between the men (39 per cent) and the women (32 per cent). Of course the consequences are rather more serious if this happens to a man because a woman can

often feign arousal. The experience is also more deflating to
the man's image of himself, although the modern generation
of young women is much more aware of the possibilities of
female sexual arousal and is less likely than previous generations to be content to provide satisfaction for the man merely
as a favour.

Most of the informants found it difficult to give specific
reasons for their inability to get aroused on one or more
occasions. The largest number (12 per cent) said it was
because they were tired. Others (3 per cent) said it was something about their sexual partner that inhibited their arousal.
Some of the women (2 per cent) said fear of pregnancy seemed
to prevent sexual arousal and other women (2 per cent)
found they were worrying about their sexual performance or
their inability to reach an orgasm. Gorer (1971) has suggested
that female orgasm may be 'a cultural construct, not basically
founded on the imperatives of female anatomy'. A few men
(2 per cent) said fear of impotence actually caused it, others
(1 per cent) lost their erection while fitting on the condom or
waiting for the woman to provide a contraceptive, and a few
men (2 per cent) said they had drunk too much.

Finally they were asked if they felt that they were sexually
frustrated. It could be said that this is not a very useful question as it is very subjective and tends to invite an affirmative
answer from the men. In fact 18 per cent of the men and 10
per cent of the women said they felt sexually frustrated. In
earlier times it might have been considered unladylike for a
woman to say that she was frustrated, but female sexual
response can be just as demanding and the idea that strong
sexual impulses are an exclusively male prerogative no longer
stand up to scientific or social examination.

6.7   Sex Problems

All the men and women were asked if they had any particular problems about sex. As many people find it easier to say
no than to reveal and explain specific difficulties, the informants were then handed a card while the interviewer said:
'Here is a list of some of the difficulties other people have

mentioned. Have any of these been a problem for you?' Over half (57 per cent) the group said they had a sex problem and some of them mentioned more than one.

Of all the many problems mentioned, the one that was most frequently reported was anxiety over their own sexual performance. No fewer than 18 per cent (21 per cent men, 13 per cent women) said they were anxious about their sexual capabilities. Another fear was a waning interest in sex, especially among the women; 11 per cent said they seemed to be losing interest in sex (7 per cent men, 16 per cent women) and 5 per cent said they were getting bored with sexual activities (2 per cent men, 9 per cent women). The present day emphasis on sex in the popular press, advertisements, films, drama, fiction and magazine articles including specialist periodicals devoted to sex, all seem to produce a dual reaction in some people. On the one hand they feel that everyone else is having a more exciting sex life than they are, and on the other hand, and perhaps as a consequence, they begin to feel that sex has become too important, too dominant and too commercial. Of course this over-exposure of sex probably only applies to a minority. If the majority felt like this, the advertisers, editors and producers would take up a different theme.

'I must say I sometimes worry about my actual sexual performance. Whether I'm really doing it right, I mean.'

'I seem to lose interest occasionally. When there's something on my mind, worried about things, and so on.'

'Sometimes I'm just not interested. I don't know why.'

'I do get a bit anxious about it sometimes. You get that feeling that she's not really enjoying it and it's my fault.'

'I had a testicle removed and I thought it might spoil it a bit, but it didn't, so I stopped worrying.'

'I still do get guilt feelings of a sort. I know it's a mental thing, but I can't help it.'

'Yes, I'm anxious about having another baby.'

'I don't want to start a family, not before I'm married.'

A surprisingly large number of men (16 per cent) said they had guilt feelings about sex and this was also true of some of the women (9 per cent). Others mentioned moral problems

(5 per cent men, 6 per cent women) and some referred specifically to religious difficulties (6 per cent men, 5 per cent women). Many men and some women were concerned about masturbation (12 per cent men, 2 per cent women) or about feeling over-sexed (9 per cent men, 2 per cent women).

Table 6/4 classifies these results into three groups: (1) married, (2) those with steady partners including those living together, (3) others including divorced, separated, those with

TABLE 6/4. The marital status of those who had sex problems*

Type of problem	Marital status (men and women)				Men only	Women only
	married	steady†	others‡	total		
	257	57	62	376	%	%
Sex performance	40	13	13	66	21	13
Losing interest	30	6	4	40	7	16
Bored	14	2	2	18	2	9
Guilt feelings	24	11	13	48	16	9
Moral problems	8	6	6	20	5	6
Religious	14	5	2	21	6	5
Masturbation	17	6	6	28	12	2
Over-sexed	16	3	4	23	9	2
Others	37	8	9	54	14	15
Not known	1	2	1	4	1	1
No problems	117	21	23	161	44	41

* Some informants reported more than one problem.
† This includes those unmarried and living together.
‡ This includes divorced, separated, those with no experience and those who have had no regular partner.

no sexual experience and those with no regular partners. It shows that the married were less likely to be anxious about their sexual performance; 40 out of 257 (16 per cent) married were anxious, compared with 13 out of 57 (23 per cent) with steady partners, and 13 out of 62 (21 per cent) of the others. But they were more likely to lose interest in or become bored with sex (17 per cent married, 14 per cent steadies, 10 per cent others). The unmarried were also more likely to be concerned with moral, religious and guilt feelings (18 per cent married, 39 per cent steadies, 34 per cent others); those with the highest rates of premarital sexual intercourse were the most likely to have guilt feelings. The unmarried were more likely to be concerned about masturbation, but the proportion of married with this problem was not insignificant (7 per cent married, 11 per cent steadies, 10 per cent others). There was no difference in the marital status of those who felt over-sexed (6 per cent married, 5 per cent steadies, 5 per cent others).

It is surprising that so many young married men and women have worries about guilt feelings, religious and moral difficulties (18 per cent) and masturbation (7 per cent). It is equally surprising that so many of those who are having premarital intercourse with regular partners find their interest in sex is waning (14 per cent). But the overall impression is that the married are more likely to be concerned by a waning interest, and the unmarried by feelings of guilt. About a third of the unmarried mentioned moral problems whether or not they had a sexual partner.

About a quarter (24 per cent) of the whole group had a sex problem which they had never discussed with anyone. The others had talked about their problem to their spouses (16 per cent) or to friends (10 per cent). A very few discussed it with a doctor (2 per cent), a clergyman (1 per cent) or parents (1 per cent), or others (siblings, other relatives, employer etc.). Among the 33 per cent who did discuss it with someone, 28 per cent found it helpful and 5 per cent did not (24 per cent did not discuss it and 43 per cent did not have a problem).

The list of those who were unable to help is interesting:

6 out of 60 spouses were unhelpful (10 per cent)
7 out of 37 friends were unhelpful (19 per cent)
1 out of 4 parents were unhelpful (25 per cent)
3 out of 9 doctors were unhelpful (33 per cent)
1 out of 3 clergymen were unhelpful (33 per cent)

So only a few of those with problems about sex sought help from professionals and those who went elsewhere usually found the advice more helpful.

Well over half (57 per cent) the group had sex problems of

one kind or another; 63 per cent were unmarried and 54 per cent were married. Despite the emphasis on sex education, the high sales of sex manuals, the proliferation of advice columns in newspapers and journals, and the establishment of special advice centres for the young in many towns, it is clear that most young adults have unanswered questions and unsolved problems.

6.8   Fidelity

The replies to questions about frequency of sexual intercourse reported in section 6.5 was not limited to the number of times with one partner, even in the case of the married informants, but it was limited to their experiences in the last year. In the same way this section on fidelity and promiscuity refers to the number of sexual partners in the last twelve months. Obviously many married men and women who are now quite faithful to each other had several partners before they married, but this section reports on their sexual behaviour now and within the last year.

A total of 63 (17 per cent), 50 men (23 per cent) and 13 women (8 per cent), said they have intercourse with more than one partner. In the whole group 9 per cent (12 per cent, men, 6 per cent women) did not have any sexual intercourse in the last year, so that leaves 74 per cent (65 per cent men, 85 per cent women) who had only one partner.

Of course a certain amount of under-reporting must be expected on a subject as delicate as this and even in a friendly interview there may be some who do not feel inclined to admit to infidelity. It is impossible to estimate the extent of this under-reporting, but it is reasonable to regard these figures as a minimum.

For a very few men (1 per cent) it was just one isolated incident. For another small group (1 per cent men, 2 per cent women) only one other person was involved, although in some of these cases they were meeting regularly. Another group of men (3 per cent) were having a series of one-night stands – sexual encounters – but never more than once with the same person. The remaining group (17 per cent men, 6 per cent women) were having intercourse several times with several people.

Table 6/5 shows that the majority were unmarried, but by no means all. In fact 17 out of 257 (7 per cent) had been unfaithful to their spouses in the last year. This is quite a large figure when consideration is given to the age of these men and women; most of them have only been married a few years and in every case less than seven years. This percentage does not include the 10 who are already divorced or separated; 1

TABLE 6/5. Those who have had more than one sexual partner in the previous year

| Number of partners | Marital situation | | | | | Total | |
	Married	Div. or sep.	Living together	Steady partner	No steady	No.	%
Only one partner	240	5	3	23	6	277	74
One other, once	2	0	0	1	0	3	1
One other, several times	2	3	0	2	0	7	2
Several, once each	1	0	0	3	3	7	2
Several people, many times	12	1	2	14	17	46	12
No S.I.	0	1	0	9	26	36	9
Total	257	10	5	52	52	376	100

of these had no intercourse last year, 5 had one partner only, and 4 had more than one.

Among the 109 unmarried, 36 (33 per cent) had not had intercourse in the last year, 31 (28 per cent) had one sexual partner only, and 42 (39 per cent) had more than one partner. It is no surprise that the unmarried have more sexual partners, and even a quarter of those who said they had steady partners admitted to being quite promiscuous; but it is also important to note that 61 per cent of the unmarried had only one partner or no sexual intercourse at all.

There were 26 people in this group who were having sexual intercourse and who did not have a regular partner; 20 of these people (74 per cent) had intercourse with more than one person in the last year. On the other hand about half (44

per cent) of those with steady partners did not have intercourse with anyone else. It is sometimes said that there is a
certain type of person who becomes promiscuous because he
cannot settle down. This may well be true but there may
also be some substance in a contrary hypothesis: some girls
and boys are covertly promiscuous because they meet parental and social disapproval when they express the wish to have
overt premarital intercourse with one person. If this is true,
it may be some consolation that the social disapproval of
premarital intercourse has decreased and this may mean that
promiscuity has also decreased. The attitude towards premarital intercourse may be less prohibitory, but there is still
the strong feeling, among older generations at any rate, that
it is only permissible between two people who intend to get
married. We should recognize that not all young men and
women want to make that kind of commitment before they
have their first experience of sexual intercourse.

Leaving aside for the moment those who do not have a
regular partner and considering only the 257 who are married and the 57 who say they have a steady partner, it can be
seen in Table 6/5 that 39 of these people (12 per cent) had
more than one partner in the year; 15 of them said their
partners were usually acquaintances or pick-ups, while 24
said their partners tended to be friends and people they knew
quite well. It would be wrong to postulate much from these
small numbers, but it is worth noticing that not all extrinsic
sex is with strangers, pick-ups or prostitutes.

These 39 (31 men, 8 women) were asked if their spouse or
steady partner had found out about this intercourse with
another person. Table A6/6 summarizes the position. In fact
14 of the 39 (36 per cent) did know; 6 were said to be understanding, 5 indifferent, 1 hostile, 1 encouraged the relationship and 1 pretended not to know about it. In so far as these
39 are still married and going steady, these extrinsic sexual
adventures seem to have been received with remarkable tolerance and do not appear to have aroused much hostility.
Indeed Table A6/6 shows that 7 of the 39 did not find out
about this until their spouse or steady had volunteered the
information.

The word 'promiscuous' has been used sparingly in this section because it means so many different things to different people. In some press reports it seems to mean the same thing as premarital sexual intercourse. It is defined in the Oxford dictionary as 'indiscriminate' but also as 'sexual relations unrestricted by marriage or cohabitation'. The latter definition is not really useful and I believe it will be more helpful if its meaning in this report is confined to those who in the course of the year had several different sexual partners. On this definition, 53 (14 per cent of the whole group) were promiscuous; 13 of them were married (5 per cent of those who were married). All these men and women are young, still at the height of their sexual powers, living in a world where commercial enterprise emphasizes sexual success. Consequently I do not find these figures either surprising or depressing.

It would be a mistake to take the figures given in this section as representative of other groups, even ones of a similar age-range. These percentages cannot be used to predict the extent of infidelity or promiscuity in other samples, but they do indicate that these phenomena cannot be regarded as isolated and rare events. Whatever moral judgements one may care to make about people who are unfaithful or promiscuous, it is necessary to take into account that many thousands of people behave in this way.

6.9   The Inexperienced

Throughout this report it has been necessary to remind the reader that 17 (8 per cent) men and 9 (6 per cent) women have not at any time had sexual intercourse. These 26 (7 per cent) people were asked if they thought it was likely that they would have sexual intercourse in the next five years, by which time they would be thirty.

Most of them thought they would; 4 said they definitely would have sexual intercourse; 13 hoped they would; another 5 said they wanted to but did not feel too sure when it would happen; and the remaining 4, all men, said it was very unlikely. In some ways the latter categories are less surprising than the former. The total number of people in this country who do not intend to have sexual intercourse is probably in excess of the 2 per cent recorded in this study. It is more remarkable that there are 17 people (9 of them men) who want to have sexual intercourse and yet have not done so, despite the recent changes in attitude towards premarital sex relations.

An attempt was made to find out how far these 26 informants were involved in inceptive activities. Unfortunately it is difficult to get information about these activities because the ordinary vocabulary lacks precision; for example, 'petting' is an American expression which is used to cover a wide variety of activities from a simple caress to a situation closely resembling sexual intercourse. Inquiries about specific sexual actions cause embarrassment and increase the risk of getting no usable reply. In fact we asked specific questions because we preferred accuracy even at the risk of a low response rate. In the event only 3 found it difficult to reply.

The main questions attempted to find out if they had ever had a relationship with a girl or boy which involved undressing or touching of the sex organs. Eleven of them (7 men and 4 women) said this had never happened; 8 of the remaining had gone this far before the age of twenty-one; and 4 after that age. So about half of this small group (11 out of 26) have had practically no physical sexual experience at all.

Table 6/6 shows that these 26 people with no experience of sexual intercourse are more likely to leave school at fifteen (54 per cent compared with 49 per cent of those with sexual experience), are more likely to go to church (27 per cent compared with 15 per cent of the others) and, most notable of all, are likely to be less well paid (73 per cent were in the lowest income group compared with 31 per cent of the others). The fact that so many of these people had low earnings suggests that the lack of facilities and opportunities that money can buy may be one reason why they had no experience of sexual intercourse.

Homosexuality seems to be a less important factor. The table shows that 8 per cent of those who had not had sexual intercourse had some experience of homosexual activities and this applied to 10 per cent of the others. Of course this refers

TABLE 6/6. Those who have no experience of sexual intercourse compared with those who are experienced

	Both men and women			Men only	Women only
	No S.I. %	Others %	Total %	%	%
Age left school					
15	54	49	49	47	53
16–17	31	36	35	33	38
18+	15	15	15	20	9
Church attendance					
Never or hardly ever	73	85	85	88	79
Sometimes or weekly	27	15	15	12	21
Wages					
Under £20	73	31	34	32	24
£20–30	15	28	27	42	17
Over £30	4	16	15	24	4
NK	8	25	24	2	55
Homosexual experience					
Some	8	10	10	15	3
None	92	90	90	85	97
Number of girl/boy friends					
None	27	14	15	15	15
1–4	65	61	61	60	63
5+	8	25	24	25	22
Attitude to premarital sex					
Unqualified approval	35	61	59	66	49
Qualified approval	23	34	33	26	44
Disapproval	42	6	8	8	7
No. (100%)	26	350	376	219	157

to homosexual activities in the past; in section 6.5 it was suggested that a few of these people were still homosexually active, whereas others had stopped these activities and were now exclusively heterosexual.

There were wide differences in the extent to which this special group had contacts with the opposite sex. In an attempt to get information about the more stable relationships, all the informants were asked how many girl or boy friends they had been out with for longer than three months.

In the whole group about a quarter (25 per cent men, 22 per cent women) had five or more such relationships, many more (60 per cent men, 63 per cent women) had between one and four, and 15 per cent of both sexes had never taken out a girl or boy friend for more than three months. Table 6/6 shows that almost twice as many (27 per cent) of those with no experience of sexual intercourse had no long-term girl or boy friends compared with the others (14 per cent). Those who had not gone out with any girl or boy friends were asked if there was any reason for this. Here are some of the replies:

'I like to stay at home and look after my parents.'

'I'm a bit hard to get to know, I suppose.'

'I'm not that interested in sex. Not to that extent.'

'I get fed up with them because of their lack of interest in things in general. I get bored.'

'There are many reasons why I haven't got a girl friend. I bring home very little money. I run an expensive car. I smoke twenty cigarettes a day. It's awkward bringing girls back because my father is embarrassing. And anyway I don't know any.'

'I'm frightened, to tell the truth. It's my nerves. One doctor prescribed something to make me more forward, but another doctor stopped it. "What makes you think you are different from everyone else?" he said.'

'I've got two jobs and no time for women.'

The finding in Table 6/6 that church-going is associated with chastity is a reminder that moral considerations are still of great importance to some people. This is confirmed by questions about the informants' attitudes to premarital sexual intercourse. In the last part of Table 6/6 it is found that over half (59 per cent) gave unqualified approval (49 per cent women, 66 per cent men); a third (33 per cent) said it depended on the circumstances (44 per cent women, 26 per cent men including 2 per cent who said it was permissible for men but not for women); the remainder (8 per cent) did not approve of premarital sex (7 per cent women, 8 per cent men). The women were more likely to insist that a commitment to marriage, or at least mutual love, was a necessary prerequisite for premarital sexual intercourse.

It is obvious that people's actions are related to their attitudes, but this is not an invariable rule by any means. In this case 42 per cent of those who had not had sexual intercourse disapproved of premarital sex, but 35 per cent gave unqualified approval although they had no experience themselves. This is in line with the earlier finding in this report that lack of sexual experience is not always a matter of choice, but is sometimes simply because the man or woman has not been given the chance and has not known how to set about creating the opportunities. People living in large urban centres tend to believe that sex is available to all just for the asking, but others who live in smaller, less anonymous areas find there are important social and community barriers to premarital sexual behaviour, no matter how permissive attitudes appear to be.

These results suggest that those who have neither married nor had premarital sexual intercourse by the age of twenty-five may be influenced by personality factors in the sense that they may have little contact with the opposite sex and some of them may be homosexual. There are also signs that moral attitudes still restrict the sexual behaviour of a few people. But another influence, and perhaps the most important one, is lack of facilities and opportunities.

6.10 Marriage

For the majority of people at this age marriage is the most important single event in their lives. This section deals with some of the basic facts about these marriages and the following section inquires into some of the sexual problems that have arisen.

In this group 137 men (63 per cent) and 130 women (83 per cent) have married. A further 14 men (6 per cent) and 5 women (3 per cent) are formally engaged to be married. Another 47 men (21 per cent) and 17 women (11 per cent) say they hope to get married one day, but not necessarily to the person they are going out with at present. So this adds up to a total of 350 (93 per cent) people who have been or intend to be married. This leaves 3 per cent (8 men and 3 women) who say they definitely do not want to get married, and 4 per cent (13 men and 2 women) who have not made up their minds.

Among those who have been married 2 men and 6 women have separated, while 1 man and 1 woman have divorced. These 10 men and women are counted as married in the remaining calculations in this section.

In the earlier discussion on birth control (Chapter 4) the disadvantages of a forced marriage were noted. Some of these disadvantages were economic (e.g. marrying before it is possible to find a house or flat of their own) or emotional (e.g. the restrictions of parenthood soon after marriage). But what is likely to have the most detrimental effect is when pressure is put upon a couple to get married even though they hardly know each other. Pregnancy is not a sufficient reason for compelling a couple to marry. In this group 16 out of 267 (6 per cent) had married someone they had known for less than six months and 39 (15 per cent) had known their wife or husband for less than a year before they had married. But over half (55 per cent) had known their spouse for more than two years before the wedding and a few (4 per cent) said they had more or less grown up together.

Formal engagements are said to be less fashionable at the present time and 16 per cent of all those married said they did not get engaged. The same number (16 per cent) were engaged for less than six months, but the most usual time (58 per cent) was between six months and two years. The others (9 per cent) were engaged for more than two years and indeed some of them gave this as the reason for getting married.

'We'd been engaged for three years and that's long enough.'

'We were courting for five years and we'd saved up. We wanted to be on our own. We were never alone and I got fed up with that.'

'I felt the need to marry after I'd been engaged for two years.'

The converse of the forced or hurried marriage is the situation in which the girl and boy start meeting when they are still young teenagers and after a long courtship they marry without really getting to know any others of the same age. It is best summed up by the phrase that the boy or girl is 'spoken for'. It happens sometimes even though it has become clear through the months and years that they do not really get on very well together. Nevertheless the engagement continues on into marriage because the boy or girl or both do not know how to bring the relationship to an end, or because relations and friends assume that they will get married and increasingly put pressure on them not to disturb an established situation. Another important factor is the feeling of insecurity that a break would bring. The longer the engagement continues, the harder it is to break. Perhaps few girls or boys consciously tell themselves that they are getting married because their spouse-to-be is better than nothing, but it is often easier to drift into what might possibly be an unsatisfactory marriage than take the risk of trying to find someone more suitable. Both the impressions of the interviewers and the replies of the informants suggest that some people get married almost by default: they do not choose their marriage partner; no other option seems to be open to them. The large number of informants who had known their spouse for a long time before they were married tends to confirm this impression.

All the informants were asked how many girl or boy friends they had been out with for longer than three months before they started to court the person they married eventually. Almost one in five (18 per cent) had no other girl or boy friends and another 15 per cent had only one other. In fact over half (53 per cent) had been out with fewer than three girl or boy friends and only 19 per cent had courted five or more before they met their spouse-to-be. It is a pity that many young people have to make such an important decision with so little experience and with few opportunities to meet potential marriage partners.

Only 9 per cent of the whole group were ever formally engaged to someone whom they did not marry. Perhaps this is just as well because a broken engagement is often the cause of distress to one of the couple if not both. But there is another factor which may have the effect of prolonging engagements and committing a person to a relationship that is unsuitable. This is the feeling, strongly held in some quarters, that pre-marital sexual intercourse is only permissible between people who intend to get married. Consequently when two people who have been having sexual intercourse decide that they do not want to get married, the sexual part of the relationship, which up to that moment was acceptable, suddenly becomes shameful.

This means that people who feel strongly about these moral issues are reluctant to admit that they have had sexual inter-course with someone who is not a suitable marriage partner. The girl may feel that her chances of finding another man for a husband have been seriously diminished because she is no longer a virgin. Outside pressures from friends, relatives and advisers (as noted in section 4.6) regard the sexual relation-ship as a way of sealing the bond between two young people. This makes it much more difficult to look at the sexual part-ner dispassionately and ask if this really is the right person to share one's life with.

The parents approved of the marriage in 82 per cent of the cases; in 11 per cent one or other side disapproved, and in 4 per cent neither side approved; in 2 per cent the parents were dead or not in contact, and in 1 per cent the parents were 'not consulted'. Young people cannot complain, therefore, that many parents attempt to restrain them in their choice of a marriage partner. Indeed disapproval was expressed in such a small number of cases that one wonders if many par-ents felt it was not their business to interfere.

These 267 people were asked if they could say why they got married. Short answers to difficult questions like this are likely to be superficial and most of the informants cannot be blamed if they answered simply that they wanted to. But there were some interesting supplementary answers to this question.

'It was the thing to do; the next step in life.'

'It was physical attraction and the need for a companion.'

'I thought it was the right thing to do at the time.'

'Well, I was in love, wasn't I? I'd been going out for four years with the same bloke.'

'It was a spur of the moment thing. I fancied her.'
'I don't really know. We'd known each other a long time.'
'I had to.'

Some of them replied that marriage seemed to be the natural extension of the relationship or that things had got so far that there was no going back; 30 (11 per cent) of those who were married gave this answer. Another 27 (10 per cent) said they married because they were expecting a baby; 10 (4 per cent) specifically mentioned social pressures and 5 (2 per cent) gave answers that implied that they feared being left on the shelf if they did not take this opportunity (3 of these were men). The remaining 73 per cent said they were in love or 'just wanted to' or gave an answer that implied that it was a silly question. Perhaps it was, but there seems to be a minority who now look back at the reasons for marrying in a rather more rueful mood.

About a third (36 per cent) of the married informants did not have any children and 31 per cent had one; 29 per cent had two, 3 per cent had three and 1 per cent had four or more. None of them reported foster or adopted children.

These 267 people produced 274 children, an average of 1·03 per couple (see Table A6/7). Peel (1972) who studied a group after five years of marriage found that his 312 couples had produced 471 children, representing an average family size at that stage of the marriage of 1·51. Our group had not, on average, been married so long, but the overall pattern of fertility seems to be similar. Taking the whole group of 376 and including the children born out of wedlock, the average is 1·27.

Everyone, including the unmarried, was asked how many children they would like to have. This question was of no interest to the 26 (7 per cent) who did not want to marry, and another 7 (2 per cent) said they did not want to have children although they were or intended to get married.

About half the group (51 per cent) wanted two children, but 13 per cent wanted four or more children. These 376 people intend to produce 868 children, an average of 2·31 per person. Peel (1972) found that his group wanted to have 2·23 children. However he found there was a marked downward revision in intended family size, although previous comparable studies had found that wives tended to raise their family size intentions after actual experience of child-bearing.

Table A6/7 compares the actual family size so far with the intended family size. This shows that these people intend to have 594 more children, probably within the next ten years. This is more than the ideal according to the views of those worried about the population explosion. It certainly is to be hoped that they do not have more children than they intend due to ignorance about contraceptive methods. Peel confirms that the biggest single reason for having more children than intended is contraceptive misuse, although there are a few cases when the cause is not misuse but misfortune, like the mother in his group whose first pregnancy was twins and her second was triplets.

6.11   Marital Problems

The men and women were asked if there were any special difficulties that had to be faced during their marriage. Most of them managed to think of at least one, and some of them (10 per cent) said that marriage had brought many problems. One in three (36 per cent) said they had no marital problems.

The most common problem (19 per cent) was financial, usually about money management, debts or quarrels about the housekeeping allowance. Housing was also a problem frequently reported (10 per cent). Several (8 per cent) said they had experienced difficulties getting on together (e.g. nagging, moaning, bossiness, moodiness, lack of communication) and 6 per cent specially mentioned sexual problems (incompatibility, frigidity, lack of interest). Other problems were about the children (7 per cent), unwanted pregnancies (5 per cent), disapproval of the spouse's parents (3 per cent) or by their parents about the spouse (2 per cent), and illness or death in the family (4 per cent). Also mentioned were problems about work (5 per cent) and difficulties caused by the wife going out to work (3 per cent). Finally there were other problems not included in this long list (4 per cent).

'If we had money now, we'd be all right. We wanted to buy a house, but we couldn't get the mortgage.'

'We moved to the country, but he wasn't happy there and we had terrible trouble getting back.'

'Our problem has been trying to have a family. We've lost two so far and the wife is now pregnant for the third time.'

'He's been away rather a lot. Work and that sort of thing.'

'The children have come a bit soon.'

'We've had so many problems we're getting a divorce.'

'It's worked out better than I thought.'

It is a varied list and it is important to realize that practical and material problems are more often a cause of strain than personal and sexual difficulties. However it is fair to say that some of the practical problems encountered early in marriage are caused, in part, by the rosy idea that love solves everything; of course, even those with an over-romantic view of marriage know this is not true, but they do not act as if they know.

Although sexual difficulties may not be as important as some other problems, this is the component in marriage that is the special concern of this study and later in the interview the married informants were asked specifically about this. It was found that 68 out of 267 (25 per cent) said they had a sexual problem at one time or another since they had been married.

The sexual problem most often mentioned arose on the honeymoon and in the earlier period of their sexual relationship; this applied to 6 per cent and seems to have been caused by ignorance and thoughtlessness as much as by inexperience. Other problems mentioned were sexual incompatibility (5 per cent), difficulty in finding mutually satisfying techniques (5 per cent), inability to relax due to fear of pregnancy (6 per cent), and difficulty in finding an acceptable contraceptive method (3 per cent).

Of the 161 married informants who had sexual intercourse before the age of twenty, 37 (23 per cent) had a problem; 31 of the 106 (29 per cent) who first had intercourse after the age of nineteen had a sexual problem. So those who started later were slightly more likely to have a problem. Of the 189 married informants who had premarital sexual intercourse, 46 (24 per cent) had a sex problem; whereas among the 78 who did not have sex before marriage, 22 (28 per cent) had a problem. Again this shows a slight tendency for the inexperienced to be more prone to sexual problems.

But the differences in these figures are slight and they do not give strong support to the argument that sex before marriage helps a person to make a good sexual adjustment when the time comes to marry and settle down. On the other hand they lend absolutely no support to the opposite theory that the best way to prepare for a happy sex life in marriage is to postpone all sexual activities until the honeymoon.

Both men and women agreed that the husband was usually more sexually experienced when they married; 48 per cent of the men and 52 per cent of the women thought this was so, and about a third (37 per cent men, 32 per cent women) thought they were about equally experienced. Only 5 per cent of the men, but 8 per cent of the women, thought the wife was more experienced. The remaining 9 per cent men and 8 per cent women said they did not know.

These figures probably exaggerate the true picture even though what little evidence there is leads us to expect the men to be more experienced than the women. There are still some men who would be reluctant to admit to their wives that they do not know much about sex, and there are still some women who would not wish to appear too expert. These figures are disturbing, even if distorted, because boys are taught so little about female sexual needs and no doubt there are some men who would question whether a woman's sexual response is his concern.

Table A6/8 shows that those who have premarital sexual intercourse are likely to be more experienced than their spouse when they marry. This is hardly surprising, but nonetheless 56 out of the 189 (30 per cent) who had premarital intercourse found they were equally experienced and 45 (24 per cent) found their spouse was even more experienced. Among the 92 who maintained that they were equally experienced, 56 (61 per cent) had had premarital intercourse (and so, presumably, had their spouses), while 36 (39 per cent) were virgins, like their spouses. So it can no longer be assumed that the first night of the honeymoon is the occasion when the man reveals the mysteries of sex to the woman.

Finally it is appropriate that this section should end with the report that about half the group (49 per cent) said they thought sex was over-rated. Furthermore another 7 per cent said they were unsure, which means that only 44 per cent were prepared to give a negative answer to this question.* It is clear, therefore, that it is possible to exaggerate the importance of sexual adjustment. Most people will be able to think of happily married couples where the sexual component is unimportant or non-existent.

But these are young married men and women. A quarter of them have encountered sexual difficulties at some time during their marriage, and some of them still have sexual problems (6 per cent) or fears about unwanted pregnancy (5 per cent). It may be impossible to prevent all these problems, but it certainly should be possible to learn from these people and to help the next generation by providing better preparation for the sexual part of marriage.

6.12   Attitudes to Premarital Sex

I am often asked if I think teenage sexual behaviour has changed since we did the research seven years ago. My guess is that behaviour has changed only slightly, but there has been a marked change in attitudes. Seven years ago people had rather more sex than they said they had. Today teenagers have rather less sex than they say they have.

But activities are influenced by attitudes and this section concentrates upon the changing views and opinions of these ex-teenagers who have now become young adults. As far as non-sexual matters are concerned, quite a gulf has developed between the new generation of teenagers and many of the men and women in this group who view the new teenagers with mixed feelings and find themselves out of sympathy with many of the new political and social ideas. But as regards

* Do you think that sex is over-rated? 54 per cent women and 46 per cent men said yes; 39 per cent women and 48 per cent men said no.

attitudes to sex most of this group have changed their opinions in the last seven years.

One of the biggest and most welcome changes is the diminishing influence of the double standard of sexual morality. One of the ancient axioms of this double standard is the idea that premarital sexual intercourse is forbidden for women but not for men. Table 6/7 compares the attitudes to this and three other statements held by this group when they were

TABLE 6/7. The attitudes of eighteen-year-old boys and girls to four statements on the double standards of sexual morality compared with their attitudes seven years later

	Attitude	Boys then %	Men now %	Girls then %	Women now %
Sexual intercourse before marriage is all right for men but not for girls	Agree	23	6	42	11
	DK	21	2	14	7
	Disagree	56	91	44	82
When it comes to sex, there is one standard for men and another for women	Agree	31	34	45	29
	DK	37	13	28	11
	Disagree	32	53	27	60
If a girl has sex before marriage, she gets a bad reputation	Agree	45	25	58	36
	DK	18	13	14	13
	Disagree	37	63	28	52
Most men want to marry a virgin	Agree	66	61	69	59
	DK	19	9	19	9
	Disagree	15	20	12	33
No. (100%)		393	206	397	143

eighteen with their opinions seven years later. This is taken from an attitude inventory which the informants were asked to complete immediately after the interview. It consisted of 28 statements and the informants were simply asked to note whether they agreed or disagreed with each one. This attitude inventory was not ready or tested before the interviews started and so the first 27 informants were not given the opportunity to complete it; these 13 men and 14 women are excluded from the calculations given in Table 6/7 and in the other percentages noted in this section.

Originally the women were equally divided in their attitude to the statement *sexual intercourse before marriage is all right for men but not for girls*. Now only a small minority (11 per cent) support this idea. The men are even more emphatic about this. Seven years ago 23 per cent agreed with the statement. Now a large majority (91 per cent) disagreed.

The second statement is *when it comes to sex, there is one standard for men and another for women* and the replies can be taken in two ways. Some have answered as if they were reporting on the existing situation whether they approved or not, but others answered according to what they thought ought to be the case and disagreement signified dissatisfaction with the existing situation. This ambiguity resulted in a large number of people who could not decide (classified as DK), especially seven years ago. As many men agree with the statement on the second survey as in the first, but many more of both sexes now disagree. Whether they were reporting ruefully on things as they are, or whether they were stating a case for women's liberation, it is clear that there has been a considerable decrease in the strength of the double-standard morality.

Seven years ago half the sample agreed that *if a girl has sex before marriage, she gets a bad reputation*. There has now been a considerable change in attitude and a majority of men (37 per cent then, 63 per cent now) and women (28 per cent then, 52 per cent now) disagree with the statement.

The last statement in Table 6/7 is not strictly a part of the double standard because some men who wish to marry a virgin expect to be equally inexperienced on their wedding day. But these are a minority. Many of those who want to marry a virgin do not preclude premarital intercourse for themselves. Likewise many women assume that sexually experienced men want to marry girls who are virgins. It is all part of the attitude that some girls are for fornicating and others are for marrying. This unattractive idea, a distinction based on social class differences, still lingers on, but less forcibly. A majority still agree with the statement that *most men want to marry a virgin*. The main change in attitude has been that those who were not sure seven years ago now signify their outright disagreement.

Attitudes to birth control have also changed. Even seven years ago 82 per cent (with very little difference between boys and girls) agreed that *young people should be taught all about birth control*. Despite this strong demand from the teenagers, the vast majority of people leaving school today have not received any instruction about birth control. Seven years later only a very small number (3 per cent) disagreed with this statement. Here is a clear case of an educational requirement which is not being provided.

There have been considerable changes in the attitudes towards homosexuality. A large number (47 per cent) of eighteen-year-old boys agreed with the statement that *all homosexuals should be severely punished*. It was clear that before the research started opinions had changed and so the word *severely* was left out of the statement in the second attitude inventory. Despite this modification, only 7 per cent of the men now agree with this statement, a reduction of 40 points. There were fewer girls who thought homosexuals should be severely punished; even seven years ago more disagreed (45 per cent) than agreed (35 per cent) with the statement. But now, like the men, only 7 per cent agree with the amended statement.

This increased tolerance towards homosexuality must be welcomed even if it does not go far enough for the pressure groups who believe that there is still a tendency to regard homosexuality as a sickness. Elsewhere* I have shown that there is little justification for this assumption, but at least it is possible to report that the earlier punitive attitude has largely disappeared.

* '. . . if homosexuality itself is a pathological condition, then it must be one of the most common psychological disorders known. It would be an illness from which over a million men and probably as many women were suffering, and would constitute a far bigger health problem than cancer, heart conditions or any other single disease . . . the increasingly prevalent idea of referring to homosexuality as a sickness is part of a common approach in modern society to regard non-conformity and mental illness as synonymous,' from Schofield, *Sociological Aspects of Homosexuality*, Longman, 1965.

People concerned about race relations sometimes suggest one component of racial prejudice is sexual fear, or perhaps sexual jealousy. During the interview everyone was asked to express an opinion about having sexual intercourse with people of different races. Several women (23 per cent) and fewer men (14 per cent) said that it was wrong. But the majority (74 per cent women, 81 per cent men) did not raise any objections. More specifically, 9 per cent of this group, all of whom were white, said they themselves had experience of sexual intercourse with someone of a different race.

Seven years ago a quarter (25 per cent) of the sample agreed with the statement that *it would be best to keep coloured people in their own districts in order to prevent too much contact with whites*. There was very little difference between the men and women either then or now. Today, 15 per cent agree, 12 per cent are unsure and 75 per cent disagree. This is a movement towards increased tolerance, but it is a reminder that even among a group of young people, one in seven will agree with a statement expressing a favourable view of apartheid.

When they were eighteen, a third of the boys (35 per cent) and nearly two out of three girls (62 per cent) agreed with the statement that *sexual intercourse before marriage is wrong*. There were several people (20 per cent boys, 14 per cent girls) who were classified as DK because they wished to qualify the statement. This left 45 per cent of the boys and 24 per cent of the girls who disagreed.

This statement was not included in the new attitude inventory because I wanted to inquire into attitudes towards premarital intercourse in rather more detail. Seven years later 66 per cent of the men and 49 per cent of the women expressed unqualified approval about premarital sexual intercourse, and only 8 per cent of the men and 7 per cent of the women positively disapproved. In so far as these findings can be compared with the statement seven years ago, this reflects a tremendous change in attitude, especially among the women. Whereas two thirds of the girls thought premarital sex was wrong at the time of the first research, nine out of ten of them no longer hold such strong views.

There remains a large proportion (26 per cent men, 44 per

cent women) who gave qualified approval to premarital intercourse, depending upon the circumstances. These 127 people were then asked this supplementary question: Do you think it is all right for two people to have sex before marriage when they are really in love? Only 13 said they disapproved and 3 were unsure. This leaves 111 people plus the 221 who gave unqualified approval, making a total of 332 (88 per cent of the whole group) who do not object to premarital sexual intercourse when the two people concerned are in love. Everyone knows that the younger generations have a more permissive view about sex, but even so this is a remarkable result. It means that premarital sexual intercourse between couples who are in love is now accepted by the vast majority in this age group, and it is the few who think it is wrong or sinful who are the exception.

The informants were asked if they objected to premarital intercourse between two people who were not in love. Over half (58 per cent) said they did not object. A few (6 per cent) were doubtful and several (36 per cent) disapproved.

This is a significant finding. All these people have been told many times that sex without love is to be deplored. Christian morality (but not the original Christian doctrine) decrees that sexual activities must be linked with love if they are to command respect. Nearly all romantic fiction assumes that two people go to bed because they are in love with each other. Even the major part of modern fiction exalts sexual activities in the name of love and explains infidelities by the irresistible power of love. Despite these and many other social pressures, repeated almost without opposition, a large number (58 per cent) of young people do not accept this moral principle. Instead they accept the evidence of their eyes and their senses. They are aware that hundreds of people separate sex from love, and are prepared to satisfy their sexual desires without pretending that it is part of a loving relationship.

There was one other question designed to elicit views on sex and love. Everyone was asked: Is it all right to have sex with one person when you are in love with another? Unlike the other attitude questions, this question was intentionally phrased in a personal way and, quite understandably, produced a much larger negative response, particularly among the married. More than two out of three people (62 per cent men, 79 per cent women) said they did not approve of this. A small proportion (14 per cent men, 8 per cent women) did not know what to think about it, but 25 per cent of the men and 13 per cent of the women said they would have sex with a person even though they were in love with someone else.

This demonstrates how people are much more tolerant in their attitudes than in their behaviour. Even in this case where a degree of infidelity is implied, a considerable minority seemed to feel that it was possible to partake in sexual activities without prejudicing the continuation of another more important loving relationship.

6.13   Variations in Sexual Behaviour

The findings reported in this chapter make it clear that a wide variation in sexual behaviour is to be found even in a small group of people of the same age living in the same country. Some of the men and women have never had sexual intercourse and others take very little interest in sex; together they make up a not inconsiderable proportion of the group. Others started early and continue to have an active sex life, and another sub-section of this group started late but now have frequent sexual intercourse.

Although the first experience of sexual intercourse was usually before marriage, there were many exceptions; in between those who had premarital sex with several people, and those who had no sex until they were married is another large subsection who only had sex with their spouse-to-be. Although infidelity is unusual in this group of young marrieds, it is by no means unknown. People may complain that the results of this research are based on only a small number of people, but even a group of this size has produced remarkable individual variations in sexual behaviour. This diversity must emphasize that any narrow sexual ethic or any restrictive moral code is bound to leave a large number of people out of the reckoning.

Some of the findings are unsurprising and confirm the

results reported in the earlier research. But some of the other findings are rather unexpected. It is remarkable that so many people, married or otherwise, still seem to have sexual problems, especially anxiety about their own sexual performance or the worry that sex is getting less and less interesting. Every week thousands of words are written in books and articles in an attempt to solve these problems. Thousands of words are spoken by professional people and by volunteers in advice centres about sexual difficulties. Yet many of the people in this group have never talked to anyone about their sexual problems and those who confided in others often felt that the advice was unhelpful. It looks as if we are still a long way from obtaining the necessary expertise.

I end by noting four of the less obvious conclusions to be drawn from this chapter.

There is no doubt that premarital sexual intercourse is now an acceptable form of behaviour in the eyes of most people. Those concerned with the dissemination of contraceptive advice and education must take this into account. Campaigns against the spread of VD must be tailored to fit into the existing situation, not to rail impotently against it. Authorities who have to make social policy decisions about problems such as abortion, adoption and unmarried mothers must be aware of current sexual attitudes.

There are many areas where help is still needed. Apart from the obvious requirements, such as more contraceptive services, more venereologists and more facilities for abortions, it is clear that more personal and indirect needs are not being provided. Educational authorities must share some of the blame for the finding that the first experience of sex is so often disappointing, and that so many people still have sexual problems even when they are twenty-five and married. Much of the advice given to young people is negative. A more positive approach must include the provision of suitable facilities. It may be a disappointment to the romantically inclined, but one of the possible conclusions to be drawn from this chapter is that money and opportunity have something to do with sexual happiness. People who are concerned about leisure facilities should not pretend that sex does not exist. If it is known that young people are going to make love and have sex, perhaps there are better places than the bushes of an urban park, the floor of a disused building or the back row of a cinema.

Although this group of informants is in no sense particularly sophisticated or permissive, a large number of them have made a distinction between sex and love. Many of them do not subscribe to the immutable theory that sex without love is immoral. Attitudes to sex have undergone a considerable change in the last few years and, although this is not always reflected in changes of behaviour, there is now a considerable body of opinion that believes it is possible to find sexual pleasure without spoiling more important relationships. Some of the people who hold this view are happily married.

The evidence suggests that many young people do not get a wide enough range from which to select a suitable mate. The choice is getting more restricted, not less. One reason for this is the attitude that premarital sex is only acceptable as a prelude to marriage. The effect of this is that premarital intercourse confers an obligation on the two participants and limits their opportunities of finding a suitable marriage partner. Young people should be encouraged to meet a large number of other young people before being required to commit themselves. In some quarters premarital sexual intercourse is more binding than an engagement ring.

7. Social Policy

7.1 A Review of the Results

A follow-up research has two important advantages. In the first place we have a large amount of information about the people from whom the sample was drawn. This has made it possible to check our relatively small sample against the sampling frame. We discovered that those we did not contact hardly differed from those we interviewed. We also found that those who refused to agree to a second interview were more likely to be working-class and were more inhibited sexually, but the bias is quite small.

The second advantage is that we can assess how these people have changed in seven years. Although there were many expected changes as they have grown from teenagers to adults, it was impossible to make predictions about future activities and attitudes from a study of the original interview schedule. Those who had received sex education did not differ noticeably from those who had not; there was no striking difference in the teenage activities of those who now used contraceptives and those who did not, or between those who got a venereal disease and those who did not. Those with early sexual experience did not marry earlier, nor were they more active sexually at the age of twenty-five. Those with homosexual experience were not more likely to become exclusively homosexual.

Many other comparisons between the old and new interview schedules were made but are not in this report because no trend could be discovered. The main lesson to be learnt from these comparisons is that it is dangerous to make predictions about the future behaviour of an individual from a study of his sexual acts and attitudes as a teenager.

As in all large researches, many of the results confirm what we already knew or suspected. The new information is fragmentary and it is not easy to see the complete picture. Indeed it is rarely possible to see the whole picture and only a zealot would try to explain sexual behaviour from the results of one research. But it is possible to fit a few more bits of the jigsaw into place although, as always in a study of human activities, there are still many gaps and some pieces do not appear to fit anywhere.

Certain aspects of the sexual scene have become clearer, while some past assumptions are now seen to be open to doubt. Throughout the last five chapters I have suggested ways in which the results might influence social policy. The next five sections of this chapter are not a summary of the findings, but a brief review of those results which may cause us to modify our ideas about the sexual scene. In the last two sections of the report, I look ahead to see how these results may apply to future developments.

7.2 Sex Education

The main impression left by Chapter 2 is that the demand for good, sensible, straightforward sex education is great and is not being met. Indeed there is considerable dissatisfaction with the sex education they got, or did not get, and this gap is being filled after school by commercial promotions. Although it is said that things are better now, there is little doubt that the emphasis is wrong and the teaching is inadequate.

The idea that sex education can be left to the parents does not stand up to examination. Most would find it embarrassing and many do not have the necessary knowledge; four out of ten of the married informants said they did not know all they needed to know about sex – hardly a persuasive argument for the parent as a sex educator. The majority would prefer to learn about sex at school from the teacher; even those who want to learn about it first from their parents believe that the school has much to contribute. When we have managed to get sex education working properly in the schools, then perhaps the next generation of parents will find it easier to help their children and answer their questions as they arise.

Setting up a relevant course of sex education is not such a difficult task as some people like to make out, although it does require careful preparation and special training for the teacher. Most of the basic facts can be presented quite simply. For example, just about everything a person needs to know is contained in *Boy Girl – Man Woman* (Claesson, 1971), a book of less than 150 pages. Nor is it necessary to tread delicately round the emotional subjects. In another good book, *Learning to Live with Sex* (Birkitt, 1972), the subject of masturbation is dealt with in sixteen unequivocal lines. Some people who read these lines will complain about the lack of moral guidance, but they would be mistaken. It is explained that masturbation is not unusual and nothing to be ashamed of, and that is certainly a moral statement.

As for motivation, this research has made it clear that the pupils want to learn and know they need to learn. It is perhaps more important to try to understand the motives of those who oppose sex education, because there is always the danger that an attempt to make it better will bring to life powerful reactionary forces. Thus the end result would be that the sex education received by the pupils would be even less relevant than it is today.

There is no evidence to show that sex education has a damaging effect. Unfortunately there are few signs that sex education, as given at present, has much influence at all on behaviour either for good or for bad. There are slight indications that it may have some effect on attitudes, and it may help young people to become more aware of problems likely to be encountered on the sexual scene. It is certain that there is no positive correlation between sex education and sexual maladjustments such as promiscuity, venereal diseases and unwanted pregnancies. The plain fact is that sex education cannot be blamed for anything because to all intents and purposes it has hardly been tried; the timid attempts currently being made in most schools are, as these informants made clear, not worth the name of sex education.

Those who advocate a diminution of sex education should

not expect to return to the situation that existed twenty or more years ago. The gap will be filled by publishers, film makers and others who seek to turn the demand for sex education into saleable commodities. It is difficult for educationalists to have much influence on the contents of these products. The criterion is profitability. It is strange that the people who worry most about pornography and other commercial excesses of the sexual scene are prepared to leave, by default, the sex education of our children to commercial entrepreneurs.

It has been shown in this chapter that most schoolchildren acquire more sexual myths than knowledge. Sex education is given too late and the folklore already acquired acts as a block to further learning. The equation *sex=smut* is a product of our schools and the opponents of sex education have not suggested anything that will change this situation.

The most frequent criticism of relevant sex education programmes is that not enough weight is put upon the moral aspects. But the sexual and ethical codes are changing quite rapidly and an inflexible moral stance would not be helpful to the pupils, nor would they find it acceptable. The critics always complain about the lack of emphasis on love, but adolescents learn about romantic love from many other sources. The higher forms of selfless love are better taught by example than in a classroom, although progress is being made in developing the techniques of moral education.

In any case I deny that good courses of sex education are devoid of moral content. On page 58 I suggested several moral guidelines that are essential parts of modern sex education. In addition I believe it is quite immoral if we do not help boys and girls to understand the strength of their sexual drive, and it is culpable to assume that young people will not have sexual intercourse before marriage when all the evidence suggests that most of them will.

7.3 *Venereal Diseases*

The moral aspects are also often emphasized during discussions about VD. Indeed the last section (3.11) of Chapter 3 has been entitled 'The Fear of Success' because many people have the feeling that the successful elimination of the venereal diseases would be a mixed blessing. In fact it was shown in this research (section 3.6) that there is no justification for the assumption that a young person who catches VD will be promiscuous, and the VD rates are not a good measurement of the moral state of the nation. But there is a moral aspect that deserves more emphasis. It is immoral to spread a highly infectious disease and there is room for research into possible coercive measures.

The VD figures continue to rise and the moralists go on wagging their fingers, but again I want to suggest that the situation is not so daunting as people will have us believe. There is a receptive audience anxious to learn how to avoid the worry and embarrassment of catching the disease. Those most likely to spread the disease are also those who are most eager to get to know about it. The medical scientists have been quite successful in finding a simple and satisfactory form of treatment.

The campaigns against VD have been fairly successful at warning people of the dangers. What is needed now is a change of emphasis. Nearly everyone is now aware of the problem and the publicity campaigns should now concentrate upon making the symptoms better known. The next important step is to make sure that people recognize it when they have got it. Syphilis is decreasing and NSU in increasing, so less is required on the horrific details and more on the method of treatment. This research has shown that most people have acquired their limited knowledge more or less by chance and therefore the opportunity exists for providing information before they acquire misinformation.

People are still reluctant to go to a VD clinic. We must find out why so many prefer to go to a general practitioner when the clinics are better equipped to deal with these diseases. It is important that those running the clinics should succeed in breaking down the barriers that keep people away. There is some doubt if even half this group would go to a VD clinic at the first sign of infection. A majority did not know where their local VD clinic was situated and many did not know

how to get the address. Various suggestions are made in
section 3.8 to combat the negative attitude towards clinics.

It is important that future campaigns should make it clear
that the treatment is not painful. Above all it should be
clearly stated that VD is a curable disease. People who are
worried about sexual laxity may be reluctant to speak plainly
about this, but they must not be allowed to confuse the situation. If everyone who caught VD recognized the symptoms
and immediately went to the clinic, the problem would be far
less serious. This is obvious, but you would not think so if you
listened to some of the wary and admonitory statements about
the treatment of the venereal diseases.

7.4 Contraception

The moral aspects of birth control have become less prominent in recent years, although they have not completely disappeared. The Pope remains inflexible although this research
and other surveys have shown that more and more Roman
Catholics now use contraceptives. The Secretary for Social
Services is impressed by the economic advantages of birth
control but repeats his concern that contraceptives on the
NHS might become an inducement to promiscuous living and
might threaten the security of family life; in his evidence to
the Select Committee on Science and Technology's sub-
committee on Population, Sir Keith Joseph worries about the
encouragement of 'casual breeding' and 'the flaunting of
advice and facilities for the unmarried couple'. In section 4.7
the motives of those who exaggerate the dangers of the pill
are questioned. As many of the side-effects are caused by
nervousness associated with taking the pill, the publicity
given to these fears is self-fulfilling.

This report has shown that the gap between the first sexual
intercourse and the regular use of contraceptives is the cause
of much distress and harm. This raises difficult moral problems for those who distribute contraceptives. But the stance
taken in this report is a long way from being amoral. It is a
cause for concern that the young teenager and those who are
least able to look after an unwanted baby are the two groups

that are least likely to be provided with contraceptives.

Freedom of choice is denied to some women because they are not well enough informed to question the man's decision. One of the more revealing results of this research is that the male sometimes regards the pill as a threat to his dominant role. Male attitudes to contraceptives make it clear that more time and money must be spent on persuading men of the importance of contraception. Despite the new liberation movements, many women still think that birth control is the man's business.

Many other suggestions are made in Chapter 4 for a change of emphasis in future campaigns. There is no ideal contraceptive and people should be given a wider choice. Women are more likely to be influenced by social workers or neighbours than by advertising or pamphlets. They are more likely to accept the idea when it becomes official government policy. A change of terminology might be considered; 'family planning' was once a good euphemism and it has undoubtedly helped to make birth control more acceptable, but perhaps it has now outlived its usefulness.

One of the most pressing requirements is an improvement in distribution. The results given in section 4.6 show that it is still difficult for some people to get the contraceptives they require. There is a need for better retail outlets. Free supplies should not be restricted to the poor. Many people who can afford to buy contraceptives will spend the money on something else and if, as a result, they produce unwanted children, it is the community that loses both socially and financially. Improvements could be made in the clinics whether run by voluntary organizations or statutory bodies. Unmarried clients with regular boy friends may be able to cope with the situation, but the feckless girls are sometimes put off by tactless questions.

Another problem is the medical orientation that surrounds the distribution of contraceptives for the female, so much so that the client thinks of herself as a patient although she is not sick just because she is fertile. Cartwright and Waite (1972) found that only a few general practitioners had been on a family planning course and many doctors revealed a rather worrying ignorance about contra-indications to pre-scribing the pill; yet nearly half said they would advise patients who were suffering no demonstrable side effects to stop taking the pill after a certain length of time, although neither the Family Planning Association nor the Inter-national Planned Parenthood Federation recommend such a policy. The disadvantages of this medical orientation have been mentioned several times in Chapter 4. Instead of repeat-ing these points, I quote a forthright paragraph from Dr Black (1972) which appeared in the Family Planning Associa-tion's own journal.

We are already experiencing the consequences of medical intransigence, which has often effectively limited the availability of birth control services. On the insistence of medical advisers, only a doctor may perform an abortion or vasectomy, fit the loop or in most countries even prescribe the pill. Yet the technical skills and knowledge required for any one of these minor pro-cedures are minimal and can be adequately learnt by repetition. The sanctity of 'professional standards', however much they may restrict the health and social benefits of birth control to a privi-leged few, are held to be inviolate. The idea that a nurse or a medical auxiliary should perform, fit or prescribe is considered profane, despite ample empirical and scientific evidence of their ability to achieve comparable medical results.

Finally I want to suggest, as I have in preceding sections of this chapter, that the task is not beyond us. As the main rea-son for not using contraceptives is inertia, this presents the birth control campaigners with a fine opportunity. Opinions against birth control are not strongly held and attitudes can be modified. Although negative attitudes to birth control certainly exist, this research shows that over half this group say that contraceptives either add to their sexual pleasure or make no difference to it. It is encouraging to find that less reliable methods are less popular. The cost of providing con-traceptives is not large and several cost/benefit analyses show that in the end the community would gain if contraceptives were free. This is hopeful because, for the politicians, financial arguments are sometimes decisive where humane considera-tions have failed to convince.

7.5   Premarital Pregnancies

The moral aspect is very important in the matters considered in Chapter 5. Religion still plays a big part in moral pronouncements even if it has less influence on behaviour. Although people now profess more tolerance towards unmarried mothers, illegitimacy still attracts considerable social disapproval. People tend to feel sympathetic towards 'the girl who has slipped up' but differentiate between her and 'the bad girl who is irresponsible'. An added complication is that some doctors attempt to impose their moral views on their patients.

The first priority, whatever one's moral persuasion, must be the prevention of unwanted pregnancies. Responses based on the old adage 'you've made your bed, now you must lie on it' are inappropriate when the birth of an innocent child is involved. Although there is an obvious connection between the frequency of sexual intercourse and the chance of a premarital pregnancy, attempts to reduce the illegitimacy and abortion rates by denouncing sex before marriage are unlikely to be effective. Sometimes there are deep-seated personality causes for a premarital pregnancy, but this research has shown that the main reason is that young people do not start using birth control methods at the same time as they start to have sexual intercourse.

As well as more enlightened efforts to prevent unplanned premarital pregnancies, more thought should be given to the consequences. A forced marriage is often the least satisfactory solution. Of the teenage girls marrying in 1960, 9 per cent had become divorced by 1970. Yet parents, friends and even professional advisers still put pressure on the girl to marry the putative father.

Unmarried girls who become pregnant should have the options clearly explained to them. The advantages as well as the disadvantages of abortion, adoption or keeping the child should be put in a straightforward way. The putative father should also be given this information. There must be something wrong if middle-class girls are more likely to have an abortion, and working-class girls are more likely to have a shot-gun wedding.

Abortion is a hornet's nest of controversy. Apart from strong moral considerations which depend in the main on varying definitions of 'life', there are also medical disagreements. Contraception will not provide the individual with complete freedom from unwanted fertility in the immediate future. Consequently abortion is a necessary adjunct to birth control. One cannot logically oppose the former and support the latter. Indeed, for reasons explained in section 5.9, the abortion rate is likely to go up before it goes down, even if more people use contraceptives.

Long-term physical complications (such as prematurity and still-birth) are rare although not unknown, but the psychological effects of abortion have been grossly exaggerated. The greatest single cause of distress is the delay caused by the medical profession and the present law; Tietze (1963) maintains that the amount of psychological disturbance is directly proportional to the delay. Unfortunately medical consultants have been slow to adopt the new out-patient abortion techniques. The training and orientation of gynaecologists have always been those of surgeons. Consequently they still tend to think of a termination as a surgical operation. Menstrual regulation will eliminate most of the delay and will be much cheaper, an important consideration for the NHS.

Again I want to suggest that the situation is far from hopeless. One encouraging aspect is that those who most want to avoid a premarital pregnancy are also those whose pregnancies are most disadvantageous for the community. Furthermore we have been able to isolate the stage when most distress is caused, so we must now devote more concern and resources to those who have just started to have sexual intercourse.

The new out-patient abortion techniques will eliminate not only the delay, but the need for a diagnosis in many cases. Perhaps the greatest advantage of all is that the new techniques will silence many of the ethical objections and will reduce much of the controversy which has always surrounded the termination of unwanted pregnancies.

7.6　Sexual Intercourse

Sexual behaviour has changed in the last few years, but attitudes have changed still more. Premarital sexual intercourse is acceptable to 88 per cent of this group when the couple are in love; even when they are not in love 58 per cent do not disapprove; 25 per cent men and 13 per cent women said it was acceptable to have sexual intercourse with one person and be in love with another. Gorer (1971) asked the question in a different way but found a similar change in attitude; 40 per cent men and 34 per cent women thought a woman could be in love with two men at once, and 40 per cent of all his informants thought a man could be in love with two women simultaneously. Being 'in love' obviously means different things to different people.

One change of attitude to be welcomed is the declining influence of the double standard of sexual morality. But it has not disappeared altogether and most of the informants in this group expected the man to take the lead on the honeymoon night. Unfortunately boys are hardly ever taught anything about female sexual needs.

Premarital sexual intercourse is accepted by most young people, but it is still difficult for them to use birth control because the first experience is often unpremeditated and the girls do not find it easy to get contraceptives. If the gap between first experience of sexual intercourse and regular use of contraceptives is to be closed, girls must be prepared beforehand. There will be opposition to this suggestion, but not from the young people concerned because 97 per cent of the informants thought that birth control should be part of sex education in schools.

In Chapter 6 it was noted that some young people drift into marriage with little enthusiasm for their mate because they do not know how to get out of the commitment. The most usual attitude to premarital intercourse, which only approves of sex with the person you intend to marry, makes it more difficult to break off the engagement. Gorer (1971) found that 88 per cent women and 46 per cent men married the person with whom they first had sexual intercourse.

As for extramarital relations, the results given in Chapter 6 are probably minimum figures. The number who have been unfaithful to their spouse is small (7 per cent) but not insignificant, especially as these are the early years of the marriage. About a third of the unmarried had more than one partner in the year, but by no means always with strangers, pick-ups or prostitutes. Promiscuous sexual behaviour sometimes involves close friends and some infidelities are known and accepted by the spouses. Extrinsic sex requires a special research of its own. All that can be said here is that infidelity and promiscuity are not rare and cannot be made to disappear by condemnation alone.

Many pronouncements do not seem to take into account that sex is vastly enjoyable. The informants in this research do not make this mistake. Although the first experience was not always a success, nearly all of them now enjoy their sex life including those who are promiscuous. A considerable minority (25 per cent men and 20 per cent women) said they were not getting enough sex; some of these were married, but most of them were single. The biggest restriction on sexual activities is the lack of facilities and opportunities that money can buy.

Although most people enjoyed sex and there was a demand from some for more, it is sad to report that a large number had sexual problems of one kind or another. The most frequently reported was anxiety over their own sexual performance. Others feared they were losing interest in sex, despite the emphasis on sexual matters in Western civilization, or perhaps because of it, for about half the group thought sex was over-rated. This over-exposure of sex leaves many people with the impression that everyone else's sex life is far more exciting than their own.

The results reported in Chapter 6 do not give much support to the traditional moralities. There is no support for the idea that sex is best if you wait until you are married; premarital intercourse neither helps nor hinders sexual adjustment. There is no support for the notion that sex is rarely satisfactory unless both are in love. More often than not, casual sex adventures are enjoyed. However, this research

confirms the findings of the earlier study that premarital
sexual intercourse is often an extension of a loving relationship. Perhaps the most important finding is that there is a
very wide variation in sexual behaviour and this must always
be taken into account. Any narrow moral code is going to
leave most people out of the reckoning.

7.7   *A Situation of Instability*

In several places in this report and particularly in section
2.14, I have noted that the attitudes to sex of these young
adults are dissimilar to the views of older generations. The
sexual code of ethics is changing rapidly and this situation of
instability is going to continue for a long time. We must learn
to respond to the process of change. We still need to know the
basic facts, but we must also learn to apply these in a fast-
changing situation.

The new generations question the old sexual ethics and
traditional moralities. Nor surprisingly, they find some of
them inappropriate to present-day conditions. Of course
many of the values of the traditional moralities still apply,
including the fundamental Christian values. But the traditional attitudes to sex are not immutable, as even a cursory
examination of Christian teaching soon reveals. But it is
wrong to assume that these new attitudes to sex are amoral.
The sexual behaviour of most young adults is strictly governed by strongly held ideas of right and wrong.

In a new situation people behave in a new way and so fail
to fulfil old expectations. This causes anxieties. In separate
sections (2.17, 3.11, 4.6–4.8, 5.8) of earlier chapters I have
attempted to understand and explain these anxieties. It is not
necessarily bad to be beset by anxieties, for they help us to
prepare for a situation that is changing. Furthermore anxieties alert us to the possibilities of trouble and it is sensible to
try to redirect a change if you happen to think it is going the
wrong way. It is, however, fruitless to try to create and live
in a static unchanging situation.

Unfortunately most of the opposition to current changes on
the sexual scene is misinformed. Statistics on illegitimacy,

premarital conceptions and venereal diseases are used as arguments against birth control and sex education, although these rates started to increase twenty years ago when there were only a few family planning clinics, when the pill was unknown and when there was hardly any sex education in the schools. The idea in the Longford report that sex education should be left to the parents simply ignores the facts of the situation.

Perhaps the hardest thing to understand about these critics is their belief that somehow sex can be kept a secret from the young. They are unable to comprehend that this void will be filled by misinformation. Despite the commercial exploitation of sex – the strip clubs, blue films, hard pornography, sex supermarkets – it is the *lack*, not the *surfeit*, of knowledge that is the cause of distress to young people.

The other common mistake is to think that there is only one answer. What may have been the solution for yesterday in one situation may not be the solution for today in another situation. Sexual activities are not homogeneous. Attitudes to sex vary according to regions, religion, backgrounds, sections of society and sex. What is appropriate for one individual is unsuitable for another. Pair bonding may be the complete sexual solution for most people, but not for everyone. It is absurd to think there is one solution for so many problems.

7.8 Population and Sex

I have tried to suggest in the preceding sections of this chapter that we should not be daunted or overawed. Considerable progress can be made in improving the standard of sex education, the control of VD, the provision of birth control services and the prevention of unwanted pregnancies, without spending huge sums of money or waiting for official government approbation. A more serious problem and one that is far less easy to solve is the increase in population in this country, as in other parts of the world.

This is not a research about population but it would be wrong to ignore the subject altogether when the control of the birth rate is so closely allied to the problems discussed in this chapter. It is important to refer to it in a report on the sexual behaviour of young British adults because so many people seem to think that the population explosion is some-one else's problem; often you will hear them say that we need not worry because the birth rate in this country is declining; all this means is that the population is still increasing but not so rapidly as a few years ago.

The facts are alarming. The best estimates show that the population is still rising and there is no sign that our numbers will stabilize. The population will increase from 55 million in 1971 to 63 million in 2001. This will require us to build the equivalent of twenty-five new towns the size of Nottingham. The intentions of this group of informants is to have an aver-age 2·3 children per family. An average family size of 2·1 is necessary to bring about an eventually stable population.

There are approximately 3,700 million people in the world. It took from the beginning of man to about AD 1830 for the world population to reach its first 1,000 million inhabitants. The second 1,000 million was added in a hundred years, and the third in thirty years. The fourth 1,000 million will be reached by 1975. This unprecedented growth is the result of developments in medical science which led to a decline in the death rate. But in most areas of the world birth rates remain high. If the present rate is maintained the population of the world will have doubled (nearly 8,000 million) by the end of the century.

According to a United Nations publication (1971): 'Population growth alone will call for increases in food sup-plies of 40 per cent over the period 1965–1980 and 120 per cent over the period 1965–2000. Considering the need for better nutrition and the effect of increasing income on food demand, the actual increases in food supplies called for will be much larger.' Britain is quite unable to feed her present population. Half our food is bought from other countries. What is going to happen if these countries keep the food they grow and have none left to sell to us?

As in all countries in the world, over-population in Britain is a hindrance to economic and social development and a threat to individual well-being. Ehrlich (1970) notes the strong connection between population growth and major environmental problems: 'As the populations of many municipalities grow, their sewage treatment facilities, though once adequate, are quickly outgrown. Funds for new facilities can be obtained only at the expense of those needed for better schools, police departments, water systems, roads, and other public services. Inevitably, it seems, the available funds are insufficient to meet all of these needs, which are created in part by increases in population.'

Already too many people live too close together with the resulting acute shortage of housing and inadequate access to medical services. Over-crowding is an increasing problem in this country. The density of population in England is four times that of China and seventeen times that of the USA. Ehrlich (1970) suggests that overcrowding also affects mental health: 'rates for violent crimes have been shown to be positively correlated with actual population densities in American cities . . . The rises in assault and robbery with higher density were particularly striking, although murder and rape both also reflected the trend . . . Incidence of divorce, suicide, child abuse, and various forms of mental breakdown are higher in urban areas.'

A reduction in population requires some kind of fertility control programme and this implies much more than better birth control services or a more liberal law on abortion. It probably requires the realignment of tax structures so that they no longer favour large families, educational campaigns aimed at changing social attitudes towards child-bearing, and even the retraction of social and legal sanctions towards other forms of sexual behaviour, such as inceptive and homosexual activities.

No doubt a fertility programme would be unpopular and perhaps even impossible in a democratic community. But according to a National Opinion Poll (in the *Daily Mail* on 9 February 1972) many people recognize that there is a problem; 54 per cent thought that Britain's present population was too big and 65 per cent thought the government should try to slow down population growth. In fact the government does not have a population policy. To take no action is to take strong action, for every day the problem grows larger.

Even if advice, contraceptives, vasectomy and abortion are freely available to all who want them, this is unlikely to solve the problem of over-population. But it might avoid, or at least postpone, the day when we have to resort to measures of compulsion.

New attitudes to sex deserve encouragement for another reason. Perhaps it is less fundamental than the problem of over-population, but in some ways it is a more congenial and compelling reason: many people do not develop their full sexual potential, or to put it more frankly, they do not get as much pleasure from sex as they deserve.

It seems to me to be quite wrong that so many people have to fumble their way to sexual satisfaction without guidance from the educational authorities; it is wrong that, in the present state of contraceptive knowledge, so many people's enjoyment of sex is spoilt by the fear of an unplanned pregnancy; it is wicked that sexual maladjustments like illegitimacy and venereal disease are prevalent when a little more concern and effort would reduce them, even if it is not possible to eliminate these problems altogether.

People who get VD are not criminal; people who have premarital pregnancies are not mentally sick; people who want contraceptives are not patients. They are clients or customers and they are exercising their right to choose. This means they need to have relevant information, because the choice they do not know about is the choice they will never make. Perhaps their choice is not what you would choose, but their right to make a choice should not be denied unless there are very good reasons. In these circumstances at least, it is better to try to change the situation than attempt to change the people.

Appendix A. Tables

TABLE A1/1. Age left school: the original sample compared with the extracted group (i.e. those who were re-interviewed)

Age left school	BOYS			GIRLS		
	Original sample %	Extracted group %	Difference %	Original sample %	Extracted group %	Difference %
15 and under	47	46	−1	55	53	−2
16	25	25	—	25	23	−2
17	8	10	+2	9	12	+3
18 and over	4	4	—	4	5	+1
Still at school	16	15	−1	7	7	—
No. (100%)	393	219	—	397	157	—

TABLE A1/2. Religious denominations: the original sample, the extracted group and the second interview

Denomination	Original sample %	Extracted group %	Difference %	Second interview %	Difference %
	BOYS				
C of E	56	56	—	53	−3
Non-Com	7	9	+2	6	−3
RC	11	11	—	9	−2
Jewish	7	9	+2	8	−1
Other	2	0	−2	0	—
None	16	14	−2	22	+8
DK	1	1	—	2	+1
No. (100%)	393	219	—	219	—
	GIRLS				
C of E	63	61	−2	59	−2
Non-Com	9	6	−3	4	−2
RC	16	21	+5	19	−2
Jewish	6	7	+1	6	−1
Other	1	1	—	1	—
None	4	3	−1	10	+7
DK	1	1	—	1	—
No. (100%)	397	157	—	157	—

TABLE A1/3. The source of knowledge about conception: the original sample, the extracted group and the second interview

| Source of knowledge | BOYS | | | GIRLS | | |
| | First interview | | Second interview | First interview | | Second interview |
	Original sample %	Extracted group %	%*	Original sample %	Extracted group %	%*
Mother	5	4	8	29	28	24
Father	5	5	10	2	1	7
Teacher	13	11	5	17	18	8
Sibling	1	1	1	3	3	4
Clergyman	0	0	0	0	0	1
Other adults	3	3	—	2	2	—
School friends	60	62	63	37	40	65
Workmates	3	3	11	3	2	16
Books	8	8	26	5	4	20
Others	2	2	4	2	2	10
Self taught	—	—	24	—	—	24
No. (100%)	393	219	219	397	157	157

* At the second interview informants were allowed to give more than one answer so percentages add up to more than one hundred.

TABLE A1/4. Sexual experience: the original sample compared with the extracted group

| Sexual experience | BOYS | | | GIRLS | | |
	Original sample %	Extracted group %	Difference %	Original sample %	Extracted group %	Difference %
Small amount of experience	36	34	−2	43	41	−2
Some experience but no sexual intercourse	35	38	+3	42	41	−1
Experienced including sexual intercourse	29	28	−1	15	18	+3
No. (100%)	393	219	—	397	157	—

TABLE A2/1. Age of first sexual intercourse: those who received sex education compared with those who did not

Sex education	AGE OF FIRST SEXUAL INTERCOURSE				
	14–17 %	*18–21* %	*22+* %	*None* %	*Total*
None	21	24	12	3	60
Some	11	16	9	4	40
Total	32	40	21	7	100
No. (100%)	123	151	77	25	376

TABLE A2/2. The number of sexual partners in the last year analysed by type of sex education

Number of partners	TYPE OF SEX EDUCATION			
	None	*Poor*	*Adequate*	*Total*
Men:				
One partner	98	22	23	143
More than one	34	8	8	50
NK or NA	17	4	5	26
Total	149	34	36	219
Women:				
One partner	69	35	30	134
More than one	5	4	4	13
NK or NA	4	3	3	10
Total	78	42	37	157

TABLE A4/1. The different contraceptive methods known to the men and women in this group

Contraceptive method	Men %	Women %	Total %
Pill	97	100	98
Condom	97	93	96
Cap	68	75	71
Coil	61	83	70
Withdrawal	45	46	45
Safe period	36	50	42
Chemical	34	36	35
Sterilization	25	20	23
Douche	9	9	9
None	1	1	1
No. (100%)	219	157	376

TABLE A4/2. The number who used birth control before and after marriage

When birth control first used	Men	Women	Total	% of all married	% of whole group
After marriage	57	64	121	45	32
When engaged	7	7	14	5	4
Before marriage	53	38	91	34	24
Never used	20	21	41	15	11
Not married	82	27	109	—	29
Totals	219	157	376	99	100

TABLE A6/1. Premarital sexual intercourse and the age they left school

	AGE LEFT SCHOOL			
Sexual experience	15	16	17+	Total
Premarital S.I.	131	62	79	272
S. I. after marriage	42	22	14	78
No experience of S.I.	13	3	10	26
Total	186	87	103	376

TABLE A6/2. Premarital sexual intercourse and those who got A levels

	A LEVELS		
Sexual experience	None	1+	Total
Premarital S.I.	219	53	272
S.I. after marriage	72	6	78
No experience of S.I.	17	9	26
Total	308	68	376

TABLE A6/3. Premarital sexual intercourse and social class

	SOCIAL CLASS				
Sexual experience	Middle	Non-manual	Manual	NK	Total
Premarital S.I.	84	70	110	8	272
S.I. after marriage	18	24	30	6	78
No experience of S.I.	8	10	6	2	26
Total	110	104	146	16	376

TABLE A6/4. The present heterosexual frequencies of those who have had homosexual experience in the past

Frequency of sexual intercourse	HOMOSEXUAL ACTIVITY		Total
	Some	None	
Never	2	24	26
None	2	8	10
1–4	1	10	11
5–24	8	28	36
25–50	5	45	50
50+	18	208	226
DK	0	17	17
Total	36	340	376

TABLE A6/5. The number who did not enjoy sexual intercourse among married and unmarried men and women

	DO YOU ENJOY SEXUAL INTERCOURSE?			Total
	Yes	No	DK	
Married	251	6	—	257
Divorced or separated	8	2	—	10
Living together	5	0	—	5
Steady	47	5	—	52
No steady	22	4	—	26
No S.I.	—	—	26	26
Total	333	17	26	376

TABLE A6/6. The spouses and steady partners who know that the informants have had sexual intercourse with another person

Extent of knowledge	MARITAL STATUS		Total no.	%
	Married	Steady		
Found out	2	5	7	18
Was told	2	5	7	18
DK	13	12	25	64
Total No.	17	22	39	—
%	44	56	—	100

TABLE A6/7. The actual number of children among 267 married couples and the intended family size among 376 men and women, all aged twenty-five

Number of children	ACTUAL NUMBER		INTENDED NUMBER	
	Per family	In total	Per family	In total
None	96	0	7	0
1	83	83	15	15
2	77	154	192	384
3	9	27	84	252
4	1	4	43	172
5	0	0	3	15
6	1	6	5	30
DK	0	0	1	—
N/A	—	—	26	0
Total	267	274	376	868
Average	1·03	—	2·31	—

TABLE A6/8. The more experienced partner in the marriage and their premarital sexual experience

Sexual intercourse	THE MORE EXPERIENCED					
	Informant	Spouse	Equal	DK	NA	Total
Premarital	72	45	56	16	83	272
After marriage	5	29	36	8	—	78
None	—	—	—	—	26	26
Total	77	74	92	24	109	376

Appendix B. Methodology

B.1 Finding the Informant

The sample for the first research was drawn from seven areas. As the earlier study had shown very few differences between the areas, the sample for the second interviews was taken from three of these areas. When the first research was carried out the register of electors did not contain the names of people under twenty-one and so the original random sample was drawn from school attendance lists and from lists especially made for the research.

It is known that this sample is representative of the teenage population seven years ago.* If it had been possible to see all these people again, it would have been equally representative of young adults now aged about twenty-five. However it is inevitable that some of these people could not be traced and others were not interviewed for other reasons. The question to be decided is how far representation has been lost by these reduced numbers.

The old interview schedules were locked up at the HEC headquarters and were only identified by a code name. Confidentiality was considered to be so important that it was quite an elaborate procedure to break the code seven years later. The code led to the old progress sheets kept in another place, which in turn led to another list of names miles away from the original schedules.

There were 790 people who were identified and eligible for an interview. Sometimes the interviewer went round to the last known address, but this was so time-consuming that more often a survey agency was employed to make the first call. In

* The sampling procedures are explained in detail on pages 276–83 of *The Sexual Behaviour of Young People*.

fact 84 per cent had moved since the first interview and in many cases the agency was not able to get the new address. This left the research team with a difficult and expensive tracing task which is described briefly in section 1.2.

Eventually a letter was sent to each individual at his* present or last known address, reminding him that he had agreed to another interview and mentioning that someone would be calling to arrange a convenient time for an interview. Each letter was signed by the person who was to carry out the interview and (s)he* called a few days later even if the individual had not replied. This call attempted to establish if the person eligible for interview was (1) still living there, or (2) had moved to a new address, or (3) had moved but the present residents did not know the new address. But sometimes the house was empty or demolished; on other occasions the house appeared to be occupied but there was never anyone at home even after frequent calls at different times of the day. After a series of calls, never less than three, each individual was put into one of the eight categories listed in Table B/1.

This table shows that 85 per cent of the group were traced and, if time and money had been limitless, about 557 (70 per

TABLE B/1. The result of attempts to trace 790 informants seven years after the interview

Result	No.	%
Not traced, address unknown	117	15
Dead, disabled or in hospital	7	1
Traced, but away from interviewing area	106	13
Traced, but living abroad	11	1
Traced, but away for long period	45	6
Traced, but no reply	19	2
Refused	109	14
Interviewed	376	48
Total	790	100

* As elsewhere in this report the masculine pronouns are used for stylistic simplicity but in fact there was an equal number of women in the original sample and an equal number of female interviewers.

cent) could, in theory, have been interviewed. In fact 376 (about 2 in 3) of them were interviewed. Attempts to interview the others had to be abandoned because they lived too far away, or they could not be contacted for other reasons.

B.2   The Refusals

In addition a further 109 (14 per cent) were contacted but refused to agree to an interview. Refusals are inevitable in this kind of research, especially when they already know that we are likely to ask personal questions about their sexual behaviour. Nevertheless every effort was made to try to persuade each refuser to change his mind. If this attempt was unsuccessful, the interviewers were required to do their best to find out the reason for the refusal.

The proportion who refused is not large for this type of research, but in any case the number of refusals is less important than the type of refusal. If they all refuse for a similar reason, or if it is a particular type of person who always refuses, then there is the danger that the results will be biased. Table B/2 classifies the reason for refusing into seven categories.

TABLE B/2. Reasons given for refusing to agree to a second interview

Reason	Men No.	Women No.	Total No.	Total %
No reason given	16	15	31	28
Not interested	10	15	25	23
No time	7	5	12	11
Relative refused	6	5	11	10
Too personal	5	7	12	11
Resent intrusion	2	0	2	2
Other reasons	5	11	16	15
Total	51	58	109	100

The largest proportion (28 per cent) did not feel inclined to give any reason despite pressure from the interviewers. Another large group (23 per cent) said that they were not interested, or that they had no time (11 per cent). In other cases (10 per cent) it was a relative, usually the wife or husband, who would not let the informant give the interview. Specific reasons for refusing were less frequent although some (11 per cent) thought it was too personal and a few (2 per cent) said they resented the intrusion.

There was not much difference between men and women except that the women seemed to be less interested. But for both sexes the main reason for refusing was apathy. This probably includes those who refused to give a reason as well as those who said they were not interested. It possibly also applies to those who said they had no time because the interviewers always said that they could return at any time of the day or evening, so that a time and place for an interview could have been fixed if the informant had been at all willing.

Each refusal was written up as a short report and discussed among the research team to see what could be learnt from the episode. On the following pages are fourteen extracts from the notes made by the interviewers after receiving a refusal. Many people have remarked that we were fortunate to have such interesting work, and this is true, but the following notes will demonstrate that there were times when the situation was embarrassing, depressing, or even a little frightening. Patience and persistence were requirements on this job, but there were other moments when tact and sensitivity were essential.

The wife answered the door and she went to explain to him. He was working on his car at the back and sent a message through her that he was not interested. She was sympathetic and twice went back to argue with him, but he refused to come in and speak to me.

A shy little thing opened the door and said she didn't want to do it. Not very forcefully, so I persuaded her to make an appointment for Monday. When I arrived for the interview her husband came to the door. He looked very nervous and explained that he and his wife had discussed the whole thing together and didn't want people interfering in their private lives, and that his wife was frightened to say no. He was trying to be angry, but I felt they were genuinely upset by the idea and that if I pushed it, some crisis would follow. I felt rather awful, myself. So I explained that we had no wish to intrude where we were not wanted and left it at that.

Mother asked me not to bother her daughter who was in hospital and had just lost her baby. I decided any further attempts to persuade her would be wrong.

The door was answered by his wife who wanted to know what it was all about. 'Oh, he wouldn't want to do anything like that.' Eventually she reluctantly agreed to tell me when he'd be in, but he wasn't when I called. After two more calls the wife said he wasn't interested in doing it.

She was very rude. She just slammed the door in my face after saying it was none of my business. The husband was there as well, looking aggressive.

She had been recently widowed and did not want to talk about her life at all. She was very nice, but a little upset so I did not want to press her.

The wife answered and called upstairs to her husband. It seemed like they had just been having a row. She said it was 'those research people'. He shouted down from the top of the stairs that he wasn't interested. We had a difficult conversation with me talking up the stairs, but he wouldn't come down and nothing I said would change his mind.

He just couldn't be bothered with me. He kept on watching TV while I talked to him, lying on the couch with no shirt on. He was beginning to get a bit annoyed with my interrupting the programme, so I left.

He looked like a champion wrestler with a big black beard. He gave me an odd sort of grin while I was talking to him. He kept on saying, 'What's in it for me?' or 'How much is it worth?' In the end he became aggressive and looked dangerous. I really thought I'd be thrown out.

She was very cheerful and listened while I explained things. She agreed it would be very important and helpful, that only people who'd been interviewed before could be interviewed again, that we needed every possible interview, and then she said, 'No one's forced to do it, are they?' 'No, but . . .' 'Well, I'm not doing it.'

There seemed to be a large number of young children milling around in the small garden. The wife poked her head out of the bedroom window and eventually the husband opened the door. He was very thin and a bit careworn, but said he was willing to cooperate. I suggested a date at his house but he said that was impossible, so I made an appointment for him to come to the office. But he never turned up and when I returned to the house the wife said he hadn't the time to go for an interview.

There was lots of moving of curtains, but no one answered the door. Eventually mother came round from the back door and said her son was not in. At later visits mother or sister said he was out, didn't want to be bothered, had no time, and often stayed away for days. I feel sure he was there when I called, but I couldn't do anything more.

This is the second time I've had a long discussion down one of those door-answering devices. It's hard to be convincing shouting into that thing alongside the door post.

She said, 'Surely you can find someone else' and so I explained why it had to be her, but she couldn't see what I was getting at.

B.3   *Possible Bias from Lost Informants*

It is clear that the greatest loss in numbers is not through refusals, but because it was beyond the financial resources of the research to find and interview about a third of the original sample. It is important to see how far this has biased the results. Tables B/3, B/4 and B/5 are a selection from the many tabulations made to check on this possible source of bias.

The information on these three tables is derived from the original interview. Table B/3 shows the age the 790 infor-

TABLE B/3. Age of leaving school analysed by those who were interviewed, those who refused and those who were not contacted

Age left school	Not contacted %	Refused %	Interviewed %	Total %
At fifteen	50	58	49	51
At sixteen	26	26	24	25
Seventeen and over	23	17	27	24
No. (100%)	305	109	376	790

mants left school, divided into three groups. The first column includes those not traced, those who lived too far away and those who could not be contacted when the interviewer called. If this column (labelled 'not contacted') is compared with the fourth column (which is the whole group of 790), it can be seen that there are very few differences. Almost exactly half left at fifteen, a quarter at sixteen and another quarter after that age. It is reasonable to suppose that as far as education is concerned, there is very little difference between those who were not contacted and the whole group.

However, when one looks at those who were contacted and compares those who refused (the second column) with those who were interviewed, a difference begins to emerge. It is clear that the better educated are more likely to agree to an interview. Among the interviewed, 49 per cent left at fifteen, 24 per cent at sixteen and 27 per cent at a later age. Among the refusers, more (58 per cent) left at fifteen, and fewer (17 per cent) left after sixteen.

A similar trend can be detected in Table B/4 in which the 790 individuals are put into three socio-economic groups

TABLE B/4. Socio-economic class analysed by those who were interviewed, those who refused and those who were not contacted

Social class of father	Not contacted %	Refused %	Interviewed %	Total %
Middle class	27	21	29	27
Others	53	55	51	52
Working class	20	24	20	21
No. (100%)	305	109	376	790

according to the occupation of their fathers; professional, managerial and supervisory are classified as middle-class; semi-skilled and unskilled manual workers are classified as working-class; and all the others (some of whom would perhaps call themselves middle- or working-class) are put into a mid-group named 'others'. The table shows that the middle class are more likely to agree to an interview and the working class are more likely to refuse. Those who were not traced are somewhere in between these two groups, but closer to those interviewed than those who refused.

Table B/5 shows the results of four other items taken from the interview schedule of seven years ago. The first shows a variation from the trend noted in Tables B/3 and B/4. In this case the not-contacted group do not come between the refusers and the interviewed. Those who came from broken homes (where one or both parents were dead or absent at the time of the first interview) changed their residence more often and so were more difficult to trace. A quarter of all those not contacted were from broken homes compared with 17 per cent of those who refused and 19 per cent of those who agreed to be interviewed.

There are only small differences between the three groups when their police record is considered. It might have been thought that those who got into trouble with the police would have been more difficult to interview, but the opposite is the case; those who were interviewed were more likely to have been in some sort of trouble with the police compared with the others. The earlier research noted a statistical association between those who had early sexual experience and those who got into trouble with the police. It was found that teenagers who were extrovert, adventurous and inclined to get into trouble were likely to have a higher level of sex activity. This is confirmed by the third item in Table B/5.

In the earlier research everyone was put into one of five categories of sex experience. Stages I and II had no or limited experience; stage III had inceptive experience; stages IV and V had experienced sexual intercourse with one or more partners. This table shows there was surprisingly little difference in the sex experience of those who were interviewed and those who were not traced. But those who refused to be interviewed again were much less experienced when they were teenagers. There are clear indications that the late starters and the more inhibited were less likely to agree to a second interview.

This was also shown in questions about attitudes to sex; one example of which is the last item in Table B/5. The boys were asked if they would like their wife to be a virgin when they married and the girls were asked if they would like to be

TABLE B/5. Four items from the first schedule analysed by those who were interviewed, those who refused and those who were not contacted

	Not contacted %	Refused %	Interviewed %	Total %
Parental background				
Two parents	75	83	81	79
Broken home	25	17	19	21
Trouble with police				
No	74	73	70	72
Yes	26	27	30	28
Stages of sex experience				
I and II	39	42	38	39
III	38	39	39	39
IV and V	23	18	23	22
Attitudes to premarital virginity				
Important	70	80	65	69
Not or DK	30	20	35	31
No. (100%)	305	109	376	790

a virgin on their wedding day. Two out of three (69 per cent) said this was an important consideration. (In the event less than half are likely to achieve this ambition.) Those who agreed to a second interview had the more relaxed views; those who were not contacted were similar to the over-all total and those who refused were the least permissive.

A comparison of the first and fourth columns of Tables B/3, B/4 and B/5 reveals a quite remarkable similarity in the percentages. This leads to the conclusion that the large number (38 per cent) who were not traced or who could not be contacted for other reasons has not biased the results of the research at all. But the smaller number (14 per cent) of people who were traced but refused to be interviewed again were more likely to be working-class, less well educated, more introvert, less permissive in their attitudes, and less adventurous in their sexual activities. The differences are not great but it should be remembered that this research has tended to exaggerate the sexual propensities of the young adults in this country.

B.4 Selecting the Questions

It goes almost without saying that a large number of people were consulted before the research started. Much of the advice received is valuable and has been acted upon, but one of the disadvantages of this procedure is that nearly everyone has suggestions for additional questions. Experience warns us that interviews that go over the hour bring response rate problems and some selection has to be made. Our problem was that the topics which we most wanted to cover in detail were all sensitive subjects and these kinds of questions should not be asked until the informant is relaxed and settled. When a friendly relationship has been established and the answers have begun to flow, then the sensitive questions are more likely to get valid replies. Most of the essential background material had been collected at the first interview and so it was not necessary to ask questions about home background and schooling again. Nevertheless over forty questions were asked on nonsexual subjects such as leisure activities, friends, marriage and changes since the last interview. Some of these might be regarded as 'waste' questions as far as the analysis is concerned, but they were useful because it got the informant talking and enabled the interviewer to gain his confidence.

Eventually it was decided that the main questions should concentrate on five problem areas: sex education; venereal disease; contraception; premarital pregnancies; sexual intercourse. Batches of questions on these topics were put together into questionnaire form for testing. Following a procedure devised and carried out with success for other researches (Schofield, 1969), a series of pilot interviews were conducted so as to check that the questions were meaningful and unambiguous. During this pilot stage the interviewer would go back over the questionnaire and ask the volunteers (who were about the same age as the informants) about the wording of the questions so as to be sure there had been no misunderstanding. Some of these volunteers were social scientists and thus were able to make useful suggestions. A number of these pilot interviews were tape-recorded and these were studied and discussed by the research team, from the point of view of both questionnaire construction and interviewer training.

The attitude inventory was given to the informants immediately after the interview. This required less testing because it consisted of twenty-eight of the fifty statements given at the original interview seven years ago. Nevertheless they were tested to see if the wording was still meaningful and some were deleted because they no longer seemed relevant to young adults.

As a result of what was learnt during the pilot stage, the questionnaire was re-drafted incorporating the revisions and then the schedule was again tested to see that the questions flowed naturally so that the interest of the informant could be maintained. It was a difficult schedule for the interviewer to administer because large blocks of questions had to be skipped according to the experiences of the informant. The period when the informant was filling in the attitude inventory was valuable for the interviewer who was able to make a quick check over the schedule to see if there were any inconsistencies or ambiguous answers.

B.5 The Interviews

The interviewers were especially recruited and trained for this research. They were all about the same age as the informants, and they were also graduates with some social science training and interviewing experience. They had to be trained in the special interview techniques required when dealing with sensitive subjects. Almost as important they had to learn how to make a good first impression on the doorstep. It was difficult to acquire this art of gentle persuasion, especially as anything that approached the style of the high pressure salesman produced a poor response. It was also important to remember that no one was under any obligation to be interviewed; and the right to privacy is more important than the author's understandable desire to produce useful research results.

A small team of specialist interviewers was recruited instead of professionals such as are used in most survey organizations

because the majority of high calibre and experienced interviewers are women. As in the earlier research it was decided
that women should interview women, and men should interview men. The indications are that this arrangement is preferable, although perhaps not essential.

It was an important aspect of the research method that the
informant should be alone so that he or she should feel free to
answer honestly and frankly. In a few cases (4 per cent) we
were unable to get them alone. A temporary office was established in each interviewing area to which informants could
come if their home conditions were not suitable. This is particularly important when seeking to interview men because
they are usually only to be found at home during the evening
when the whole family is present.

At the end of each interview the informant was ranked for
various factors and Table B/6 gives these results. Of course

TABLE B/6. Ranking on five point scales of the behaviour of the
informants during the interview

Factor	Rating scale (%)				
Talkative . . . reserved	27	29	22	17	5
Serious . . . flippant	35	42	18	5	1
At ease . . . nervous	28	38	20	12	2
High validity . . . low	33	39	21	4	2

these are nothing more than subjective assessments made by
the interviewer, but they give some general indications. The
table shows that most people took the interviews seriously
although some were much more talkative than others. Even
allowing for the subjective tendency to give a favourable
ranking, it appears that most people were at ease during the
interview despite the personal nature of the questions.

The completed interview schedules were coded, punched
and tabulated in the usual way and a detailed analysis of the
responses was made. Hundreds of tables were examined and
a particular study was made between the replies on the first
schedule and the answers given seven years later. Table A1/2
is an example of the answers being given to the same question

asked at both interviews. In this case the replies reflect the dwindling interest in religion and fewer men now say they belong to a particular denomination. But apart from the increase in the number who say they have no particular allegiance, the proportions among the various denominations are similar. Despite the long time interval and even though some of the informants had quite forgotten about the first interview, there were few major inconsistencies.

B.6 Validity

The most relevant question of all is to query the truthfulness of the answers we received and it is always the question that a social researcher cannot answer with certainty. The most he can do is to ensure that the design of the research and the administration of the interview increase the chances of getting valid responses. A person who gives truthful answers about his shopping habits or voting intentions may well hesitate before he decides to be equally frank about his sex experiences. This may be obvious to all, but it is surprising how many surveys on sexual attitudes assume that people will answer all questions with equal candour.

The answers reported here are nearly always the results from a good interview carried out in a friendly situation. It is fair to assume that few of the informants intentionally deceived the interviewer. The difficulty is that some people unintentionally deceive themselves. Answers, particularly to attitude questions, often contain an element of good resolutions. Everyone knows that what people say is not always the same as what people do. All the researcher can do is (1) to make it clear that nothing is to be gained by the informant impressing the interviewer, and (2) provide the conditions in which it is easier to tell the truth than to lie.

The interviewer was required to estimate the truthfulness of the answers immediately after each interview. Table B/6 shows that only 6 per cent were given a low rating and in 72 per cent of the cases the responses were rated as having high validity. Of course this is a subjective judgement but it should not be disregarded altogether.

There is some relationship between validity and interest; the informant is much more likely to tell the truth if he finds the interview worth his time and trouble. Only 4 per cent said they found the interview less interesting than previously, and 45 per cent said it was more interesting; the others said they found it equally interesting on both occasions (20 per cent) or could not remember enough about the first interview to give an opinion (31 per cent).

The overwhelming majority agreed to (yet) another interview at a later date and only 3 per cent definitely refused. This is an indirect measure of validity because an informant is unlikely to waste his time if he does not place some value on the help he is prepared to give to the research. One person agreed to be interviewed again with these words: 'I suppose so, but I don't want to make a career of it.' I have much sympathy with those who expressed reluctance but agreed to help. A long interview is an imposition and can only be justified if the results are properly considered and used. Another informant said: 'I don't like people like you snooping around other people's personalities', but he agreed to be interviewed again. I also have much sympathy for that remark and for another informant who said: 'Sex is something to do, not talk about.'

It is reasonable to conclude that the group we interviewed is representative. Tables 1/1 to 1/3, A1/1 to A1/4 and B/3 to B/5 all show that those who were not traced or not contacted were not very different from those we did see. Every investigator dealing with human groups knows that he is unlikely to get a 100 per cent response. The most that can be done is to get as much information as possible about those who have refused. In this research we know a great deal about the refusals, and we know that the less well educated and the less sexually active are under-represented in the interviewed group. But we also know that this bias is quite small and the results given in this report present a fairly accurate portrait of the sexual behaviour of young adults.

References

BAIRD, DUGALD, 'A Fifth Freedom?', *British Medical Journal*, 13 November 1965.

BARNES, KENNETH, *The Facts of Life*, BMA, 1966.

BIRKITT, ANN, *Learning to Live with Sex*, Family Planning Association, 1972.

BLACK, TIMOTHY, 'Institutional checks to family planning', *Family Planning*, 21, 2, 1972.

BROOK, CASPER, 'The cost effectiveness of family planning', *Family Planning Miscellany*, Family Planning Association, 1968.

CALLAHAN, D., *Abortion Law, Choice and Morality*, Macmillan, 1970.

CARTWRIGHT, ANN, 'General Practitioners and Family Planning', *Medical Officer*, 120, 43, 1968.

CARTWRIGHT, ANN, *Parent and Family Planning Services*, Institute of Community Studies, Routledge and Kegan Paul, 1970.

CARTWRIGHT, ANN and WAITE, MARJORIE, 'General Practitioners and Contraception in 1970–71', *Journal of the Royal College of General Practitioners*, 22, 2, 1972.

CAUTHERY, PHILIP and COLE, MARTIN, *The Fundamentals of Sex*, W. H. Allen, 1971.

CLAESSON, BENT, *Boy Girl – Man Woman*, Calder and Boyars, 1971.

CLARK, M., 'Sequels of Unwanted Pregnancy', *The Lancet*, 501, 31 August 1968.

COMFORT, ALEX, *The Anxiety Makers*, Nelson, 1967.

D'AGAPEYEFF, JEREMY, 'Release: A Progress Report', Release, 1972.

DALLAS, DOROTHY, *Sex Education in School and Society*, National Foundation for Education Research, 1972.

DALSACE, J. and DOURLEN-ROLLIER, A., *L'Avortement*, Casterman, 1970.

DAVIS, GEOFFREY, 'Menstrual Regulation', *Family Planning Journal*, 21, 3, 1972.

DAWKINS, J., *Teach Your Child About Sex*, Pearson, 1964.

DOUGLAS, J. W. B., *The Home and the School*, MacGibbon and Kee, 1964.

DUNWOODY, JOHN, SERVICE, ALASTAIR and STUTTAFORD, TOM, *A Birth Control Plan for Britain*, Birth Control Campaign, 1972.

EHRLICH, PAUL and EHRLICH, ANNE, *Population Resources Environment: Issues in Human Ecology*, W. H. Freeman, 1970.

GORER, GEOFFREY, *Sex and Marriage in England Today*, Nelson, 1971.

HACKER, ROSE, *The Opposite Sex*, Pan, 1963.

HILL, MAURICE and LLOYD-JONES, MICHAEL, *Sex Education: The Erroneous Zone*, National Secular Society, 1970.

HITCHENS, R. A. N. and JAMES, E. B., 'Premarital Intercourse, Venereal Disease and Young People: Recent Trends', *Public Health*, 79:5, pp. 258–70, 1965.

LAING, W., 'The costs and benefits of family planning to public authorities responsible for the health and welfare services', *P.E.P.* Broadsheet 534, 1972.

LAMBERT, JOAN, 'Survey of 3,000 Unwanted Pregnancies', *British Medical Journal*, 156, 16 October 1971.

LITTLE, ALAN, 'A Sociological Portrait: education', *New Society*, 482, 1971.

MCCORICE, and HALL, 'Sexual Behaviour and Contraceptive Practice of Unmarried Female Undergraduates at Aberdeen University', *British Medical Journal*, 694, 17 June 1972.

MORTON WILLIAMS, J. and HINDELL, K., 'Abortion and Contraception: A Study of Patients' Attitudes', *P.E.P.* Broadsheet 536, 1972.

PARE, C. M. B. and RAVEN, H., 'Follow-up of Patients Referred for Termination of Pregnancy', *The Lancet*, 635, 28 March 1970.

PEAKER, G., *Plowden Children Four Years Later*, National Foundation for Educational Research, 1971.

PEEL, JOHN, 'The Hull Family Survey. I. The survey couples', *Journal of Biosocial Science*, 2, 45, 1970.

PEEL, JOHN, 'The Hull Family Survey. II. Family planning in the first five years of marriage', *Journal of Biosocial Science*, 4, 333, 1972.

PEEL, JOHN and POTTS, MALCOLM, *Textbook of Contraceptive Practice*, Cambridge University Press, 1969.

POTTS, MALCOLM, *Against Nature: The Use and Misuse of Birth Control*, Darwin Lecture, 1970.

POTTS, MALCOLM, 'Post-conceptive control of fertility', *International Journal of Gynaecology and Obstetrics*, 8, pp. 957–70, 1970.

ROGERS, REX, 'The Effects of Sex Education', *New Society*, 453, 1971.

SCHOFIELD, MICHAEL, *The Sexual Behaviour of Young People*, Longman, 1965.

SCHOFIELD, MICHAEL, *Sociological Aspects of Homosexuality*, Longman, 1965.

SCHOFIELD, MICHAEL, *Society and the Young School Leaver*, HMSO, 1967.

SCHOFIELD, MICHAEL, *Social Research*, Heinemann, 1969.

SCLARE, A. B. and GERAGHTY, B. P., 'Therapeutic Abortion: A Follow-up Study', *Scottish Medical Journal*, 16, 438, 1971.

SEGLOW, JEAN, KELLMER-PRINGLE, MIA and WEDGE, PETER, *Growing Up Adopted*, National Foundation for Educational Research, 1972.

TIETZE, C., 'Intrauterine Contraceptive Rings: History and Statistical Appraisal', *Excerpta Medica. Netherlands International Congress*, 54, 1963.

WARD, AUDREY, 'General Practitioners and Family Planning in Sheffield', *Journal of Biosocial Science*, 1, 15, 1969.

WREN-LEWIS, JOHN, *What Shall We Tell the Children?* Constable, 1971.

Legalised Abortion, The Royal College of Obstetricians and Gynaecologists, *British Medical Journal*, 850, 2 April 1966.

Survey on Abortion, National Opinion Polls, Abortion Law Reform Association, 1966.

Children and their Primary Schools: Central Advisory Council for Education, (The Plowden Report), HMSO, 1967.

Human Fertility and National Development, United Nations, 1971.

Family Planning in Great Britain, Office of Health Economics, 1972.

Pornography: The Longford Report, Coronet, 1972.

Report of the Population Panel (Cmnd. 5258), HMSO, 1973.

Index

Abortion:
    complications, 155–7, 211
    contraception, 123–4, 153–7
    cost of, 146–7
    education, 140
    extent of, 26, 141–8
    illegal, 90–1, 142, 144–5, 147, 150, 154–6
    sex education, 26, 46, 48, 54, 57
    sex induced, 136, 139, 141–2
    social policy, 200, 209, 217–218
    statistics, 90, 210
    veneral diseases, 70
Adolescence, 52
Adoption, 123, 136, 141, 144, 149, 152–3, 158, 200, 210
Advertisements, 64, 100, 122, 130–1, 175, 208
Advice centres, 178
Analysis, 18–20, 238
Antibiotics, 63–4, 77
Attitude inventory, 17–18, 54, 194, 237
Attitudes to:
    illegitimacy, 159
    premarital sexual intercourse, 184, 193–9
    sex, 42–3, 46, 146, 160, 182–183, 215, 234

Baird, Sir Dugald, 156

Barnes, Kenneth, 52
Bias, 15, 202, 232–3, 240
Biology, 53, 57
Birkett, Ann, 204
Birth Control Campaign, 116
Birth control, see Contraception
Black, Timothy, 209
Books on sex education, 29, 31–32, 35, 51–3, 66, 68–9, 220
Boy/girl friends, 41, 70, 75, 143, 183–4
British Medical Association, 128
British Medical Journal, 128
Broken homes, 71, 118, 234
Brook, Casper, 132
Brook clinics, 126

California, 53
Callahan, D., 155
Cap, 91, 98–9, 101–2, 113, 222
Cartwright, Ann, 90, 91, 94, 102, 103, 129, 208
Cauthery, Philip, 63
Central Council for Health Education, 11
Chemists, 101, 149
Children:
    illegitimate, 123, 136
    number of, 37, 99, 153, 189–191, 216, 225
    sex education, 45, 50, 53, 59

China, 89, 217
Choice, 158–9, 185, 201, 208, 210, 218
Christian doctrine, 198, 214
Church of England, 120, 169, 219
Civil liberties, 86, 89, 129, 151
Claesson, Bent, 204
Clark, M., 156
Clergymen, 24, 92, 177, 220
Clinic:
  family planning, 92–4, 101, 103–4, 126–9, 167, 208, 215
  VD, see Venereal diseases
Coil, 91, 98–9, 111–13, 132, 222
Cole, Martin, 63
Comfort, Alex, 88
Commercial exploitation, 51–54, 175, 203, 205, 215
Communes, 50
Conception, 35
Condom:
  distribution, 95, 101–2, 111, 127–8, 132
  effectiveness, 125, 131
  extent of use, 90–2, 96, 98–9, 107
  myths, 112–14
  orgasm, 114, 174
  sex education, 26, 85, 222
  venereal diseases, 63, 82, 120
Contact tracing, 82, 86–7
Contraception, 26, 41–2, 44–5, 57–8, 90–133, 145, 150–1, 153–7, 190–1, 200, 207–9, 211, 218
Contraceptive pill, see Pill
Contraceptives:
  age first used, 94–7, 122–4, 131, 139, 151, 168, 207
  cost of, 101–2, 111–12, 127–128, 131–2, 208–9

distribution of, 100–4, 126–129, 131, 154, 158, 208
  medical orientation, 93, 102, 128–32, 208–9
Crab lice, 66, 72–3
Criminal abortions, see Abortions, illegal

D'Agapeyeff, Jeremy, 147
Dallas, Dorothy, 53
Dalsace, J., 154
Davis, Geoffrey, 157
Dawkins, J., 52
Denmark, 155
Diagrams, 52–3
Diaphragm, see Cap
Dirty jokes, 35
Divorce, 48, 136, 170, 176, 179, 210, 217
Doctors, 24, 144, 147, 155, 157, 177, 208, 210
Domiciliary services, 116
Double standard of morality, 58, 194–5, 212
Douglas, J. W. B., 47
Drinking, 56, 74, 119, 121, 174
Drugs, 56

Education:
  effects of, 33, 38, 47–9, 50–51, 140
  Minister of, 53
Education system, 56, 58
Ehrlich, Paul, 216, 217
Eickhoff, L., 56
Engagements, 186–7, 201, 212

Family:
  influence of, 47–9, 50, 53
  size of, 153, 190, 216, 225
Family Planning Association, 87, 100, 102, 103, 116, 126, 130, 167, 209

Female sexual needs, 50, 115, 212

Fertility, 117, 124, 189, 217

Films, 31, 53–4, 175, 205, 215

Forced marriages, 124, 136, 141, 146, 149–52, 186, 210

Forum, 52

France, 154

General practitioners, training of, 94, 206

Girl friends, *see* Boy/girl friends

Gonorrhoea, 48, 61–3, 65–6, 72–3, 77, 82, 84, 86–7

Gorer, Geoffrey, 90, 99, 107–8, 115, 174 212

Guilt feelings, 106, 156, 162–3, 175, 176–7

Gynaecologists, 145, 156–7, 211

Hacker, Rose, 52

Harris, Alan, 57

Headmasters, 57–9

Health Education Council, 9, 11, 64, 65, 87, 101, 227

Hill, Maurice, 29, 51–2, 69

Hindell, Keith, 124–5, 156

Hitchens, R. A. N., 81

Home background, 153, 161

Homosexuality, 43, 75, 83, 171, 182–3, 185, 196, 202, 217, 224

Hospitals, 145, 147, 154

Hungary, 155

Hysterectomy, 157

Illegitimacy, 48, 54, 65–7, 90, 123, 136, 140, 143–4, 150, 152, 167, 210, 214, 218

Inceptive experience, 121, 182, 234

Independent Broadcasting Association, 100

Infidelity, 40, 50, 74, 88, 178–181, 198–9, 213, 225

Information:
   demand for, 26–7, 34, 54–5, 89, 91, 212
   source of, 27–30, 47, 52, 68–69, 85, 92–3, 220

International Planned Parenthood Federation, 130, 155, 209

Interview, 12–13, 18, 54, 172, 202, 227–9, 238–9

Interviewers, 9, 12, 14, 17, 18, 141, 187, 227, 229, 233 236–9

Intra-uterine device, *see* Coil

James, E. B., 81

Jews, 120, 169, 219

Joseph, Sir Keith, 207

Kellmer-Pringle, Mia, 153, 158

Laing, W. A., 132

Lambert, Joan, 104, 135, 167

Little, Alan, 47

Lloyd-Jones, Michael, 29, 51–52, 69

Longford, Lord, 35, 53, 172, 215

Loop, *see* Coil

Love, 151, 166, 172, 189, 198–199, 201, 205, 212, 213–14

LRC International, 127

Marital problems, 43, 148, 190–3

Marriage:
   adultery, 178–81
   attitude to, 50, 96, 162, 168–169
   commitment, 186–8, 212

Marriage: (*cont.*)
  contraceptives, 90, 95, 110,
    125
  incidence, 36, 161, 185–9,
    224
  sexual experience before, 40,
    86, 96, 162, 168–9
  sexual frequencies within,
    170–1
Masturbation, 52, 57, 176–7,
    204
Medical entrepreneurs, 147
Menstrual regulation, 153, 157,
    211
Menstruation, 26
Methodology, 14–19, 227–40
Middle class, *see also* Social
    class, 23, 99, 138–9, 144–6,
    150, 158, 168–9, 210, 233
Minorities, 58–9, 150, 173, 199,
    213
Miscarriages, 26, 123, 141
Misinformation, 29, 69, 85,
    163, 206, 215
Moral aspects:
  birth control, 103, 124, 128,
    159, 207–8
  premarital pregnancy, 147,
    156–7, 210–11
  problems, 175–7, 198
Moral education, 26, 38, 49,
    58, 205, 213–14
Morton Williams, Jean, 124–5,
    156
Motivation, 204

National Children's Bureau,
    152, 158
National Health Service, 85–6,
    100, 126, 142–3, 145–7,
    207
Non-Conformists, 120, 169, 219
Non-gonococcal urethritis, 66

Non-specific urethritis, 61–3,
    66, 72–3, 84, 206
Nuffield Foundation, 11, 55

Office of Health Economics,
    127
Opinion polls, 53, 56, 144, 156,
    217
Oral contraceptive, *see* Pill
Orgasm, 26, 174
Original sample, 15–17, 193,
    202, 219, 220, 227–8
Over-population, *see* Popula-
    tion

Pair bonding, 215
Pare, C. M. B., 156
Parental background, *see* Home
    background
Parents and sex education, 28,
    30–7, 42, 203, 220
Peaker, G., 47
Pediculosis pubis, *see* Crab lice
Peel, John, 102, 107, 109, 128,
    130, 189–90
Permissive society, 65, 105,
    140, 156, 185, 198, 235
Petting, 182
Pill:
  dangers of, 106–9, 207
  difficult to obtain, 95, 111,
    126, 209
  extent of use, 63, 82, 96, 98–
    100, 111–13
  fear about, 104–9, 125
  information about, 26, 124,
    222
Pilot interviews, 236–7
Plowden Report, 47
Population, 50, 117, 133, 154,
    190, 207, 215–18
Pornography, 35, 53–4, 205,
    215

Posters, 68–70
Potts, Malcolm, 102, 107, 109, 130, 153
Predictions, 202
Pregnancy Advisory Services, 146
Pregnancy testing agencies, 148–9
Premarital conceptions, 91, 150–1, 167, 215
Premarital pregnancies, 40, 46, 119, 123, 134–59, 210–212
Premarital sexual intercourse:
    attitudes to, 49, 177, 184, 192–9, 212
    contraception, 123–4
    frequency, 170–2
    incidence, 96, 160–2, 166–9, 223
    opposition to, 23, 69, 104, 200–1
    sex education, 39, 45
Premature ejaculation, 114
Privacy, 129, 230, 237
Promiscuity:
    abortion, 143
    contraception, 102, 120, 127
    incidence, 138, 178–81, 213
    sex education, 39–40, 45, 56–57, 204
    terminology, 181
    venereal diseases, 63, 73–5, 81, 88, 206
Prostitution, 56, 75–6, 81, 180
Protective, see Condom
Puberty, 52
Public lavatories, 76, 79–80, 85
Publicity campaigns, 30, 65, 80–6, 89, 129–30, 200, 206, 217
Publishers, 51–2, 100, 205

Racial discrimination, 43, 58, 197
Raven, H., 156
Refusals, 14–15, 202, 229–35, 240
Religion:
    church attendance, 71, 118–119, 182–4
    denomination, 17, 120, 169, 219
    influence of, 90, 93, 169, 176–7, 198, 210, 214, 239
Research, 57, 130–3, 203, 236
Retail outlets, 100–2, 208
Reuben, David, 52
Rhythm method, see Safe period
Rogers, Rex, 49, 53
Roman Catholics, 93, 120–1, 169, 207, 219
Royal College of Obstetricians and Gynaecologists, 156–7

Safe period, 91, 98–9, 112–13, 121, 222
Schofield, Michael, 11, 48, 93, 121, 196, 227, 236
School:
    age left, 17, 22–3, 119, 140, 168, 182, 219, 223, 232
    curriculum, 48, 55
    GCE, 22, 24, 48, 118, 122, 168, 223
    teachers, 23, 25, 28, 31, 42, 48, 54, 55, 58, 77, 92, 203, 220
    type of, 21, 53, 118
Sclare, A. B., 156
Seglow, Jean, 152–3, 158
Sex education, 20–60, 69, 124, 164, 202–5, 215, 221
Sex manuals, 52, 178, 200

Sexual adventures, extrinsic, 180, 213

Sexual Behaviour of Young People, 11, 48, 160, 227

Sexual enjoyment, 105, 112–116, 148, 163, 171–4, 200–201, 209, 213, 218, 224

Sexual intercourse:
first experience, 39, 43, 92–5, 122–4, 131, 137, 139, 151, 160–4, 167–8, 180, 191, 199, 207, 221
frequency, 45, 137–9, 145, 160–1, 169–71, 224

Sexual knowledge, 36–8, 42, 45–6

Sexual maladjustments, 48, 54, 57, 204, 218

Sexual myths, 29, 51, 112–17, 142, 205

Sexual partners, 39, 86–8, 92, 114, 165–6, 172–3, 177–181, 221

Sexual problems, 35, 49, 174–178, 190–2, 200, 213

Sexually transmitted diseases, 61–2, 64

Sheath, *see* Condom

Shot gun marriages, *see* Forced marriages

Social class, 15–17, 21–3, 71, 119, 140–1, 158, 168, 195, 223, 233

Social policy, 200, 202–18

Steady, *see* Boy/girl friends

Sterilization, 91, 98, 111–13, 116, 209, 218

Students, 124, 140

Sweden, 48, 57, 155

Syphillis, 44, 61–2, 65–6, 72–3, 82, 86–9, 206

Teachers, *see* School: teachers

Tehran, 154

Television, 31, 49, 53, 56, 65, 68–9

Terminations, *see* Abortion

Terminology, 129–30, 181, 208

Tietze, C., 211

Tracing, 12–14, 227–9

Traditional moralities, 213–14

Trouble with police, 71, 74, 120, 234

Turkey, 154

Twain, Mark, 28

United Nations, 216

United States, 155, 217

Unmarried mothers, 136, 140, 144, 150, 152, 158–9, 200

Unwanted pregnancies, 90–1, 95, 103–4, 121, 123, 127, 134–59, 167, 190, 204, 215

Vacuum aspiration, 147, 156–7

Validity, 238–40

Vasectomy, *see* Sterilization

Vending machines, 103, 131

Venereal diseases:
campaigns, *see* Publicity campaigns
clinics, 62, 64, 66, 76–80, 84–86, 206
compulsory inspections, 82–83, 86
incidence, 40, 61–89, 120
research, 78, 81, 86–7, 206, 218
sex education, 46, 56–7, 202, 204
statistics, 61–3, 89, 206, 215
stigma, 81–4
symptoms, 26, 44, 63, 65, 67–72, 73, 83, 206

Venereal diseases: *(cont.)*
  treatment, 64, 75–7
  vaccine, 78, 86–7

Waite, Marjorie, 129, 208
Ward, Audrey, 94
Wedge, Peter, 153, 158

Withdrawal, 90–2, 98–9, 103,
  107, 112–13, 222
Working class, *see also* Social
  class, 23, 139, 145–6, 150,
  152, 158, 169, 211, 233
World birth rates, 216
Wren-Lewis, 59